SHIPWRECKED HERITAGE:
A Commentary on the UNESCO Convention on Underwater Cultural Heritage

Second Edition

Patrick J. O'Keefe

Honorary Professor, University of Queensland

A.M.; Ph.D. (Sydney); LL.M. (A.N.U.); M.A. (City of London Polytechnic);LL.B. (Queensland); B.A. (Queensland);
F.S.A.; A.S.A.L.S.; F.A.H.A.

First published in Great Britain in 2014,
by the Institute of Art and Law Ltd, Pentre Moel, Crickadarn, Builth Wells, LD2 3BX, UK
Tel: 01982 560666; E-mail: info@ial.uk.com

ISBN: 978-1-903987-33-9

Cover image: Loss of HMS 'Victory', 4 October 1744

The Loss of HMS *Victory*, 4 October 1744, is a dramatic night scene in the van de Velde tradition. The actual ship, which in her day was recognized as 'the finest ship in the world', was wrecked and lost with all hands on the Caskets, near the island of Alderney in the English Channel after becoming separated from the rest of the English fleet in a gale.

Copyright: National Maritime Museum, Greenwich, London

© Patrick J. O'Keefe and Institute of Art and Law 2014
Second edition (first edition published in 2002)

The author asserts his rights to be identified as such in accordance with the Copyright, Designs and Patents Act 1988.

All rights reserved. No part of this book may be reproduced or transmitted in any form or by any means, electronic or mechanical, including photocopying, recording or any information, storage or retrieval system without prior permission of the publisher, except in accordance with the provisions of the Copyright, Designs and Patents Act 1988 or under the terms of a licence

This book is dedicated

to Connor
last but by no means least
and to Tara
for her loving care of family and others

TABLE OF CONTENTS

Table of Cases	vii
Table of Statutes	viii
Table of International Instruments	ix
Text of the Underwater Convention	xi
Operational Guidelines	xxiii

INTRODUCTION — 1

1. Background — 1
2. The Value of Underwater Cultural Heritage — 3
3. Protection of Value — 5
    3.1 Legislation — 5
    3.2 Salvage — 6
        3.2.1 Rewards and Amnesties — 9
        3.2.2 Proposals for International Regimes — 10
4. The Law of the Sea Regime — 12
5. The ILA Draft — 14
6. Action by UNESCO — 16
    6.1. Negotiations — 17
7. Events Since Adoption — 22
    7.1. UNESCO — 22
        7.1.1. Operational Guidelines — 22
        7.1.2. Manual for Activities Directed at Underwater Cultural Heritage — 23
        7.1.3. Training Manual — 23
        7.1.4. Code of Ethics — 23
    7.2. United Nations — 23

INTERPRETING THE UNDERWATER CONVENTION

1. Introduction to Treaty Interpretation — 27
2. Retroactivity — 28
3. Analysis of Individual Articles — 29
    Preamble — 29
    Article 1 – Definitions — 33
    Article 2 – Objectives and General Principles — 38
    Article 3 – Relationship Between This Convention and the United Nations Convention on the Law of the Sea — 45
    Article 4 – Relationship to Law of Salvage and Law of Finds — 48
    Article 5 – Activities Incidentally Affecting Underwater Cultural Heritage — 51
    Article 6 – Bilateral, Regional or Other Multilateral Agreements — 52
    Article 7 – Underwater Cultural Heritage in Internal Waters, Archipelagic Waters and Territorial Sea — 56
    Article 8 – Underwater Cultural Heritage in the Contiguous Zone — 61
    Article 9 – Reporting and Notification in the Exclusive Economic Zone and on the Continental Shelf — 62
    Article 10 – Protection of Underwater Cultural Heritage in the Exclusive Economic Zone and on the Continental Shelf — 67
    Article 11 – Reporting and Notification in the Area — 72
    Article 12 – Protection of Underwater Cultural Heritage in the Area — 74

Article 13 – Sovereign Immunity	77
Article 14 – Control of Entry Into the Territory, Dealing and Possession	78
Duty of States Parties	79
Entry into the territory	79
Dealing or possession	80
Which State?	81
Limitation periods	81
Article 15 – Non-Use of Areas Under the Jurisdiction of States Parties	82
Article 16 – Measures Relating to Nationals and Vessels	83
Article 17 – Sanctions	84
Article 18 – Seizure and Disposition of Underwater Cultural Heritage	86
Article 19 – Co-operation and Information-Sharing	90
Article 20 – Public Awareness	93
Article 21 – Training in Underwater Archaeology	95
Article 22 – Component Authorities	98
Article 23 – Meetings of State Parties	100
Article 24 – Secretariat for this Convention	103
Article 25 – Peaceful Settlement of Disputes	104
Article 26 – Ratification, Acceptance, Approval or Accession	109
Article 27 – Entry into Force	110
Article 28 – Declaration as to Inland Waters	111
Article 29 – Limitations to Geographical Scope	112
Article 30 – Reservations	114
Article 31 – Amendments	115
Article 32 – Denunication	117
Article 33 – The Rules	117
Article 34 – Registration with the United Nations	118
Article 35 – Authoritative Texts	118

ANNEX: RULES CONCERNING ACTIVITIES DIRECTED AT UNDERWATER CULTURAL HERITAGE   119

I. General principles: Rules 1-8	121
II. Project design: Rules 9-13	135
III. Preliminary work: Rules 14-15	137
IV. Project objective, methodology and techniques: Rule 16	138
V. Funding: Rules 17-19	139
VI. Project duration – timetable: Rules 20-21	142
VII. Competence and qualification: Rules 22-23	143
VIII. Conservation and site management: Rules 24-25	145
IX. Documentation: Rules 26-27	147
X. Safety: Rule 28	147
XI. Environment: Rule 29	147
XII. Reporting: Rules 30-31	148
XIII. Curation of Project Archives: Rules 32-34	150
XIV. Dissemination: Rules 35-36	154

CONCLUSION   157

SELECTED BIBLIOGRAPHY   161

INDEX   171

TABLE OF CASES

Bemis v. RMS Lusitania 884 F.Supp. 1042 (1995) 7, 48

Columbus-America Discovery Group v. Atlantic Mutual Ins'ce Company 974 F.2d 450 (1992) 7

Columbus-America Discovery Group v. Atlantic Mutual Ins'ce Company 203 F.3d 291 (2000) 11

Columbus-America Discovery Group v. Sailing Vessel 742 F.Supp. 1327 (1990) 11

In re 'La Lavia' (1996) I.L.R.M. 194 139

Malaysian Historical SalvorsSdn, Bhd v. Government of Malaysia (ICSID Arbitration Award) <https://icsid.worldbank.org/ICSID/FrontServlet?requestType=CasesRH&actionVal=showDoc&docId=DC654_En&caseId=C247> 8

Malaysian Historical SalvorsSdn, Bhd v. Government of Malaysia (ICSID Annulment Decision) <https://icsid.worldbank.org/ICSID/FrontServlet?requestType=CasesRH&actionVal=showDoc&docId=DC1030_En&caseId=C247> 9

RMS Titanic Inc. v. Wrecked and Abandoned Vessel 435 F.3d 521 8

RMS Titanic Inc. v. Wrecked and Abandoned Vessel 742 F. Supp. 2d 784 8

RMS Titanic v. Haver (1999) A.M.C. 1330 48

RMS Titanic v. Wrecked and Abandoned Vessel 924 F.Supp. 714 (1996) 140

RMS Titanic v. Wrecked and Abandoned Vessel (1996) A.M.C. 2497 131

RMS Titanic v. Wrecked and Abandoned Vessel 9 F.Supp.2d 624 (1998) 48

Robinson v. The Western Australian Museum (1977) 51 A.L.J.R. 806 8

Sea Hunt, Inc. v. Unidentified, Shipwrecked Vessel or Vessels 22 F.Supp.2d 521 (1998); 2000 A.M.C. 2113 59

The M.V. 'Louisa' Case: (Saint Vincent and the Grenadines v. Kingdom of Spain) International Tribunal for the Law of the Sea 28 May 2013 <http://www.itlos.org/fileadmin/itlos/documents/cases/case_no_18_merits/judgment/C18_Judgment_28_05_13-orig.pdf> 106

US v. Steinmetz 763 F.Supp.1293 (1991) 58

Webb v. Ireland (1988) Irish Law Reports Monthly 8: 565 9

TABLE OF STATUTES

AUSTRALIA
Protection of Movable Cultural Heritage Act 1986 — 79, 87
Historic Shipwrecks Act 1976 — 9, 46, 55, 57, 84

(WESTERN AUSTRALIA)
Maritime Archaeology Act 1973 — 5
Museum Act Amendment Act 1964. — 5

CHINA
Law on the Protection of Cultural Relics — 57

CYPRUS
Antiquities Law — 57

DENMARK
Act No. 203 of 31 May 1963 on Protection of Historic Wrecks — 5

MOROCCO
Dahir of 8 April 1981 — 46

NORWAY
Protection of Antiquities Act 1951 — 35

SPAIN
Law 60/1962 of 24 Dec. 1962 — 6

SWEDEN
Act Concerning Ancient Monuments and Finds 1988 — 57

SWITZERLAND
Loi fédérale sur le transfert international des biens culturels 2005 — 80

UNITED KINGDOM
Protection of Wrecks Act 1973 — 6, 34, 57, 74
Protection of Military Remains Act 1986 — 6, 34, 43
Dealing in Cultural Objects (Offences) Act 2003 — 79

USA
Abandoned Shipwreck Act — 57
National Marine Sanctuary Act — 46
Sunken Military Craft Act — 42, 46

TABLE OF INTERNATIONAL INSTRUMENTS

COUNCIL OF EUROPE

Recommendation 848 (1978) on the underwater cultural heritage	9
Recommendation 1486 (2000) on Maritime and Fluvial Heritage	11
European Convention on Human Rights	50, 86
European Convention on Protection of the Archaeological Heritage (Revised) 1992	11, 34, 57, 98, 148

ICOMOS

Charter for the Protection and Management of the Archaeological Heritage	135

INTERNATIONAL

Vienna Convention on the Law of Treaties 1969	27, 55
Protocol concerning Specially Protected Areas and Biological Diversity in the Mediterranean 1995	52
Geneva Convention and Statute on the International Regime of Maritime Ports (1923)	82

UNESCO

Convention on the Means of Prohibiting and Preventing the Illicit Import, Export and Transfer of Ownership of Cultural Property 1970	1, 31, 36, 78, 81, 105, 114, 158
Recommendation on International Principles Applicable to Archaeological Excavations 1956	10
Convention concerning the Protection of the World Cultural and Natural Heritage 1972	31, 112
Recommendation concerning the Preservation of Cultural Property Endangered by Public or Private Works 1968	51

UNIDROIT

Convention on Stolen or Illegally Exported Cultural Objects 1995	78, 81, 85

UNITED NATIONS

United Nations Convention on the Law of the Sea 1982	2, 12, 33, 47, 56, 62, 63, 67 *et seq.*, 72, 82, 105 *et seq.*

UNCLOS, see United Nations Convention on the Law of the Sea 1982
LOSC, see United Nations Convention on the Law of the Sea 1982

CONVENTION ON THE PROTECTION OF THE UNDERWATER CULTURAL HERITAGE 2001

Entry into force: 2 January 2009

The General Conference of the United Nations Educational, Scientific and Cultural Organization, meeting in Paris from 15 October to 3 November 2001, at its 31st session,

Acknowledging the importance of underwater cultural heritage as an integral part of the cultural heritage of humanity and a particularly important element in the history of peoples, nations, and their relations with each other concerning their common heritage,

Realizing the importance of protecting and preserving the underwater cultural heritage and that responsibility therefor rests with all States,

Noting growing public interest in and public appreciation of underwater cultural heritage,

Convinced of the importance of research, information and education to the protection and preservation of underwater cultural heritage,

Convinced of the public's right to enjoy the educational and recreational benefits of responsible non-intrusive access to *in situ* underwater cultural heritage, and of the value of public education to contribute to awareness, appreciation and protection of that heritage,

Aware of the fact that underwater cultural heritage is threatened by unauthorized activities directed at it, and of the need for stronger measures to prevent such activities,

Conscious of the need to respond appropriately to the possible negative impact on underwater cultural heritage of legitimate activities that may incidentally affect it,

Deeply concerned by the increasing commercial exploitation of underwater cultural heritage, and in particular by certain activities aimed at the sale, acquisition or barter of underwater cultural heritage,

Aware of the availability of advanced technology that enhances discovery of and access to underwater cultural heritage,

Believing that co-operation among States, international organisations, scientific institutions, professional organizations, archaeologists, divers, other interested parties and the public at large is essential for the protection of underwater cultural heritage,

Considering that survey, excavation and protection of underwater cultural heritage necessitate the availability and application of special scientific methods and the use of suitable techniques and equipment as well as a high degree of professional specialization, all of which indicate a need for uniform governing criteria,

Realizing the need to codify and progressively develop rules relating to the protection and preservation of underwater cultural heritage in conformity with international law and practice, including the UNESCO Convention on the Means of Prohibiting and Preventing the Illicit Import, Export and Transfer of Ownership of Cultural Property of 14 November 1970, the UNESCO Convention for the Protection of the World Cultural and Natural Heritage of 16 November 1972 and the United Nations Convention on the Law of the Sea of 10 December 1982,

Committed to improving the effectiveness of measures at international, regional and national levels for the preservation *in situ* or, if necessary for scientific or protective purposes, the careful recovery of underwater cultural heritage,

Having decided at its twenty-ninth session that this question should be made the subject of an international convention,

Adopts this second day of November 2001 this Convention.

Article 1 – Definitions

For the purposes of this Convention:

1. (a) "Underwater cultural heritage" means all traces of human existence having a cultural, historical or archaeological character which have been partially or totally under water, periodically or continuously, for at least 100 years such as:
    (i) sites, structures, buildings, artefacts and human remains, together with their archaeological and natural context;
    (ii) vessels, aircraft, other vehicles or any part thereof, their cargo or other contents, together with their archaeological and natural context; and
    (iii) objects of prehistoric character.

   (b) Pipelines and cables placed on the seabed shall not be considered as underwater cultural heritage.

   (c) Installations other than pipelines and cables, placed on the seabed and still in use, shall not be considered as underwater cultural heritage.

2. (a) "States Parties" means States which have consented to be bound by this Convention and for which this Convention is in force.

   (b) This Convention applies *mutatis mutandis* to those territories referred to in Article 26, paragraph 2(b), which become Parties to this Convention in accordance with the conditions set out in that paragraph, and to that extent "States Parties" refers to those territories.

3. "UNESCO" means the United Nations Educational, Scientific and Cultural Organization.

4. "Director-General" means the Director-General of UNESCO.

5. "Area" means the seabed and ocean floor and subsoil thereof, beyond the limits of national jurisdiction.

6. "Activities directed at underwater cultural heritage" means activities having underwater cultural heritage as their primary object and which may, directly or indirectly, physically disturb or otherwise damage underwater cultural heritage.

7. "Activities incidentally affecting underwater cultural heritage" means activities which, despite not having underwater cultural heritage as their primary object or one of their objects, may physically disturb or otherwise damage underwater cultural heritage.

8. "State vessels and aircraft" means warships, and other vessels or aircraft that were owned or operated by a State and used, at the time of sinking, only for government non-commercial purposes, that are identified as such and that meet the definition of underwater cultural heritage.

9. "Rules" means the Rules concerning activities directed at underwater cultural heritage, as referred to in Article 33 of this Convention.

Article 2 – Objectives and general principles

1. This Convention aims to ensure and strengthen the protection of underwater cultural heritage.

2. States Parties shall co-operate in the protection of underwater cultural heritage.

3. States Parties shall preserve underwater cultural heritage for the benefit of humanity in conformity with the provisions of this Convention.

4. States Parties shall, individually or jointly as appropriate, take all appropriate measures in conformity with this Convention and with international law that are necessary to protect underwater cultural heritage, using for this purpose the best practicable means at their disposal and in accordance with their capabilities.

5. The preservation *in situ* of underwater cultural heritage shall be considered as the first option before allowing or engaging in any activities directed at this heritage.

6. Recovered underwater cultural heritage shall be deposited, conserved and managed in a manner that ensures its long-term preservation.

7. Underwater cultural heritage shall not be commercially exploited.

8. Consistent with State practice and international law, including the United Nations Convention on the Law of the Sea, nothing in this Convention shall be interpreted as modifying the rules of international law and State practice pertaining to sovereign immunities, nor any State's rights

with respect to its State vessels and aircraft.

9. States Parties shall ensure that proper respect is given to all human remains located in maritime waters.

10. Responsible non-intrusive access to observe or document *in situ* underwater cultural heritage shall be encouraged to create public awareness, appreciation, and protection of the heritage except where such access is incompatible with its protection and management.

11. No act or activity undertaken on the basis of this Convention shall constitute grounds for claiming, contending or disputing any claim to national sovereignty or jurisdiction.

Article 3 – Relationship between this Convention and the United Nations Convention on the Law of the Sea

Nothing in this Convention shall prejudice the rights, jurisdiction and duties of States under international law, including the United Nations Convention on the Law of the Sea. This Convention shall be interpreted and applied in the context of and in a manner consistent with international law, including the United Nations Convention on the Law of the Sea.

Article 4 – Relationship to law of salvage and law of finds

Any activity relating to underwater cultural heritage to which this Convention applies shall not be subject to the law of salvage or law of finds, unless it:
(a) is authorized by the competent authorities, and
(b) is in full conformity with this Convention, and
(c) ensures that any recovery of the underwater cultural heritage achieves its maximum protection.

Article 5 – Activities incidentally affecting underwater cultural heritage

Each State Party shall use the best practicable means at its disposal to prevent or mitigate any adverse effects that might arise from activities under its jurisdiction incidentally affecting underwater cultural heritage.

Article 6 – Bilateral, regional or other multilateral agreements

1. States Parties are encouraged to enter into bilateral, regional or other multilateral agreements or develop existing agreements, for the preservation of underwater cultural heritage. All such agreements shall be in full conformity with the provisions of this Convention and shall not dilute its universal character. States may, in such agreements, adopt rules and regulations which would ensure better protection of underwater cultural heritage than those adopted in this Convention.

2. The Parties to such bilateral, regional or other multilateral agreements may invite States with a verifiable link, especially a cultural, historical or archaeological link, to the underwater cultural heritage concerned to join such agreements.

3. This Convention shall not alter the rights and obligations of States Parties regarding the protection of sunken vessels, arising from other bilateral, regional or other multilateral agreements concluded before its adoption, and, in particular, those that are in conformity with the purposes of this Convention.

Article 7 – Underwater cultural heritage in internal waters, archipelagic waters and territorial sea

1. States Parties, in the exercise of their sovereignty, have the exclusive right to regulate and authorize activities directed at underwater cultural heritage in their internal waters, archipelagic waters and territorial sea.

2. Without prejudice to other international agreements and rules of international law regarding the protection of underwater cultural heritage, States Parties shall require that the Rules be applied to activities directed at underwater cultural heritage in their internal waters, archipelagic waters and territorial sea.

3. Within their archipelagic waters and territorial sea, in the exercise of their sovereignty and in recognition of general practice among States, States Parties, with a view to co-operating on the best methods of protecting State vessels and aircraft, should inform the flag State Party to this Convention and, if applicable, other States with a verifiable link, especially a cultural, historical or archaeological link, with respect to the discovery of such identifiable State vessels and aircraft.

Article 8 – Underwater cultural heritage in the contiguous zone

Without prejudice to and in addition to Articles 9 and 10, and in accordance with Article 303, paragraph 2, of the United Nations Convention on the Law of the Sea, States Parties may regulate and authorize activities directed at underwater cultural heritage within their contiguous zone. In so doing, they shall require that the Rules be applied.

Article 9 – Reporting and notification in the exclusive economic zone and on the continental shelf

1. All States Parties have a responsibility to protect underwater cultural heritage in the exclusive economic zone and on the continental shelf in conformity with this Convention.

Accordingly:
(a) A State Party shall require that when its national, or a vessel flying its flag, discovers or intends to engage in activities directed at underwater cultural heritage located in its exclusive economic zone or on its continental shelf, the national or the master of the vessel shall report such discovery or activity to it;
(b) in the exclusive economic zone or on the continental shelf of another State Party:
  (i) States Parties shall require the national or the master of the vessel to report such discovery or activity to them and to that other State Party;
  (ii) alternatively, a State Party shall require the national or master of the vessel to report such discovery or activity to it and shall ensure the rapid and effective transmission of such reports to all other States Parties.

2. On depositing its instrument of ratification, acceptance, approval or accession, a State Party shall declare the manner in which reports will be transmitted under paragraph 1(b) of this Article.

3. A State Party shall notify the Director-General of discoveries or activities reported to it under paragraph 1 of this Article.

4. The Director-General shall promptly make available to all States Parties any information notified to him under paragraph 3 of this Article.

5. Any State Party may declare to the State Party in whose exclusive economic zone or on whose continental shelf the underwater cultural heritage is located its interest in being consulted on how to ensure the effective protection of that underwater cultural heritage. Such declaration shall be based on a verifiable link, especially a cultural, historical or archaeological link, to the underwater cultural heritage concerned.

Article 10 – Protection of underwater cultural heritage in the exclusive economic zone and on the continental shelf

1. No authorization shall be granted for an activity directed at underwater cultural heritage located in the exclusive economic zone or on the continental shelf except in conformity with the provisions of this Article.

2. A State Party in whose exclusive economic zone or on whose continental shelf underwater cultural heritage is located has the right to prohibit or authorize any activity directed at such heritage to prevent interference with its sovereign rights or jurisdiction as provided for by international law including the United Nations Convention on the Law of the Sea.

3. Where there is a discovery of underwater cultural heritage or it is intended that activity shall be directed at underwater cultural heritage in a State Party's exclusive economic zone or on its continental shelf, that State Party shall:
(a) consult all other States Parties which have declared an interest under Article 9, paragraph 5, on how best to protect the underwater cultural heritage;
(b) co-ordinate such consultations as "Co-ordinating State", unless it expressly declares that it does not wish to do so, in which case the States Parties which have declared an interest under Article 9, paragraph 5, shall appoint a Co-ordinating State.

4. Without prejudice to the duty of all States Parties to protect underwater cultural heritage by way of all practicable measures taken in accordance with international law to prevent immediate danger to the underwater cultural heritage, including looting, the Co-ordinating State may take all practicable measures, and/or issue any necessary authorizations in conformity with this Convention and, if necessary prior to consultations, to prevent any immediate danger to the underwater cultural heritage, whether arising from human activities or any other cause, including looting. In taking such measures assistance may be requested from other States Parties.

5. The Co-ordinating State:
(a) shall implement measures of protection which have been agreed by the consulting States, which include the Co-ordinating State, unless the consulting States, which include the Co-ordinating State, agree that another State Party shall implement those measures;

(b) shall issue all necessary authorizations for such agreed measures in conformity with the Rules, unless the consulting States, which include the Co-ordinating State, agree that another State Party shall issue those authorizations;
(c) may conduct any necessary preliminary research on the underwater cultural heritage and shall issue all necessary authorizations therefor, and shall promptly inform the Director-General of the results, who in turn will make such information promptly available to other States Parties.

6. In co-ordinating consultations, taking measures, conducting preliminary research and/or issuing authorizations pursuant to this Article, the Co-ordinating State shall act on behalf of the States Parties as a whole and not in its own interest. Any such action shall not in itself constitute a basis for the assertion of any preferential or jurisdictional rights not provided for in international law, including the United Nations Convention on the Law of the Sea.

7. Subject to the provisions of paragraphs 2 and 4 of this Article, no activity directed at State vessels and aircraft shall be conducted without the agreement of the flag State and the collaboration of the Co-ordinating State.

Article 11 – Reporting and notification in the Area
1. States Parties have a responsibility to protect underwater cultural heritage in the Area in conformity with this Convention and Article 149 of the United Nations Convention on the Law of the Sea. Accordingly when a national, or a vessel flying the flag of a State Party, discovers or intends to engage in activities directed at underwater cultural heritage located in the Area, that State Party shall require its national, or the master of the vessel, to report such discovery or activity to it.

2. States Parties shall notify the Director-General and the Secretary-General of the International Seabed Authority of such discoveries or activities reported to them.

3. The Director-General shall promptly make available to all States Parties any such information supplied by States Parties.

4. Any State Party may declare to the Director-General its interest in being consulted on how to ensure the effective protection of that underwater cultural heritage. Such declaration shall be based on a verifiable link to the underwater cultural heritage concerned, particular regard being paid to the preferential rights of States of cultural, historical or archaeological origin.

Article 12 – Protection of underwater cultural heritage in the Area
1. No authorization shall be granted for any activity directed at underwater cultural heritage located in the Area except in conformity with the provisions of this Article.

2. The Director-General shall invite all States Parties which have declared an interest under Article 11, paragraph 4, to consult on how best to protect the underwater cultural heritage, and to appoint a State Party to co-ordinate such consultations as the "Co-ordinating State". The Director-General shall also invite the International Seabed Authority to participate in such consultations.

3. All States Parties may take all practicable measures in conformity with this Convention, if necessary prior to consultations, to prevent any immediate danger to the underwater cultural heritage, whether arising from human activity or any other cause including looting.

4. The Co-ordinating State shall:
(a) implement measures of protection which have been agreed by the consulting States, which include the Co-ordinating State, unless the consulting States, which include the Co-ordinating State, agree that another State Party shall implement those measures; and
(b) issue all necessary authorizations for such agreed measures, in conformity with this Convention, unless the consulting States, which include the Co-ordinating State, agree that another State Party shall issue those authorizations.

5. The Co-ordinating State may conduct any necessary preliminary research on the underwater cultural heritage and shall issue all necessary authorizations therefor, and shall promptly inform the Director-General of the results, who in turn shall make such information available to other States Parties.

6. In co-ordinating consultations, taking measures, conducting preliminary research, and/or issuing authorizations pursuant to this Article, the Co-ordinating State shall act for the benefit of humanity as a whole, on behalf of all States Parties. Particular regard shall be paid to the preferential rights of States of cultural, historical or archaeological origin in respect of the underwater cultural heritage concerned.

7. No State Party shall undertake or authorize activities directed at State vessels and aircraft in the Area without the consent of the flag State.

Article 13 – Sovereign immunity
Warships and other government ships or military aircraft with sovereign immunity, operated for non-commercial purposes, undertaking their normal mode of operations, and not engaged in activities directed at underwater cultural heritage, shall not be obliged to report discoveries of underwater cultural heritage under Articles 9, 10, 11 and 12 of this Convention. However States Parties shall ensure, by the adoption of appropriate measures not impairing the operations or operational capabilities of their warships or other government ships or military aircraft with sovereign immunity operated for non-commercial purposes, that they comply, as far as is reasonable and practicable, with Articles 9, 10, 11 and 12 of this Convention.

Article 14 – Control of entry into the territory, dealing and possession
States Parties shall take measures to prevent the entry into their territory, the dealing in, or the possession of, underwater cultural heritage illicitly exported and/or recovered, where recovery was contrary to this Convention.

Article 15 – Non-use of areas under the jurisdiction of States Parties
States Parties shall take measures to prohibit the use of their territory, including their maritime ports, as well as artificial islands, installations and structures under their exclusive jurisdiction or control, in support of any activity directed at underwater cultural heritage which is not in conformity with this Convention.

Article 16 – Measures relating to nationals and vessels
States Parties shall take all practicable measures to ensure that their nationals and vessels flying their flag do not engage in any activity directed at underwater cultural heritage in a manner not in conformity with this Convention.

Article 17 – Sanctions
1. Each State Party shall impose sanctions for violations of measures it has taken to implement this Convention.

2. Sanctions applicable in respect of violations shall be adequate in severity to be effective in securing compliance with this Convention and to discourage violations wherever they occur and shall deprive offenders of the benefit deriving from their illegal activities.

3. States Parties shall co-operate to ensure enforcement of sanctions imposed under this Article.

Article 18 – Seizure and disposition of underwater cultural heritage
1. Each State Party shall take measures providing for the seizure of underwater cultural heritage in its territory that has been recovered in a manner not in conformity with this Convention.

2. Each State Party shall record, protect and take all reasonable measures to stabilize underwater cultural heritage seized under this Convention.

3. Each State Party shall notify the Director-General and any other State with a verifiable link, especially a cultural, historical or archaeological link, to the underwater cultural heritage concerned of any seizure of underwater cultural heritage that it has made under this Convention.

4. A State Party which has seized underwater cultural heritage shall ensure that its disposition be for the public benefit, taking into account the need for conservation and research; the need for reassembly of a dispersed collection; the need for public access, exhibition and education; and the interests of any State with a verifiable link, especially a cultural, historical or archaeological link, in respect of the underwater cultural heritage concerned.

Article 19 – Co-operation and information-sharing
1. States Parties shall co-operate and assist each other in the protection and management of underwater cultural heritage under this Convention, including, where practicable, collaborating in the investigation, excavation, documentation, conservation, study and presentation of such heritage.

2. To the extent compatible with the purposes of this Convention, each State Party undertakes to share information with other States Parties concerning underwater cultural heritage, including discovery of heritage, location of heritage, heritage excavated or recovered contrary to this Convention or otherwise in violation of international law, pertinent scientific methodology and technology, and legal developments relating to such heritage.

3. Information shared between States Parties, or between UNESCO and States Parties, regarding the discovery or location of underwater cultural heritage shall, to the extent compatible with their national legislation, be kept confidential and reserved to competent authorities of States Parties as long as the disclosure of such information might endanger or otherwise put at risk the preservation of such underwater cultural heritage.

4. Each State Party shall take all practicable measures to disseminate information, including where feasible through appropriate international databases, about underwater cultural heritage excavated or recovered contrary to this Convention or otherwise in violation of international law.

Article 20 – Public awareness
Each State Party shall take all practicable measures to raise public awareness regarding the value and significance of underwater cultural heritage and the importance of protecting it under this Convention.

Article 21 – Training in underwater archaeology
States Parties shall co-operate in the provision of training in underwater archaeology, in techniques for the conservation of underwater cultural heritage and, on agreed terms, in the transfer of technology relating to underwater cultural heritage.

Article 22 – Competent authorities
1. In order to ensure the proper implementation of this Convention, States Parties shall establish competent authorities or reinforce the existing ones where appropriate, with the aim of providing for the establishment, maintenance and updating of an inventory of underwater cultural heritage, the effective protection, conservation, presentation and management of underwater cultural heritage, as well as research and education.

2. States Parties shall communicate to the Director-General the names and addresses of their competent authorities relating to underwater cultural heritage.

Article 23 – Meetings of States Parties
1. The Director-General shall convene a Meeting of States Parties within one year of the entry into force of this Convention and thereafter at least once every two years. At the request of a majority of States Parties, the Director-General shall convene an Extraordinary Meeting of States Parties.

2. The Meeting of States Parties shall decide on its functions and responsibilities.

3. The Meeting of States Parties shall adopt its own Rules of Procedure.

4. The Meeting of States Parties may establish a Scientific and Technical Advisory Body composed of experts nominated by the States Parties with due regard to the principle of equitable geographical distribution and the desirability of a gender balance.

5. The Scientific and Technical Advisory Body shall appropriately assist the Meeting of States Parties in questions of a scientific or technical nature regarding the implementation of the Rules.

Article 24 – Secretariat for this Convention
1. The Director-General shall be responsible for the functions of the Secretariat for this Convention.

2. The duties of the Secretariat shall include:
(a) organizing Meetings of States Parties as provided for in Article 23, paragraph 1; and
(b) assisting States Parties in implementing the decisions of the Meetings of States Parties.

Article 25 – Peaceful settlement of disputes
1. Any dispute between two or more States Parties concerning the interpretation or application of this Convention shall be subject to negotiations in good faith or other peaceful means of settlement of their own choice.

2. If those negotiations do not settle the dispute within a reasonable period of time, it may be submitted to UNESCO for mediation, by agreement between the States Parties concerned.

3. If mediation is not undertaken or if there is no settlement by mediation, the provisions relating to the settlement of disputes set out in Part XV of the United Nations Convention on the Law of the Sea apply *mutatis mutandis* to any dispute between States Parties to this Convention concerning the interpretation or application of this Convention, whether or not they are also Parties to the United Nations Convention on the Law of the Sea.

4. Any procedure chosen by a State Party to this Convention and to the United Nations Convention on the Law of the Sea pursuant to Article 287 of the latter shall apply to the settlement of disputes under this Article, unless that State Party, when ratifying, accepting, approving or acceding to this Convention, or at any time thereafter, chooses another procedure pursuant to Article 287 for the purpose of the settlement of disputes arising out of this Convention.

5. A State Party to this Convention which is not a Party to the United Nations Convention on the Law of the Sea, when ratifying, accepting, approving or acceding to this Convention or at any time thereafter shall be free to choose, by means of a written declaration, one or more of the means set out in Article 287, paragraph 1, of the United Nations Convention on the Law of the Sea for the purpose of settlement of disputes under this Article. Article 287 shall apply to such a declaration, as well as to any dispute to which such State is party, which is not covered by a declaration in force. For the purpose of conciliation and arbitration, in accordance with Annexes V and VII of the United Nations Convention on the Law of the Sea, such State shall be entitled to nominate conciliators and arbitrators to be included in the lists referred to in Annex V, Article 2, and Annex VII, Article 2, for the settlement of disputes arising out of this Convention.

Article 26 – Ratification, acceptance, approval or accession
1. This Convention shall be subject to ratification, acceptance or approval by Member States of UNESCO.

2. This Convention shall be subject to accession:
(a) by States that are not members of UNESCO but are members of the United Nations or of a specialized agency within the United Nations system or of the International Atomic Energy Agency, as well as by States Parties to the Statute of the International Court of Justice and any other State invited to accede to this Convention by the General Conference of UNESCO;
(b) by territories which enjoy full internal self-government, recognized as such by the United Nations, but have not attained full independence in accordance with General Assembly resolution 1514 (XV) and which have competence over the matters governed by this Convention, including the competence to enter into treaties in respect of those matters.

3. The instruments of ratification, acceptance, approval or accession shall be deposited with the Director-General.

Article 27 – Entry into force
This Convention shall enter into force three months after the date of the deposit of the twentieth instrument referred to in Article 26, but solely with respect to the twenty States or territories that have so deposited their instruments. It shall enter into force for each other State or territory three months after the date on which that State or territory has deposited its instrument.

Article 28 – Declaration as to inland waters
When ratifying, accepting, approving or acceding to this Convention or at any time thereafter, any State or territory may declare that the Rules shall apply to inland waters not of a maritime character.

Article 29 – Limitations to geographical scope
At the time of ratifying, accepting, approving or acceding to this Convention, a State or territory may make a declaration to the depositary that this Convention shall not be applicable to specific parts of its territory, internal waters, archipelagic waters or territorial sea, and shall identify therein the reasons for such declaration. Such State shall, to the extent practicable and as quickly as possible, promote conditions under which this Convention will apply to the areas specified in its declaration, and to that end shall also withdraw its declaration in whole or in part as soon as that has been achieved.

Article 30 – Reservations
With the exception of Article 29, no reservations may be made to this Convention.

Article 31 – Amendments
1. A State Party may, by written communication addressed to the Director-General, propose amendments to this Convention. The Director-General shall circulate such communication to all States Parties. If, within six months from the date of the circulation of the communication, not less than one half of the States Parties reply favourably to the request, the Director-General shall present such proposal to the next Meeting of States Parties for discussion and possible adoption.

2. Amendments shall be adopted by a two-thirds majority of States Parties present and voting.

3. Once adopted, amendments to this Convention shall be subject to ratification, acceptance, approval or accession by the States Parties.

4. Amendments shall enter into force, but solely with respect to the States Parties that have ratified, accepted, approved or acceded to them, three months after the deposit of the instruments referred to in paragraph 3 of this Article by two-thirds of the States Parties. Thereafter, for each State or territory that ratifies, accepts, approves or accedes to it, the amendment shall enter into force three months after the date of deposit by that Party of its instrument of ratification, acceptance, approval or accession.

5. A State or territory which becomes a Party to this Convention after the entry into force of amendments in conformity with paragraph 4 of this Article shall, failing an expression of different intention by that State or territory, be considered:
(a) as a Party to this Convention as so amended; and
(b) as a Party to the unamended Convention in relation to any State Party not bound by the amendment.

Article 32 – Denunciation
1. A State Party may, by written notification addressed to the Director-General, denounce this Convention.

2. The denunciation shall take effect twelve months after the date of receipt of the notification, unless the notification specifies a later date.

3. The denunciation shall not in any way affect the duty of any State Party to fulfil any obligation embodied in this Convention to which it would be subject under international law independently of this Convention.

Article 33 – The Rules
The Rules annexed to this Convention form an integral part of it and, unless expressly provided otherwise, a reference to this Convention includes a reference to the Rules.

Article 34 – Registration with the United Nations
In conformity with Article 102 of the Charter of the United Nations, this Convention shall be registered with the Secretariat of the United Nations at the request of the Director-General.

Article 35 – Authoritative texts
This Convention has been drawn up in Arabic, Chinese, English, French, Russian and Spanish, the six texts being equally authoritative.

Done in Paris this 6th day of November 2001 in two authentic copies bearing the signature of the President of the thirty-first session of the General Conference and of the Director-General of the United Nations Educational, Scientific and Cultural Organization, which shall be deposited in the archives of the United Nations Educational, Scientific and Cultural Organization and certified true copies of which shall be delivered to all the States and territories referred to in Article 26 as well as to the United Nations.

The foregoing is the authentic text of the Convention duly adopted by the General Conference of the United Nations Educational, Scientific and Cultural Organization during its thirty-first session, which was held in Paris and declared closed the third day of November 2001.

IN WITNESS WHEREOF we have appended our signatures this sixth day of November 2001.

The President of the General Conference   The Director-General

ANNEX
RULES CONCERNING ACTIVITIES DIRECTED AT UNDERWATER CULTURAL HERITAGE

I. General principles

Rule 1. The protection of underwater cultural heritage through *in situ* preservation shall be considered as the first option. Accordingly, activities directed at underwater cultural heritage shall be authorized in a manner consistent with the protection of that heritage, and subject to that requirement may be authorized for the purpose of making a significant contribution to protection or knowledge or enhancement of underwater cultural heritage.

Rule 2. The commercial exploitation of underwater cultural heritage for trade or speculation or its irretrievable dispersal is fundamentally incompatible with the protection and proper management of underwater cultural heritage. Underwater cultural heritage shall not be traded, sold, bought or bartered as commercial goods.

This Rule cannot be interpreted as preventing:
(a) the provision of professional archaeological services or necessary services incidental thereto whose nature and purpose are in full conformity with this Convention and are subject to the authorization of the competent authorities;
(b) the deposition of underwater cultural heritage, recovered in the course of a research project in conformity with this Convention, provided such deposition does not prejudice the scientific or cultural interest or integrity of the recovered material or result in its irretrievable dispersal; is in accordance with the provisions of Rules 33 and 34; and is subject to the authorization of the competent authorities.

Rule 3. Activities directed at underwater cultural heritage shall not adversely affect the underwater cultural heritage more than is necessary for the objectives of the project.

Rule 4. Activities directed at underwater cultural heritage must use non-destructive techniques and survey methods in preference to recovery of objects. If excavation or recovery is necessary for the purpose of scientific studies or for the ultimate protection of the underwater cultural heritage, the methods and techniques used must be as non-destructive as possible and contribute to the preservation of the remains.

Rule 5. Activities directed at underwater cultural heritage shall avoid the unnecessary disturbance of human remains or venerated sites.

Rule 6. Activities directed at underwater cultural heritage shall be strictly regulated to ensure proper recording of cultural, historical and archaeological information.

Rule 7. Public access to *in situ* underwater cultural heritage shall be promoted, except where such access is incompatible with protection and management.

Rule 8. International co-operation in the conduct of activities directed at underwater cultural heritage shall be encouraged in order to further the effective exchange or use of archaeologists and other relevant professionals.

II. Project design

Rule 9. Prior to any activity directed at underwater cultural heritage, a project design for the activity shall be developed and submitted to the competent authorities for authorization and appropriate peer review.

Rule 10. The project design shall include:
(a) an evaluation of previous or preliminary studies;
(b) the project statement and objectives;
(c) the methodology to be used and the techniques to be employed;
(d) the anticipated funding;
(e) an expected timetable for completion of the project;
(f) the composition of the team and the qualifications, responsibilities and experience of each team member;
(g) plans for post-fieldwork analysis and other activities;

(h) a conservation programme for artefacts and the site in close co-operation with the competent authorities;
(i) a site management and maintenance policy for the whole duration of the project;
(j) a documentation programme;
(k) a safety policy;
(l) an environmental policy;
(m) arrangements for collaboration with museums and other institutions, in particular scientific institutions;
(n) report preparation;
(o) deposition of archives, including underwater cultural heritage removed; and
(p) a programme for publication.

Rule 11. Activities directed at underwater cultural heritage shall be carried out in accordance with the project design approved by the competent authorities.

Rule 12. Where unexpected discoveries are made or circumstances change, the project design shall be reviewed and amended with the approval of the competent authorities.

Rule 13. In cases of urgency or chance discoveries, activities directed at the underwater cultural heritage, including conservation measures or activities for a period of short duration, in particular site stabilization, may be authorized in the absence of a project design in order to protect the underwater cultural heritage.

III. Preliminary work

Rule 14. The preliminary work referred to in Rule 10(a) shall include an assessment that evaluates the significance and vulnerability of the underwater cultural heritage and the surrounding natural environment to damage by the proposed project, and the potential to obtain data that would meet the project objectives.

Rule 15. The assessment shall also include background studies of available historical and archaeological evidence, the archaeological and environmental characteristics of the site, and the consequences of any potential intrusion for the long-term stability of the underwater cultural heritage affected by the activities.

IV. Project objective, methodology and techniques

Rule 16. The methodology shall comply with the project objectives, and the techniques employed shall be as non-intrusive as possible.

V. Funding

Rule 17. Except in cases of emergency to protect underwater cultural heritage, an adequate funding base shall be assured in advance of any activity, sufficient to complete all stages of the project design, including conservation, documentation and curation of recovered artefacts, and report preparation and dissemination.

Rule 18. The project design shall demonstrate an ability, such as by securing a bond, to fund the project through to completion.

Rule 19. The project design shall include a contingency plan that will ensure conservation of underwater cultural heritage and supporting documentation in the event of any interruption of anticipated funding.

VI. Project duration – timetable

Rule 20. An adequate timetable shall be developed to assure in advance of any activity directed at underwater cultural heritage the completion of all stages of the project design, including conservation, documentation and curation of recovered underwater cultural heritage, as well as report preparation and dissemination.

Rule 21. The project design shall include a contingency plan that will ensure conservation of underwater cultural heritage and supporting documentation in the event of any interruption or termination of the project.

VII. Competence and qualifications

Rule 22. Activities directed at underwater cultural heritage shall only be undertaken under the direction and control of, and in the regular presence of, a qualified underwater archaeologist with scientific competence appropriate to the project.

Rule 23. All persons on the project team shall be qualified and have demonstrated competence appropriate to their roles in the project.

VIII. Conservation and site management

Rule 24. The conservation programme shall provide for the treatment of the archaeological remains during the activities directed at underwater cultural heritage, during transit and in the long term. Conservation shall be carried out in accordance with current professional standards.

Rule 25. The site management programme shall provide for the protection and management *in situ* of underwater cultural heritage, in the course of and upon termination of fieldwork. The programme shall include public information, reasonable provision for site stabilization, monitoring, and protection against interference.

IX. Documentation

Rule 26. The documentation programme shall set out thorough documentation including a progress report of activities directed at underwater cultural heritage, in accordance with current professional standards of archaeological documentation.

Rule 27. Documentation shall include, at a minimum, a comprehensive record of the site, including the provenance of underwater cultural heritage moved or removed in the course of the activities directed at underwater cultural heritage, field notes, plans, drawings, sections, and photographs or recording in other media.

X. Safety

Rule 28. A safety policy shall be prepared that is adequate to ensure the safety and health of the project team and third parties and that is in conformity with any applicable statutory and professional requirements.

XI. Environment

Rule 29. An environmental policy shall be prepared that is adequate to ensure that the seabed and marine life are not unduly disturbed.

XII. Reporting

Rule 30. Interim and final reports shall be made available according to the timetable set out in the project design, and deposited in relevant public records.

Rule 31. Reports shall include:
(a) an account of the objectives;
(b) an account of the methods and techniques employed;
(c) an account of the results achieved;
(d) basic graphic and photographic documentation on all phases of the activity;
(e) recommendations concerning conservation and curation of the site and of any underwater cultural heritage removed; and
(f) recommendations for future activities.

XIII. Curation of project archives

Rule 32. Arrangements for curation of the project archives shall be agreed to before any activity commences, and shall be set out in the project design.

Rule 33. The project archives, including any underwater cultural heritage removed and a copy of all supporting documentation shall, as far as possible, be kept together and intact as a collection in a manner that is available for professional and public access as well as for the curation of the archives. This should be done as rapidly as possible and in any case not later than ten years from the completion of the project, in so far as may be compatible with conservation of the underwater cultural heritage.

Rule 34. The project archives shall be managed according to international professional standards, and subject to the authorization of the competent authorities.

XIV. Dissemination

Rule 35. Projects shall provide for public education and popular presentation of the project results where appropriate.

Rule 36. A final synthesis of a project shall be:
(a) made public as soon as possible, having regard to the complexity of the project and the confidential or sensitive nature of the information; and
(b) deposited in relevant public records.

OPERATIONAL GUIDELINES FOR THE CONVENTION ON THE PROTECTION OF THE UNDERWATER CULTURAL HERITAGE

CHAPTER I. INTRODUCTION
A. THE CONVENTION

1. Context and Content of the Convention

1) The Convention on the Protection of the Underwater Cultural Heritage (hereinafter "the Convention") was elaborated by the UNESCO Member States as a response to the growing damage done by human activities endangering submerged archaeological sites, including the damage that might arise from activities under their jurisdiction incidentally affecting underwater cultural heritage. These are for instance dredging, pipeline construction, mineral extraction, trawling and port works. The Convention also responds to the deep concerns regarding the increasing commercial exploitation of underwater cultural heritage, and in particular by certain activities aimed at the sale, acquisition or barter of underwater cultural heritage.

2) The Convention intends to enable States to better protect underwater cultural heritage, by setting high protection standards and by facilitating State cooperation. The protection standards of the Convention are comparable to that granted by other UNESCO Conventions or national legislation on cultural heritage on land. Nevertheless, they are specifically tailored to the treatment of traces of human existence found under water, having a cultural, historical or archaeological character and respect their peculiarities regarding, among others, their fragility, accessibility and underwater environment.

3) In the long term the Convention is intended to achieve the appropriate legal protection of underwater archaeological sites wherever they are located. It should enable States Parties to collaborate and adopt a common approach to heritage preservation and ethical scientific management of submerged sites. Its goal is to harmonize the protection of submerged heritage with that of heritage on land and provide archaeologists, State authorities and site management institutions with norms on how to treat it.

4) The Convention contains minimum requirements. Each State Party, if it so wishes, may choose to develop even higher standards of protection, for example by also protecting on a national level remains submerged less than 100 years. Among others, the Convention:

- sets out basic principles for protecting underwater cultural heritage;
- contains provisions for an international cooperation scheme; and
- provides practical Rules on how to intervene on and research underwater cultural heritage sites.

5) The Convention does not regulate the ownership of underwater cultural heritage nor does it prejudice the rights, jurisdiction or

Article 3 of the Convention		duties of States Parties under international law, including the United Nations Convention on the Law of the Sea (hereinafter "UNCLOS"). When a doubt arises with regard to the interpretation and the application of the Convention, the latter shall be interpreted and applied in the context of and in a manner consistent with international law, including UNCLOS.

2. The Scope of Application of the Convention

	6)	The Convention applies, as regulated in its text and with the limitations contained therein, to the entire jurisdiction of its States Parties, unless a reservation is made under its Article 29. This applies to internal waters, archipelagic waters, the territorial seas, the contiguous zones, the exclusive economic zones (hereinafter 'EEZ') and the continental shelves. It also applies to the Area (the seabed and ocean floor and subsoil thereof, beyond the limits of national jurisdiction). The Convention protects as well heritage that has been or is only periodically submerged by water, partially or totally for at least 100 years, as for instance, wrecks or remains of human dwellings located on land, but periodically inundated by the tides.
Article 33 of the Convention **Article 28 of the Convention**	7)	The Rules concerning activities directed at underwater cultural heritage, contained in the Annex of the Convention (hereinafter "the Rules"), are an integral part of the Convention. They apply automatically on entry into force of the Convention for a State Party to maritime waters as provided in the Convention. Any State Party or territory may declare at any time that the Rules shall apply to its inland waters not of a maritime character.
Article 29 of the Convention	8)	At the time of expressing its consent to be bound by the Convention, a State or territory may make a declaration to the Director-General of UNESCO that the Convention shall not be applicable to specific parts of its territory, internal waters, archipelagic waters or territorial sea, and shall identify therein the reasons for such declaration. Such State shall, to the extent practicable and as quickly as possible, promote conditions under which the Convention will apply to the areas specified in its declaration, and to that end shall also withdraw its declaration in whole or in part as soon as that has been achieved.

B. STATES PARTIES TO THE CONVENTION

1. General Remarks

	9)	States are encouraged to become party to the Convention by ratifying, accepting, approving (legal acts open to Member States of UNESCO) or acceding to (legal act open to States not members of UNESCO and territories as defined by Article 26.2 (b)) of the Convention. A list of States Parties to the Convention as well as of declarations and reservations made is available on the UNESCO website www.unesco.org/en/underwater-cultural-heritage.
	10)	While fully respecting the sovereignty or jurisdiction of the States or territories where the underwater cultural heritage is situated, States Parties to the Convention recognize the collective interest of the international community to cooperate in the protection of this heritage. States Parties to the Convention, have, among others the responsibility to:
		i. individually or jointly, take all appropriate measures in conformity with the Convention and with international law that are necessary to protect underwater cultural heritage, using for this purpose the best practicable means at their

Article 2.4 of the Convention		disposal, in particular those foreseen in the Rules, and in accordance with their capabilities;
Article 2.2 of the Convention	ii.	cooperate in the protection of underwater cultural heritage;
Article 2.7 and 16 of the Convention	iii.	prevent intrusive activities directed at underwater cultural heritage aiming at commercial exploitation and avoid commercial exploitation of underwater cultural heritage.
	11)	States Parties to the Convention are encouraged to ensure the participation of a wide variety of professionals, site managers, local and regional governments, local communities, underwater archaeologists, conservation specialists, non-governmental organizations ('NGOs') and the public at large in the protection of the underwater cultural heritage and the implementation of the Convention.
Article 22.1 of the Convention	12)	States Parties are encouraged to bring together their underwater cultural heritage experts at regular intervals to discuss the proper implementation of the Convention.

2. Competent Authorities

Article 22.1 of the Convention	13)	States Parties shall establish competent authorities or reinforce the existing ones where appropriate, with the aim of providing for the establishment, maintenance and updating of an inventory of underwater cultural heritage, the effective protection, conservation, presentation and management of underwater cultural heritage, as well as research and education to ensure the proper implementation of the Convention.
Article 22.2 of the Convention	14)	States Parties shall communicate to the Director-General the names and addresses of their competent authorities relating to underwater cultural heritage. They should immediately inform him/her about any change in the details communicated.
	15)	The Director-General shall make available to all States Parties an updated list with the name and addresses of the competent authorities of all the States Parties to the Convention, through the website www.unesco.org/en/underwater-cultural-heritage.
Articles 8-13 of the Convention	16)	All reports, notifications or information to be sent to States Parties, as provided in the Convention, shall be addressed to the competent national authorities through diplomatic channels.

C. THE MEETING OF STATES PARTIES

Article 23 of the Convention	17)	The Meeting of States Parties to the Convention is its main organ. It is convened in ordinary session by the Director-General at least once every two years. At the request of a majority of States Parties, the Director- General convenes an extraordinary session. The agenda for an extraordinary session includes only those questions for which the session has been convened.
	18)	The functions and responsibilities of the Meeting and the management of its session are regulated by the Convention complemented by its Rules of Procedure, which are available in electronic format at the website: www.unesco.org/en/underwater-cultural-heritage, or in hard copy through the Secretariat.

D. SUBSIDIARY BODIES OF THE MEETING OF STATES PARTIES

1. The Scientific and Technical Advisory Body

	19)	The first Meeting of States Parties to the Convention established a Scientific and Technical Advisory Body to the Meeting of States Parties to the Convention (hereinafter "the Advisory Body"), in

Article 23.4 of the Convention		accordance with Article 23.4 of the Convention. Its functions and responsibilities are regulated by its Statutes available in electronic format at the website: www.unesco.org/en/underwater-cultural-heritage, or in paper version through the Secretariat.

2. Other Subsidiary Bodies

Rule 4 of the Rules of Procedure of the Meeting of States Parties	20)	Further subsidiary bodies may be established by the Meeting of States Parties as deemed necessary. They will be composed of States Parties. Their composition and their terms of reference, including their mandate and duration of office, will be defined at the time of their establishment.

E. THE SECRETARIAT

Article 24 of the Convention	21)	The Secretariat for the Convention is ensured by UNESCO. It organizes the sessions of the Meeting of States Parties and its Advisory Body and assists States Parties in the implementation of the decisions taken. The working languages of the Secretariat are English and French.

F. THE PRESENT OPERATIONAL GUIDELINES

22) The present Operational Guidelines can neither be understood as a subsequent agreement nor as rewriting, amending or interpreting the Convention. They merely aim to facilitate its implementation by giving practical guidance. In case of doubt, the text of the Convention prevails as interpreted according to the general rules of interpretation codified in the Vienna Convention of the Law of Treaties of 1969.

23) The Operational Guidelines may be revised by the Meeting of States Parties to the Convention whenever deemed necessary.

24) The key users addressed by the present Operational Guidelines are:

	ii.	the Advisory Body;
Articles 26 and 29 of the Convention	iii.	any subsidiary body that the Conference of the States Parties might create;
	iv.	UNESCO and the Secretariat to the Convention;
	v.	the International Seabed Authority;
	vi.	concerned intergovernmental organisations ('IGOs') and/or their specialised agencies or organs;
	vii.	concerned NGOs, in particular those accredited to work with and be consulted by the Advisory Body; and
Article 12.2 of the Convention	viii.	site managers, archaeologists, interested parties and partners in the protection of underwater cultural heritage.

25) Irrespective of its legal nature or denomination, any entity dedicated to or supporting the commercial exploitation of the underwater cultural heritage shall not be considered a user addressed by the present Operational Guidelines.

CHAPTER II. STATE COOPERATION

A. NOTIFICATIONS

Article 9.3 and 11.2 of the Convention	26)	State Parties notify the Director-General of UNESCO as promptly as possible through diplomatic channels of a discovery of underwater cultural heritage or an activity directed at it. When the concerned underwater cultural heritage is located in the Area, they notify in addition, the Secretary-General of the International Seabed Authority. In making its notification a State shall use the forms attached to the present Guidelines. It shall use:

a) Form 1 for notifying a discovery; and
b) Form 2 for notifying an activity.

B. DECLARATIONS OF INTEREST

27) A State Party wishing to declare its interest in being consulted on how to ensure the protection of a specific underwater cultural heritage shall send its declaration through diplomatic channels and using Form 3 attached to the present Guidelines:

Article 9.5 of the Convention
a) to the State Party in which's EEZ or on which's continental shelf the concerned heritage is located;

Article 11.4 of the Convention
b) to the Director-General of UNESCO if the heritage is located in the Area.

28) In declaring its interest to be consulted, a State Party should inform on its link to the underwater cultural heritage concerned by accompanying its declaration by:
   a.) the results of scientific expertises;
   b.) historic documentation; or
   c.) any other adequate documentation.

CHAPTER III. OPERATIONAL PROTECTION
A. THE PROTECTION OF UNDERWATER CULTURAL HERITAGE

Article 19.1 of the 2001 Convention
29) States Parties cooperate and assist each other in the protection and management of underwater cultural heritage, including, where practicable, collaborating in the investigation, excavation, documentation, conservation, study and presentation of such heritage. Such protection includes all necessary measures to avoid the commercial exploitation of underwater cultural heritage through trade, speculation or even barter. The underwater cultural heritage cannot be treated as commercial goods.

30) States Parties should, in particular, endeavour to:
   a.) share information about envisaged, on-going and completed projects;
   b.) make available expertise and expert advice;
   c.) facilitate the setting up of, and participation in, capacity-building programmes, the creation of specialized museums, the implementation of educational programmes (at an undergraduate, graduate and postgraduate level) and the exchange of exhibitions; and
   d.) put in place mechanisms and measures facilitating and enhancing the sharing of expertise and best practices.

B. THE RULES

Article 33 of the Convention
31) The Rules concerning activities directed at underwater cultural heritage are an integral part of the Convention. They set standards for all activities targeting traces of human existence in the sense of Article 1.1 of the Convention.

C. UNDERTAKING ACTIVITIES

Rule 22 and 23 of the Rules
32) Activities directed at underwater cultural heritage must only be undertaken under the direction and control of, and in the regular presence of, a qualified underwater archaeologist with scientific competence appropriate to the project.

33) All persons on the project team must be qualified in their respective specialisation and have demonstrated competence appropriate to their role(s) in the project.

D. RESEARCH

34) An appropriate investigation is a prerequisite for any decision concerning desired interventions and the establishment of a site protection plan.

35) States Parties are encouraged to employ a variety of archaeological sciences for investigation purposes, as for instance archaeology, namely underwater, nautical and maritime archaeology, archaeo-botany, archaeo-zoology, chemistry, cultural anthropology, dendrochronology, geology, history, historical documentation, physical and information sciences and x- raying, as appropriate, for the gathering of archaeological data.

36) They should consult appropriately qualified experts in the concerned fields.

E. IN SITU PRESERVATION AND EXCAVATION

Article 2.5 of the Convention and Rule 1 of the Rules

37) The preservation of underwater cultural heritage in situ shall be considered as the first option before allowing or engaging in any activities directed at it. Activities should be authorized in a manner consistent with protection, and for the purpose of making a significant contribution to protection, knowledge or enhancement.

38) Before deciding on preservation measures or activities, an assessment should be made of:
   a.) the significance of the concerned site;
   b.) the significance of the expected result of an intervention;
   c.) the means available; and
   d.) the entirety of the heritage known in the region.

Rule 4 of the Rules

39) Appropriate consideration needs to be given to the importance of inventories of sites.

40) Activities directed at underwater cultural heritage must use non-destructive techniques and survey methods in preference over the recovery of objects. If excavation or recovery is necessary for the purpose of scientific studies or for the ultimate protection of the underwater cultural heritage, the methods and techniques used must be as non-destructive as possible and contribute to the preservation of the remains.

41) Equally, any activity directed at underwater cultural heritage must balance the environmental impact or damage to be created, if any.

F. DOCUMENTATION AND PREPARATION OF INVENTORIES

42) Archaeological sites are fragile and sensitive to intrusion. It is important that information contained within the site is carefully recorded.

43) It is recommended that States prepare inventories of their underwater cultural heritage. They should do so in due consideration of the desirability of common standards for all national inventories of States Parties and their inter-changeability to facilitate research.

44) To inventory their underwater cultural heritage, States Parties are encouraged to require all national authorities, in particular coast guards, the navy, dredging services, research services and fishery monitoring services, to cooperate with and forward acquired information to the national competent authorities in the sense of Article 22.2. States Parties may also request assistance from any international or national specialized body, as appropriate.

G. PRESERVATION AND CONSERVATION

45) Site supervision and the physical protection of sites are recommended, where needed, to dissuade intrusion and avoid the damaging of submerged archaeological sites, including looting. States Parties should establish site management plans in conformity with Rule 25 of the Rules and encourage all national authorities undertaking or supervising activities to take the existence of underwater cultural heritage into account.

Article 2.6 of the Convention and Rule 25

46) Recovered underwater cultural heritage shall be deposited, conserved and managed in a manner that ensures its long-term preservation. Particular regard should be given to the specific needs of the conservation of artefacts recovered from underwater, as for instance the effects of oxygen influence, the impact of drying, and the development of damaging substances.

H. ACTIVITIES INCIDENTALLY AFFECTING UNDERWATER CULTURAL HERITAGE

Article 5 of the Convention

47) Each State Party shall use the best practicable means at its disposal to prevent or mitigate any adverse effects that might arise from activities under its jurisdiction incidentally affecting underwater cultural heritage.

48) States should endeavour to establish national rules for the authorization of interventions on underwater cultural heritage sites. These rules should also cover activities which only incidentally affect underwater cultural heritage sites as well as areas where it is not certain that such sites exist but there is a possibility of their presence. States are encouraged to require the approval of their national competent authorities as described in Article 22.1 of the Convention for any such intervention.

49) Where and when appropriate, local communities directly linked to the underwater cultural heritage sites should be engaged in any activity directed at this heritage.

I. PUBLICATIONS FOR SCIENCE AND THE PUBLIC

Rule 10, 26 and 27 of the Rules

50) States Parties should require that any significant activity directed at underwater cultural heritage is accompanied by a scientific publication and that the public is appropriately informed about on-going projects and the results of the research. No activity directed at underwater cultural heritage should be authorized without a programmed and affordable plan of publication according to the available financial resources. Such plan must include both information addressed to the scientific community as well as information addressed to the general public.

51) Scientific publications should permit the evaluation of the activities undertaken and the knowledge obtained by them. They should be published after the end of the activity by a reasonable deadline according to the type and scale of the activity and of the researched site.

J. CAPACITY-BUILDING

Article 21 of the Convention

52) States Parties shall cooperate in the provision of training in underwater archaeology, in techniques for the conservation of underwater cultural heritage and, on agreed terms, in the transfer of technology relating to underwater cultural heritage, including, but not limited to:

    a.) organizing and participating in regional and international training programmes;

    b.) training specialists to work in the research and protection of underwater cultural heritage; and

　　c.) creating specialized national or international institutions for the training in underwater archaeology and research in underwater cultural heritage and material conservation.

53) States Parties are encouraged to elaborate and adopt, in so far as possible, common standards to promote qualifications and competences in underwater archaeology and to exchange information thereon.

K. PUBLIC ENJOYMENT AND AWARENESS

Article 20 of the Convention

54) States Parties shall take all practicable measures to raise public awareness regarding the value and significance of underwater cultural heritage and the importance of protecting it under the Convention. They should, *inter alia*:

　　a.) cooperate in regional or international awareness raising campaigns;

　　b.) foster the publication of information on the protection and the value of underwater cultural heritage via the media and the Internet;

　　c.) facilitate community, group or public events focusing on the enhancement or protection of the underwater cultural heritage, including, in particular, programs for divers, fishermen, sailors, coastal developers and marine spatial planners;

　　d.) make available general information on underwater cultural heritage located on their territory, as appropriate;

　　e.) inform the public about activities directed at underwater cultural heritage and the recovery of artefacts from sites, including about their final storage; and

　　f.) take any other appropriate measures.

L. INFORMATION-SHARING

Article 19 of the Convention

55) Subject to Article 19.3 of the Convention, States Parties are encouraged to share information with other States Parties concerning underwater cultural heritage, including its discovery and location, heritage excavated or recovered contrary to this Convention or otherwise in violation of international law, pertinent scientific methodology and technology, and legal developments relating to such heritage by:

　　a.) sharing information on inventories and databases with authorized bodies;

　　b.) publishing, if appropriate, information on the discovery and research concerning underwater cultural heritage;

　　c.) making available to all other States Parties and UNESCO statistics on actions concerning underwater cultural heritage.

56) Each State Party should take all practicable measures to disseminate information about underwater cultural heritage excavated or recovered contrary to this Convention or otherwise in violation of international law, including, where feasible, through appropriate international databases, and cooperate to this goal with UNESCO and other intergovernmental and governmental organizations, as for example, Interpol.

M. PROMOTION OF BEST PRACTICES

57) States Parties are encouraged to propose national, regional or international programmes, projects and activities for safeguarding

underwater cultural heritage to the Meeting of States Parties for selection and endorsement by publication and designation as best practices and best reflecting the principles and objectives of the Convention and the annexed Rules.

58) In its selection and promotion of safeguarding programmes, projects and activities, the Meeting of States Parties should pay special attention to the needs of developing countries and to the principle of equitable geographic distribution.

59) Such programmes, projects and activities may be completed, in progress, or planned at the time they are proposed for selection and promotion.

N. MOBILIZATION OF NATIONAL AND INTERNATIONAL SUPPORT FOR THE CONVENTION

60) States Parties should endeavour and cooperate to mobilize international support in favour of the Convention and its principles by facilitating:

   a.) the elaboration of publications on the underwater cultural heritage, including the publication of the results of related research work;

   b.) the expositions of or on underwater cultural heritage;

   c.) the making available of information to the media;

   d.) any other appropriate means.

CHAPTER IV. FINANCING

A. FINANCING THE IMPLEMENTATION OF THE STATE COOPERATION MECHANISM

Article 10.5, 12.4 and 12.5 of the Convention

61) When a State Party implements measures of protection, issues authorizations or conducts necessary preliminary research agreed upon by a group of consulting States in the framework of Article 10.5 or Article 12.4 and 5 of the Convention, the group of consulting States Parties should decide on the common financing of such measures.

62) In deciding on the financing of measures, States Parties should take into consideration

   a) the capacity of the respective States;

Rule 17 – 19 of the Annex to the Convention

   b) the strength of the verifiable link to the concerned heritage and the interest in its protection; and

   c) the location of the concerned heritage.

63) Except in cases of immediate danger no measure should be decided to be implemented unless adequate funding is ensured.

B. THE UNDERWATER CULTURAL HERITAGE FUND

64) The Underwater Cultural Heritage Fund ("the Fund") is managed as a Special Account pursuant to Article 1.1 of its Financial Regulations. [2] The resources of the Fund consist of voluntary contributions as regulated in Article 4 of the above-mentioned Financial Regulations.

([2] The Secretariat: see RESOLUTION 8/MSP 2 and UCH/09/2.MSP/8. The latter approved financial regulations for this fund, as annexed to document UCH/09/2.MSP/8)

65) The Fund will be used as decided by the Meeting of States Parties and in conformity with the provisions and the spirit of the Convention and in complement of national efforts to finance in particular:

   a.) the functioning of the Convention and its State Cooperation Mechanism;

- b.) international cooperation projects in relation to the scope of the Convention;
- c.) the building of capacity in States Parties; and
- d.) the enhancement of the protection of the underwater cultural heritage.

66) States Parties, institutions and private entities are invited to provide support to the Convention by contributions paid to the Fund or direct financial and technical contributions to projects intended to ensure the protection of the underwater cultural heritage.

C. FINANCIAL ASSISTANCE

67) The Meeting of States Parties may receive, evaluate and approve requests for financial assistance from the Fund depending on the available resources.

68) In its decision on the attribution of funds, priority is given to requests for assistance to developing States Parties and projects enhancing State cooperation involving more than two States Parties.

69) The Meeting should base its decisions on granting assistance on the following criteria:
- a.) the amount of assistance requested is appropriate;
- b.) the proposed activities are well conceived and feasible and fully in line with the objectives of the Convention;
- c.) the project can be expected to have lasting results;
- d.) the beneficiary State Part(y/ies) share(s) the cost of the activities for which international assistance is provided, within the limits of its/their resources; and
- e.) the assistance will build or reinforce capacities in the field of safeguarding underwater cultural heritage.

70) The Advisory Body will evaluate the requests of financial assistance for projects which fall under the application of the Rules and give its recommendations to the Meeting of States Parties.

71) Interim and final reports will be submitted to the Secretariat according to the timetable set out in the funding request as approved by the Meeting of States Parties.

72) The Advisory Body will examine and evaluate the reports and submit its advice on them to the Meeting of States Parties.

D. PROCEDURE AND FORMAT

73) States Parties intending to apply for international assistance are encouraged to consult the Secretariat for the elaboration of requests. The application is to be made on the form annexed to these Guidelines. The Secretariat will verify the completeness of the information provided.

74) The complete requests for international assistance shall be submitted by States Parties to the Secretariat at least 4 months before the next ordinary session of the Meeting of States Parties.

75) Requests shall be submitted in English or French electronically or in hard copy. They shall be signed and transmitted by the National Commission for UNESCO or the State Party's Permanent Delegation to UNESCO to the following address:

> UNESCO Secretariat of the Convention on the Protection of the Underwater Cultural Heritage
> 7, place de Fontenoy, 75007 Paris, France

Tel: + 33 (0) 145684406

Fax: + 33 (0) 145685596

E-mail: u.guerin@unesco.org

76) The Secretariat shall submit the requests for international assistance concerning activities directed at Underwater Cultural Heritage to the Advisory Body. The Advisory Body shall provide its recommendations on the requests to the Meeting of States Parties for consideration and final decision at least two months before the Meeting of States Parties.

CHAPTER V. PARTNERS
A. PARTNERS IN THE IMPLEMENTATION PROCESS OF THE CONVENTION

77) Partners in the implementation process of the Convention may be:
   - a.) Governmental and government-related institutions established in the States Parties to the Convention working in activities related to the scope of the Convention;
   - b.) Centres working in activities related to the scope of the Convention and under the auspices of UNESCO, granted by the General Conference;
   - c.) NGOs accredited by the Meeting of States Parties and those having activities related to the scope and spirit of the Convention;
   - d.) Scientific institutions, museums, universities and any other similar entity whose activities are in full conformity with the principles of the Convention;
   - e.) Private entities working in full conformity with the principles of the Convention.

78) Irrespective of its legal nature or denomination, any entity supporting the commercial exploitation of underwater cultural heritage or engaged in its irretrievable dispersal is not a partner.

B. PARTNERS AT THE NATIONAL LEVEL

79) States Parties are encouraged to establish cooperation with and among non-governmental organizations, communities, groups and individuals, as well as experts, centres of expertise and research institutes to enhance the protection of the underwater cultural heritage. States Parties are encouraged to facilitate their participation, in particular with respect to:
   - a.) the identification, documentation and protection of underwater cultural heritage present on their territories;
   - b.) the establishment of inventories;
   - c.) the elaboration and implementation of programmes, projects and activities aiming at raising the awareness of the importance of underwater cultural heritage and ensuring its protection.

CHAPTER VI. ACCREDITATION OF NGOS
A. CRITERIA FOR THE ACCREDITATION OF NGO

80) In order to apply for accreditation, NGOs must comply with the following criteria:
   - a.) have statutes, objectives and activities in full conformity with the principles and objectives of the Convention;
   - b.) be engaged in activities and have recognized competence, expertise and experience in safeguarding underwater

Article 1(e) of the Stautes of the Scientific and Technical Advisory Body

cultural heritage;

c.) not be (or not have been) engaged in any activity dedicated to the commercial exploitation or the irretrievable dispersal of the underwater cultural heritage against the principles enshrined in the Convention;

d.) have a local, national, regional or international nature, as appropriate;

e.) possess operational capacities, including:
   i. a regular active membership;
   ii. an established domicile;
   iii. and a legal status according to the applicable domestic law;
   iv. having existed and having carried out appropriate activities for at least four years when being considered for accreditation.

B. PROCEDURES OF ACCREDITATION

81) The request of an NGO wishing to be accredited should be made by using the form annexed to these Guidelines and available online.

82) The Secretariat shall check the completeness of the requests and present them for consideration to the Advisory Body 3 months before each Meeting of the States Parties.

83) The Advisory Body will send the Secretariat a report with its advice concerning the accreditation, based on objective data provided by the Secretariat, by any State Party or by any other reliable source, as well as on the expertise of its members.

84) The Secretariat will submit all requests for accreditation together with the Advisory Body's report to the Meeting of States Parties for decision.

85) In taking its decision on the accreditation of NGOs, the Meeting of States Parties will pay attention to the principle of equitable geographical representation.

86) The Secretariat shall register all requests and keep up-to-date and publicly accessible a list of the NGOs accredited by the Meeting of States Parties.

C. REVIEW OF ACCREDITATION

87) The Meeting of State Parties shall review already accredited NGOs every four years as to maintaining or terminating relations with the organization in question. The Advisory Body shall report to the Meeting of the States Parties through the Secretariat on its collaboration with accredited NGOs.

88) In case of a recommendation for terminating the accreditation, the Secretariat will inform the NGO concerned which will have the opportunity to express its views in writing, which will be submitted to the Meeting of States Parties.

89) The Meeting of States Parties will take its decision based on all documents submitted for its consideration. The Meeting of States Parties may:
   a) decide to terminate the accreditation; or
   b) decide that there is no actual reason for the termination of the accreditation.

90) The Meeting of States Parties may also decide to terminate

accreditation taking into account the "Directives concerning UNESCO relations with NGOs" in the case of total absence of collaboration.

91) When deemed necessary, including the non-fulfillment of the criteria of accreditation, the Advisory Body may decide at any time to suspend the collaboration with an NGO pending a final decision by the Meeting of States Parties.

INTRODUCTION

The *Convention on the Protection of the Underwater Cultural Heritage* ('the Underwater Convention') was adopted at the 31st General Conference of UNESCO at its Plenary Session on 2nd November 2001. Eighty-seven States voted in favour, four against and there were fifteen abstentions. As there was no roll call of States present and voting, there is no official record of the way in which individual States voted. Forrest comments that those voting against were Norway, Russian Federation, Turkey and Venezuela while the abstentions included Brazil, Columbia, France, Germany, Greece, Israel, Netherlands, Paraguay, Sweden, Switzerland, United Kingdom and Uruguay.[1] The Underwater Convention was signed by the President of the General Conference and the Director-General of UNESCO on 6th November 2001.

UNESCO rules for bringing international conventions into existence require that the instrument be adopted at a General Conference. This differs from what some may regard as familiar practice. Many international conventions incorporate a signature procedure for States. Usually, this does not mean that the State signing is then a party to the convention. Under international law rules, signature merely indicates that the State concerned regards the text as a correct recording of what was agreed; intends to become a party in the future and, in the meantime, undertakes not to do anything that openly conflicts with the Convention. The State is not bound by the Convention until it ratifies (if it has signed), or accedes to it (for States which did not sign). Under UNESCO rules, adoption at the General Conference takes the place of signature and the instrument then has to be ratified or accepted. Acceptance is a term used by the United States of America but the ultimate effect in international law is the same as ratification.

Under Article 27, the Underwater Convention was not to enter into force until three months after the twentieth State deposited its instrument of ratification, acceptance, approval or accession. This occurred on 2nd January 2009. As at 15th August 2013 there are 45 States Parties. Although membership has not increased as quickly as with some of the other UNESCO cultural conventions this is a good result for a Convention that requires States to consider whether their legal position and administrative arrangements need modification before they become party. By way of comparison, the *Convention on the Means of Prohibiting and Preventing the Illicit Import, Export and Transfer of Ownership of Cultural Property* 1970, an equally complex convention, had 47 States Parties twelve years after its adoption by the UNESCO General Conference – almost the same number as the Underwater Convention over the same period. Today (August 2013) it has 123 States Parties, including most of those most vehemently opposed at the time of adoption.

1. Background

The Underwater Convention can be understood only against its physical, legal and technological background.

The physical context covers such features as rivers and lakes within the confines of the land. Girding the land masses is the sea. Between the sea shore and the deep seabed lies an underwater area known as the continental shelf. The width of this varies from just over a kilometre to a maximum of some six hundred kilometres. The depth ranges from 50 to 550 metres. The shelf drops gradually from the land mass until a point called the continental edge is reached where the continental slope falls steeply to the deep seabed. This vast area is similar to the land above water with plains, mountains and valleys. The deepest point lies in the Mariana Trench near Guam at 10,911 metres. Parts of the present seabed – such as that of the North Sea – were previously above water, either wholly or partially, since the advent of humanity.

---

[1] Forrest, C. *International Law and the Protection of Cultural Heritage* (Routledge, Abingdon, 2010) 333.

Superimposed on the physical structure of the seabed lies a legal structure establishing the rights and duties of States. Much of this is now contained in the *United Nations Convention on the Law of the Sea* 1982 (in this book the acronym UNCLOS will be used[2]). There are 165 States party to this Convention. However, this does not include a significant group of States for whom the underwater cultural heritage is particularly important because of their geographic position.[3] The United States of America, not a State Party to the Convention to date, states that it observes parts of UNCLOS as customary international law.

Based on UNCLOS, the following legal structure applies. First of all there are internal waters – water on the landward side of the baseline from which the territorial sea is measured. In general, these are treated in the same way as the land territory of the State. The baseline is normally the low water line along the coast but there can be special provision for features such as reefs and deeply indented coastlines.

From the baseline, States may then have a territorial sea up to twelve nautical miles in width. Here the State is sovereign except that the ships of other States have the right of innocent passage.

In a zone continuing out a further twelve nautical miles, States may exercise control to prevent infringement of their customs, fiscal, immigration and sanitary laws. This is known as the 'contiguous zone'.

The legal definition of the continental shelf in UNCLOS is a complex one which, for political reasons, departs from the physical concept. For example, in order to compensate States with a narrow shelf, the legal concept extends up to 200 nautical miles from the baseline even though this encroaches on the geological deep seabed. Where the physical width of the continental shelf adjacent to a State exceeds 200 miles, its maximum legal width is established following a complex formula set out in UNCLOS. In effect, this allows the 'inclusion within national jurisdiction of substantially the whole of the physical continental margin'[4] i.e. the continental shelf, slope and rise but excluding the deep oceanic floor. On the continental shelf, coastal States exercise sovereign rights for the purpose of exploring and exploiting their natural resources i.e. mineral and other non-living resources and living organisms in constant contact with the seabed.

Above the continental shelf is the exclusive economic zone or EEZ. This is 200 nautical miles wide but it gives the coastal State sovereign rights in the waters above the seabed as opposed to sovereign rights in the seabed itself. These rights include 'the protection and preservation of the marine environment' as well as those related to exploration and exploitation, conservation and management of the natural resources.

Finally, there is the 'Area' which is the 'seabed and ocean floor and subsoil thereof, beyond the limits of national jurisdiction'. The Area and its resources are the common heritage of mankind. No State can claim or exercise sovereignty or sovereign rights over any part of the Area or its resources nor appropriate any part of it.

In conclusion, there are six zones – internal waters, territorial sea, contiguous zone, continental shelf, EEZ and the Area – and in each of these, States have different rights and obligations. These rules in UNCLOS resulted from several attempts in the twentieth century to regulate the law of the sea, and the final text which sets out these zones and their elements was a very hard won compromise of diverse State interests, finalised in sessions over ten years of negotiation.

While States were creating this legal structure (UNCLOS I [1956-1958], UNCLOS II [1967], UNCLOS III [1973-1982]), the world of underwater cultural heritage to which it applies was

---

2   It is acknowledged that UNCLOS originally referred to the United Nations Conference on the Law of the Sea. Some authors use LOSC and others CLOS. UNCLOS is used here as it can now often be found referring to the Convention, including in reports of the Secretary-General of the United Nations.

3   Such as Cambodia, Columbia, Israel, Latvia, Libya, Peru, Thailand, Turkey, United States of America, Venezuela: <http://www.un.org/depts/los/reference_files/status2010.pdf>.

4   Churchill, R.R. and Lowe, A.V. *The Law of the Sea* (Manchester University Press, Manchester, 3rd edn 1999) 175.

changing through rapid developments in technology. Until the invention of the aqualung in 1943, the seabed could be reached only with great difficulty. The human body could be trained, as with sponge divers, to descend to some depth for a short period of time. Diving bells allowed limited access as did hard suits but these were cumbersome and needed considerable support facilities. The aqualung permitted any generally fit person to penetrate to a maximum of 39 metres or around 50 metres for more experienced divers. The use of saturated gasses to replace the nitrogen in the diver's blood further increased the depth that could be reached. Today it is not unusual for highly experienced recreational divers to descend to 100 metres or more. From the 1960s onward a number of manned or remote controlled submersibles have been built that allow access to depths in excess of 6,000 metres, enough to reach 98 per cent of all ocean floors. Devices for searching the ocean floor have developed enormously in recent years in both range and efficiency.

There are many dangers to underwater cultural heritage. Responses to the most significant are dealt with in detail, where appropriate, in the following pages. The significance of any particular danger depends on many factors including where the heritage lies and its composition. Natural factors include organisms in the sea and water currents. Dangers created by humans arise from fishing, construction projects and, indeed, any activity that man engages in, on, or under the ocean. A category of particular significance in the current context is the looting of sites for personal gain.

2. The Value of Underwater Cultural Heritage

On the seabed lie the accumulated remains from the activities of humanity for thousands of years. There are countless shipwrecks as well as prehistoric campsites or migration routes, sunken towns, harbour works and other constructions; not to mention objects that have fallen off vessels over the centuries. All of this material forms the underwater cultural heritage.

It has been argued that the deeper-lying wrecks should be in better condition than those in shallower waters as there is less microbiological activity causing decay in deep, cold conditions.[5] While this may be correct as a general principle, much depends on the materials used in construction of the vessel, how it sank, whether it sits on the seabed or is embedded in it, the composition of the water and so on.[6]

Wrecks, in particular, are of great importance for the study of humanity's history. The wreck gives a snapshot of that history at a particular point in time. Virtually everything on board the vessel at the moment of its sinking would have been there for a purpose. Wrecks often carry cargo which gives an idea of trade patterns, economic conditions and perhaps more. One short study on the importance of ingots for documenting long distance trade in metals comments that "ingot material from dated wrecks can be uniquely useful even in areas as apparently far removed as African art history" as there appeared to be a link between the famous Benin bronzes and a particular type of ingot manufactured in Birmingham.[7] Wrecks, at least until recent times, are also the remains of probably the most advanced technological achievement of their period.

However, underwater sites and especially wrecks can contribute to the advancement of knowledge only if they are properly examined. They are a finite source of understanding of our history. Any interference with them which does not advance that understanding is simply vandalism. To enable scientific and rational decisions to be made, the science of underwater archaeology has evolved. This is said to have begun with the excavation of the Cape Gelidonya

---

5 Bascom, W. *Deep Water, Ancient Ships: the Treasure Vault of the Mediterranean* (Doubleday, New York, 1976).
6 There are conflicting views, for example, on the fate of the *Titanic*, an iron hull resting some 4,000 metres below the surface of the Atlantic since 1912. Some argue that it will collapse in the near future while others say it will gradually deteriorate over hundreds of years: see 'Note' (2001) 54 *Archaeology* 6-7, 16.
7 Craddock, P.T. and Hook, D.R. 'Ingots from the Sea: The British Museum Collection of Ingots' (1987) 16 *International Journal of Nautical Archaeology and Underwater Exploration* 201, 205.

wreck in 1960.[8] The work was done by a team led by George F. Bass, a graduate student of classical archaeology at the University of Pennsylvania, and Peter Throckmorton, a journalist and amateur archaeologist.

It was the first underwater excavation in the Mediterranean region in which the directing archaeologist dived and excavated. Despite the difficulties presented by working underwater, the team adhered to standards of land excavation, adapting methods as necessary for the underwater environment.[9]

As underwater archaeology has evolved, however, excavation has come to be seen as at one end of the scale of a range of ways for dealing with underwater cultural heritage. At the other end is preservation *in situ*; in other words, leaving the site untouched. The reasons for taking this approach are numerous: funding for excavation may not be available; there may not be adequate facilities available for conservation, storage and display of objects raised; current techniques for excavation may not be adequate for the task. Preservation *in situ* does not mean that the site cannot be visited and photographed.

If it is decided to excavate, there will necessarily be decisions on what is going to be done. For example, the *Vasa*, currently exhibited in Stockholm, was excavated as a complete unit. The major surviving section of the *Mary Rose*, on exhibition at Portsmouth, was raised in one lift. In the case of the *Batavia*, individual planks from the port side of the ship's stern were raised, conserved and reassembled in the Maritime Museum in Fremantle, Western Australia. In all three cases, the excavation also revealed many artefacts.

The value and benefits of a comprehensive excavation, even when no major vessel like the *Vasa* is involved, is shown by that undertaken by Parks Canada at Red Bay in the province of Labrador. This followed research in Basque records in Spain which showed that in the sixteenth century there had been a previously unrecognized industry in whale oil and salt cod produced from what are now Canadian waters and taken to the Basque region of Spain. Those records showed that a galleon had sunk in Red Bay in 1565. A survey of the area was made in 1977 and the following year test excavations were made. Work began in earnest in 1978 and lasted till 1985. A five volume report was produced.[10] Robert Grenier, former President of the ICOMOS International Scientific Committee for the Underwater Cultural Heritage has stated:

> A museum built at the small fishing village of Red Bay by Parks Canada now exhibits artifacts and a partial replica of the galleon, and, importantly, it supplements the local economy devastated by the closure of the cod fishery. The museum also offers visitors the world's only existing sixteenth-century Basque whaling boat, the ancestor of modern search and rescue craft. This museum now attracts tourists from all over the world to this remote place and constitutes the village's only continuous source of income. But even at Red Bay, the notion of *in situ* preservation has been put into practice: two other sixteenth-century galleons and their accompanying artifacts we found have been left *in situ* for future generations ....[11]

A sketch of the galleon serves as the logo for the Underwater Convention.

However some excavations have been aimed solely at making a commercial profit. Such was the fate of the *Geldermahlsen*, a Dutch East Indiaman wrecked in 1752. It struck Admiral

---

8 Attempts had been made before this to investigate wrecks systematically (e.g. by Cousteau at Grand Congloué and Taillez on the Titan Reef) and techniques and tools developed but there was a lack of archaeological rigour.

9 Peachey, C. 'Cape Gelidonya Wreck' in Delgado, J. (ed.) *Encyclopaedia of Underwater and Marine Archaeology* (British Museum Press, London, 1997) 84.

10 Grenier, R., Bernier, M-A. & Stevens, W. *The Underwater Archaeology of Red Bay: Basque Shipbuilding and Whaling in the 16th Century* (Parks Canada, Ottawa, 2007). See postscript at p. 160.

11 Copy from letter dated 19 Oct. 2001 on file with the author.

Stellingwerf Reef off Bintan in Indonesian territorial waters[12] and was been found by Michael Hatcher who raised its cargo of ceramics and sold them through Christie's in Amsterdam for something in the region of £10 million. The work on the wreck has been described in these terms:

> Hatch has to recover as much as possible as quickly as possible, preferably in one season, before rivals infringe on the site, and costs escalate out of control of even very wealthy individuals and into the realms of red-tape-bound institutions and governments. He cannot spend time marking down the location of every single object on a wreck, in three dimensions. On the 'G' he did a rough archaeological survey, and John Brunner's pictures provided useful data. But photographs also played into the hands of Hatch's critics. One shot shows a diver prising open a chest, while a plank disappears into the deep. On the plank are Chinese characters. Historians would dearly like to know the exact text of that inscription.[13]

Miller has used terms such as 'mined', 'scavenged', 'strip-mining' in relation to Hatcher's operations. Almost nothing was recorded about the *Geldermalsen* and no proper conservation work was done on the artefacts raised. Many objects, including 32,500 cups and saucers, were not recovered.[14] Miller raises two other aspects of the *Geldermalsen* episode that have more general relevance: one, the role of the auction house, Christie's, and, two, that of museums and other public collections which took part in the bidding.

> Christie's was the agent provocateur that made the scavenging possible and profitable. ... Those who are concerned about the protection of shipwrecks would do well to direct attention, blame, and the harsh glare of publicity on auction houses such as Christie's of Amsterdam whose aggressive search for new sources of saleable antiquities results in the destruction of archaeological sites.[15]

The Rijks Museum in the Netherlands, along with others, boycotted the auction but the British Museum and similar institutions bought. Even in 1985, the ethics of such purchases by museums was questionable. Now it would be in direct contradiction of Paragraph 2.4 of the Code of Professional Ethics of the International Council of Museums. It should also be noted that on its insistence as alleged owner of the *Geldermahlsen*, ten per cent of the proceeds went to the Dutch Government.

> What an amazing situation, the Dutch Ministry of Finance gets 10% of the auction sale, the money goes into the coffers and the Museums have to bid on the auction market with their own budgets. How cynical.[16]

Pieces from the *Geldermahlsen* are still being traded on the Internet.

3. Protection of Value

The value of underwater cultural heritage can be protected only by a legal framework designed for that purpose. However, until the advent of the Underwater Convention, no such framework was available. The law of individual States usually applies only within the territory of the State. As we have seen, this encompasses the land mass of the State plus its territorial sea. There is a limited ability to legislate over the adjacent continental shelf. Until relatively recently, because much underwater cultural heritage lay at depths beyond easy access, States felt no need to protect it.

3.1 Legislation

A very early piece of legislation dealing specifically with protection of shipwrecks was passed in

---

12 Green, J. Review of Bowens, A. (ed.) *Underwater Archaeology: the NAS Guide to Principles and Practice* in (2009) 38 *International Journal of Nautical Archaeology* 191, 192.
13 Hatcher, M. (with Thorncroft, A.) *The Nanking Cargo* (Hamish Hamilton, London, 1987) 162.
14 Miller, G.L. 'The Second Destruction of the Geldermalsen' (1987) 47 *The American Neptune* 275.
15 Miller, above, at 278.
16 Green, J. Book review of *The Nanking Cargo* by Hatcher, M. with de Rham, M. and other books on the *Geldermalsen* sale (1988) 17 *International Journal of Nautical Archaeology and Underwater Exploration* 357, 359.

Denmark in 1963.[17] Western Australia passed legislation in 1964.[18] The *Maritime Archaeology Act* 1973 replaced this. Australia passed federal legislation in 1976 and this extended to cover events on the continental shelf.[19] However, Australia has never exercised this jurisdiction in a way which would bring it into conflict with other States. The United Kingdom passed specific legislation in 1973[20] but this only extended to the territorial sea. Its *Protection of Military Remains Act* 1986 offers protection in limited circumstances in both territorial and international waters. Many other States now have either specific legislation dealing with underwater cultural heritage or their law applying to antiquities in general covers it.[21]

3.2 Salvage

Where legislation was absent, any protection for the value of underwater cultural heritage had to be sought in other areas of law. Some saw the law of salvage as providing a means to this end. That is an ancient law. Basically it is designed to encourage the saving of life and property in danger of being lost at sea. The salvor, the person doing the saving, is entitled to a reward taken from the value of the property saved. However, salvage law varies greatly between legal systems and does not apply at all to wrecks in some systems. In Spain, for example, underwater cultural heritage is out of the stream of commerce and the law on maritime salvage is expressly excluded.[22] Under French law:

> … when a legitimate owner cannot be identified or has no heirs, … the wreck belongs to the State and is considered State property. Wrecks cannot be sold and, with rare exceptions, they cannot be subject to commercial concession [sic]. Conversely, if an unidentified wreck is discovered, the discoverer is obliged to declare the find, and has no right to ownership of the wreck. French law only provides financial compensation. This sum is fixed according to the scientific, not the commercial value, of the wreck. The typical amount is modest, between US$15,000 and US$42,000.[23]

Even where salvage law is applicable, it is defective. It did of course evolve at a time when the concept of underwater cultural heritage was unknown. As the reward is based on the commercial value of what is discovered, it encourages salvors to pursue what is of commercial value rather than historical or archaeological value.

Courts in the United States of America have used salvage law in many cases involving historic wreck. An outstanding example is the series of cases involving the *S.S. Central America* which sank in 1857 some 256 kilometres off the South Carolina coast at a depth of 2.4 kilometres. It was found in 1998 by the Columbus-America Discovery Group. A dispute arose as to whether the insurance companies that had paid out at the time of the sinking still had any interest under

---

17 *Act No. 203 of 31 May 1963 on Protection of Historic Wrecks.*
18 *Museum Act Amendment Act* 1964.
19 This early legislation is discussed in O'Keefe, P.J. & Prott, L.V. 'Australian Protection of Historic Shipwrecks' (1978) 6 *Australian Yearbook of International Law* 119.
20 *Protection of Wrecks Act* 1973.
21 O'Keefe, P.J. & Prott, L.V. *Law and the Cultural Heritage: Volume I: Discovery and Excavation* (Professional Books, Abingdon, 1984) 112-116 looks at the arguments for and against specific and general legislation in this field. Examples of national legislation can be found in Droomgoole, S. (ed.) *The Protection of the Underwater Cultural Heritage: National Perspectives in Light of the UNESCO Convention 2001* (Martinus Nijhoff, Leiden, 2006). Legislation from the Asia/Pacific region is considered in Prott, L.V. (ed.) *Finishing the Interrupted Voyage* (UNESCO, Institute of Art and Law; Paris, Builth Wells; 2006).
22 Article 22(3) of *Law 60/1962 of 24 Dec. 1962*: Aznar-Gómez, M.J. 'Spain' in Droomgoole, S. (ed.) *The Protection of the Underwater Cultural Heritage: National Perspectives in Light of the UNESCO Convention 2001* (Martinus Nijhoff, Leiden, 2006) 271, 283.
23 L'Hour, M. 'DRASSM 1996-2008: An Overview of the Accomplishments and Future of French Underwater Archaeology' in *International Meeting on the Protection, Presentation and Valorisation of Underwater Cultural Heritage – Chongqing, China* (23 to 27 Nov. 2010): <http://www.unesco.org/culture/underwater/pdf/uch_publication_chine_en.pdf>.

the principle of subrogation[24] in the gold that had been found. The Court of Appeals for the Fourth Circuit held that the law of salvage applied rather than the law of finds which would have given the Discovery Group ownership.[25] In psychological terms the Court saw the law of finds as encouraging secrecy and competition whereas salvage law, it said, emphasizes openness, co-operation and preservation of property. But the courts have had to stretch the concept of this law to apply it to historic wreck. For example, traditionally that law required the property to be in danger. How is an historic wreck in danger when it is lying on or in the seabed? The courts have tried in various ways to expand the concept beyond mere physical danger. For example, in *Bemis v. RMS Lusitania* the Court stated:

> Courts will usually find that underwater shipwrecks are in marine peril, because sunken vessels and their cargoes are in danger of being lost forever.[26]

Forrest expresses the situation in these terms:

> … those wishing to preserve the application of salvage law to the recovery of underwater cultural heritage have advocated a broad definition of the term, which relates not only to the physical threats to the objects, but also to the loss of its economic realisation.[27]

In addition to extending the concepts used in assessing salvage, the courts have attempted to apply a requirement that the archaeological and historical value of the wreck be preserved by the salvor. However, whether this has been done is assessed at the time the reward is made. By then work on the site would be finished and it would be too late to rectify any defects in carrying it out. Moreover, this technique is inherently inadequate as a court does not have the resources to supervise work on the site nor the ability to enforce its orders on persons or sites if these are beyond its jurisdiction.

The wreck of RMS *Titanic* illustrates the tensions that appear when a court grants an applicant the status of 'salvor in possession'; that is, when the court recognizes that the salvor has an exclusive right to salvage the wreck. The *Titanic*, claimed to be unsinkable, struck an iceberg and sank some 640 kilometres off the coast of Newfoundland. The wreck has only just come within the coverage of the Underwater Convention, having sunk on 15th April 2012, thus now having been underwater for more than 100 years as the Convention requires.

The wreck was found in 1985 at a depth of approximately 4,000 metres by an expedition from the Woods Hole Oceanographic Institute (United States of America) and the Institute of France for the Research and Exploration of the Sea (IFREMER). Two years later, an American corporation, Titanic Ventures, contracted with IFREMER to raise artefacts from the wreck. Thirty-two dives were made on the site and some 1,800 objects raised. Titanic Ventures then sold its salvage interests and the artefacts to RMS Titanic Inc. (RMST). In 1992, RMST was sued in the District Court for the Eastern District of Virginia by Marex Titanic Inc. which claimed salvage rights in relation to the vessel and ownership of the artefacts. The Court took jurisdiction in the case even though the vessel had not flown the American flag and it lay in international waters. The matter was resolved in favour of RMST which, in 1994, was made salvor in possession on the understanding that all artefacts recovered would be exhibited and not sold or otherwise disposed of. Maintenance of salvor in possession status requires the salvor to actually work on the wreck on a regular basis. Accordingly, RMST mounted a number of expeditions to the site and raised more artefacts.

In September 2001, RMST came up with a scheme to sell the artefacts it had raised to a specially created non-profit foundation and to various museums. It argued that this was necessary because it was no longer earning sufficient income from tourism and sale of visual images; disposal of the artefacts was necessary to protect shareholder interests in RMST and save conservation costs of US$300,000 a year. Application was made to the District Court for permission to sell the artefacts

---

24   The insurer succeeds to the interest of the insured on payment for the loss.
25   *Columbus-America Discovery Group v. Atlantic Mutual Insurance Company* 974 F.2d 450 (1992).
26   884 F. Supp. 1042, 1051 (1995).
27   Forrest, C. fn. 1 above, 303.

but the Court refused. It pointed out that the undertaking not to sell the artefacts was voluntarily given when RMST was granted salvor in possession status. In 2000 the Court was requested to allow a 'surgical incision' to be made in the hull but refused.[28] In 2004 RMST applied to have its status changed from salvor to finder but the court rejected the application.[29] In 2006 the Court of Appeal ruled that it was the law of salvage and not the law of finds that governed the case.[30] RMST then proceeded in 2007 to seek a salvage award between 90 and 100 per cent for all of its efforts in salvaging the Titanic wreck site up to 31st December 2006. The Court made the award in the amount of 100 per cent.[31] No buyer having come forward, in 2011 RMST was granted ownership of the artefacts subject to covenants and conditions.[32]

This case has been the most complex and convoluted of all cases involving salvage of an historic wreck. However, it must not be thought that the United States of America is the only State where courts have had to deal with the application of salvage law to historic wrecks. For example, in *Robinson v. The Western Australian Museum*,[33] the High Court of Australia was faced with claims to the *Vergulde Draeck*, a Dutch East Indiaman which sank in 1656 off the coast of Western Australia. The resulting judgements do not reveal any common approach among the members of the court. Two of the judges came to consider the significance of the Dutch wrecks to the history of Australia and reached opposite conclusions.[34] In Finland the finders of the *Vrouw Maria*, a ship that sank in 1771, claimed salvage rights in respect of objects raised. The court held that:

> the regulations of the Antiquities Act eliminate the possibility of applying the salvage and reward regulations of the Maritime Act to wrecks and objects discovered in wrecks, or objects evidently originating from such contexts, that are protected by the Antiquities Act.[35]

Using a salvage contract to exploit underwater cultural heritage can have the possibility of taking the parties into areas of law and policy normally far removed from those involved with such heritage. An example is that of the arbitral proceedings arising from work on the *Diana*. This was a British vessel which sank in 1817 carrying a cargo of Chinese porcelain in what are now Malaysian territorial waters. In 1991, the Government of Malaysia entered into a contract with a marine salvage company incorporated under the laws of Malaysia but, it was alleged, with the majority of its shares being held by a British national. Under the contract the company was to find the wreck, which it did, and salvage the cargo for the Government. Any finds would belong to the Government against payment to the salvage company of a proportion of what was found. There was a dispute over the amount owed to the company which alleged that it received only 40 per cent of the amount raised at auction by Christie's, rather than 70 per cent as stipulated in the contract and received no share in what the Government had withheld from auction. In 2004, the company submitted a request for arbitration to the International Centre for the Settlement of Investment Disputes.[36] It was alleged that the salvage contract amounted to an 'investment' under an agreement between the United Kingdom and Malaysia for the protection and promotion of investments. The sole arbitrator dismissed the claim on the ground that there was no 'investment'.[37] The claimants applied for an annulment of that decision and succeeded

---

28   *RMS Titanic v. Wrecked and Abandoned Vessel*, Order of the Court, 28 July 2000.
29   *RMS Titanic Inc. v. Wrecked and Abandoned Vessel*, Order of the Court, 2 July 2004.
30   *RMS Titanic Inc. v. Wrecked and Abandoned Vessel* 435 F.3d 521, 535.
31   *RMS Titanic Inc. v. Wrecked and Abandoned Vessel* 742 F. Supp. 2d 784, 788.
32   See further p.131 below.
33   (1977) 51 A.L.J.R. 806.
34   The argument concerned the constitutional validity of Western Australian legislation which had to be for the 'peace, order and good government' of the State and whether the historical significance of the wrecks brought them within such categories: O'Keefe, P.J. & Prott, L.V. fn. 19 above , 173.
35   Matikka, M. 'Finland' in Droomgoole, S. (ed.) *The Protection of the Underwater Cultural Heritage: National Perspectives in Light of the UNESCO Convention 2001* (Martinus Nijhoff, Leiden, 2006) 43, 53.
36   The ICSID was established by the *Convention on the Settlement of Investment Disputes between States and Nationals of Other States* 1965 to provide facilities for conciliation and arbitration of such disputes.
37   <https://icsid.worldbank.org/ICSID/FrontServlet?requestType=CasesRH&actionVal=showDoc&d

in 2009.[38] The episode shows that contracts of this nature can bring into operation laws well outside those normally applying to cultural heritage and ones that many would argue should have no relevance to it.[39] It also shows the financial dangers for the government in that Malaysia was ordered to pay its own costs and the full costs and expenses incurred by ICSID in connection with the annulment proceedings.

Overall, the application of salvage law to historic shipwrecks has led to many court proceedings and issues are still unresolved. It would be appropriate to adopt Forrest's own conclusion on his study of this area:

> As a body of law, it [salvage law] encourages the premature recovery of underwater cultural heritage (often without any pre-disturbance survey to investigate the archaeological importance of the site); it encourages quick and unscientific excavation techniques; and it encourages the piecemeal sale of artefacts rather than their preservation as a collection.[40]

We have seen above a court in the United States of America saying that the law of salvage 'emphasizes openness, co-operation and preservation of property'. It is said to do this through the salvage reward which gives encouragement to salvors; remove this and the incentive to be open about what has been found is removed. That conclusion is highly debatable. It will only come into play where what has been found is valuable in economic terms. If a wreck, for example, has nothing of monetary value on board, there is no incentive for the finder to report it.

3.2.1 Rewards and Amnesties

The Underwater Convention does not have any provision for rewards but these are common where finds are made on land. The ethical issues and the effectiveness of rewards are much debated. The reality of the situation where 'finders keepers' is pervasive in the public perception was expressed by Walsh J. in the case *Webb v. Ireland*:

> I fully recognize that as a matter of prudence and indeed as a way of safeguarding similar such objects as may in the future be found that it could well be regarded as expedient on the part of the State, not merely to reward such persons but generously to reward them for the sake of ensuring, or assisting in ensuring, that the objects will be disclosed to the State and will be dealt with by the State, for the benefit of the common good in accordance with the law for the time being in force.[41]

Under the Australian *Historic Shipwrecks Act* 1976 there is provision for payment of a reward. The largest reward granted was a total of Au $30,000 in 1980 to the discoverers of the SS *Rapid*.[42]

The 1978 Council of Europe Recommendation[43] on the underwater cultural heritage recommended that 'a standard system of fixed finder's monetary rewards should be established' in national legislation. The draft convention based on that Recommendation was never adopted[44] but there is nothing to stop a State Party to the Underwater Convention making provision for rewards if it so wishes. They may not even be monetary as sometimes official recognition of what a person has done in making a discovery is sufficient.

Another aspect of underwater cultural heritage administration that does not appear in the Convention is the granting of amnesties for past conduct, particularly the collecting of material from sites. There is very little or no comparative study of how these operate and how effective

---

	ocId=DC654_En&caseId=C247>.
38	<https://icsid.worldbank.org/ICSID/FrontServlet?requestType=CasesRH&actionVal=showDoc&docId=DC1030_En&caseId=C247>. It is not known whether the matter was taken further.
39	Vadi, V.S. 'Investing in Culture: Underwater Cultural Heritage and International Investment Law' (2009) 42 *Vanderbilt Journal of Transnational Law* 853.
40	Forrest, C. fn. 1 above, 320.
41	(1988) *Irish Law Reports Monthly* 8: 565,605.
42	<http://museum.wa.gov.au/sites/default/files/Coral%20Coast.pdf>.
43	Recommendation 848 (1978).
44	Page 11 below.

they are, yet from time to time States indulge their nationals in this way. Australia introduced an amnesty on 1st April 1993 for people who had discovered the location of a shipwreck or gained control of a 'relic' without reporting it.[45] Prior to this there was protection of individual wrecks on a designated basis but in 1985 the legislation was amended to provide for blanket protection of all wrecks over 75 years old. The amnesty lasted 11 months and resulted in some 20,000 artefacts being declared. Rodrigues indicates that the amnesty was underfunded and poorly resourced in terms of staff. Following up what happened to collections proved particularly difficult. However, much information was collected, some of which was very important. She gives a number of examples including that of the *Zuytdorp* – a Dutch East Indiaman which sank off Western Australia:

> … it was the discovery of the bell fragment that proved the most significant, as it helped to prove that the vessel lay against a drying reef, thereby allowing survivors to get ashore. … the Zuytdorp was lost without a trace, or satisfactory explanation, rendering the material remains on land and at sea the only known record of the event. The Zuytdorp was doubly important because preliminary indications were that the survivors had interacted with local Aborigines, making it one of the first known 'contact' events in Australia.[46]

3.2.2 Proposals for International Regimes

In light of the damage being caused to underwater cultural heritage by various activities already mentioned and the lack of an effective legal framework of protection, attempts were made to provide an international regime that States would implement on a uniform basis. These attempts took place over many years. The Underwater Convention should be seen as a step in a long journey which is not yet complete – even if it ever could be as there is always the need to improve the law and to deal with future developments.

The first international instrument to deal with underwater cultural heritage was the UNESCO *Recommendation on International Principles Applicable to Archaeological Excavations* 1956. UNESCO Recommendations have been little considered but they cannot be ignored. They constitute a significant body of legal principle and UNESCO Member States have an obligation to consider them seriously; where possible to implement them and to report on the measures they have taken in regard to them[47]. The 1956 Recommendation covered:

> Any research aimed at the discovery of objects of archaeological character, whether such research involves digging of the ground or systemic exploration of its surface or is carried out on the bed or in the sub-soil of inland or territorial waters of a Member State.

The Recommendation saw the underwater cultural heritage as subject to basically the same rules as that on land.[48]

Also in 1956, the International Law Commission commented for a draft it had produced for a Convention on the Continental Shelf that:

> It is clearly understood that the rights in question do not cover objects such as wrecked ships and their cargoes (including bullion) lying on the seabed or covered by the sand of the subsoil.[49]

At Geneva in 1958, the matter was raised in the Fourth Committee under a proposal to include

---

45 The facts that follow are taken from Rodrigues, J. 'An Amnesty Assessed. Human Impact on Shipwreck Sites: the Australian Case' (2009) 38 *International Journal of Nautical Archaeology* 153.
46 Above at 160.
47 <http://portal.unesco.org/en/ev.php-URL_ID=21681&URL_DO=DO_TOPIC&URL_SECTION=201.html>.
48 The Recommendation is discussed in O'Keefe, P.J. & Prott, L.V. *Cultural Heritage Conventions and Other Instruments: A Compendium with Commentaries* (Institute of Art and Law, Builth Wells, 2011) 209.
49 (1956) *Yearbook of the International Law Commission*, Vol. II, 298.

in the Convention's coverage 'mineral and other non-living resources'. The question was asked whether this included shipwrecks and their cargoes. The reply was that these were not resources, which were intended to include only shells and similar objects.[50]

In 1977 the Council of Europe began to examine issues concerning the underwater cultural heritage. Following a report[51] by its Education and Culture Committee, the Parliamentary Assembly recommended that the Committee of Ministers draw up a European convention on the topic.[52] An *ad hoc* Committee of Experts was appointed for this purpose. A Draft Convention was finalized in 1985 and sent to the Council of Ministers for approval. However, this was never adopted 'due to Turkey's objection to its territorial scope of application'.[53]

The Council of Europe returned to the subject in its *European Convention on Protection of the Archaeological Heritage (Revised)* 1992.[54] That Convention considers archaeological heritage as "all remains and objects and any other traces of mankind from past epochs ... which are located in any area within the jurisdiction of the parties" (Article 1). The Explanatory Memorandum to the Convention states:

> In itself this is merely stating what is inherent in any international convention. Here it emphasizes that the actual area of State jurisdiction depends on the individual States and in respect of this there are many possibilities. Territorially, the area can be coextensive with the territorial sea, the contiguous zone, the continental shelf, the exclusive economic zone or a cultural protection zone. Among the members of the Council of Europe some States restrict their jurisdiction over shipwrecks, for example, to the territorial sea while others extend it to their continental self. The Revised Convention recognizes these differences without indicating a preference one for the other.[55]

In effect, this is a recognition of the existing situation.

The Parliamentary Assembly of the Council of Europe returned to this topic with its Recommendation 1486 (2000) on Maritime and Fluvial Heritage.[56] Paragraph 13 (iv) recommended that the Council of Ministers:

> associate the Council of Europe with the elaboration by UNESCO of an international convention on the underwater cultural heritage and in the preparation at European and international level of any other legal instruments relating to the maritime and fluvial heritage.

Among its other provisions are two dealing with protection of underwater cultural heritage from commercial recovery operations; one with the encouragement of bilateral and regional agreements and another with sovereign immunity over warships and other State vessels.[57] For example, the Recommendation proposed the mitigation of 'the sovereign immunity which States retain over vessels of war and other State-owned vessels wherever they are sunk'.[58]

The International Law Association entered the field in 1988 when it established a Cultural Heritage Law Committee – one of the then twenty international committees within the Association. A

---

50 See discussion in Caflisch, L. 'Submarine Antiquities and the International Law of the Sea' (1982) 13 *Netherlands Yearbook of International Law* 3, 14.

51 Council of Europe *The Underwater Cultural Heritage: Report of the Committee on Culture and Education, Parliamentary Assembly: Council of Europe* (Doc. 4200, Strasbourg, 1978).

52 Recommendation 848 (1978).

53 Strati, A. *The Protection of the Underwater Cultural Heritage: An Emerging Objective of the Contemporary Law of the Sea* (Martinus Nijhoff, The Hague, 1995) 87.

54 European Treaty Series No. 143.

55 Council of Europe *European Convention on the Protection of the Archaeological Heritage (Revised) Explanatory Report* Doc. MPC (91) 8, 3.

56 Adopted on 9 Nov. 2000. It was based on a Report from the Committee on Culture and Education – Doc. 8867.

57 These are all matters dealt with in the Underwater Convention.

58 Page 36 below.

Report containing a Draft Convention on the Protection of the Underwater Cultural Heritage was adopted at the Association's 66th Conference in Buenos Aires and then forwarded to UNESCO for consideration. It formed the original basis for discussion leading to the Underwater Convention.

4. THE LAW OF THE SEA REGIME

In 1973 lengthy negotiations began which eventually led to the United Nations Convention on the Law of the Sea (UNCLOS). How to deal with underwater cultural heritage was raised during these negotiations. It had a low priority. Caflisch refers to a study 'on the legal regime of submarine antiquities' by the United Nations Conference on the Law of the Sea as 'cursory'.[59] Comparatively little attention was paid to what eventually became Article 149.

> All objects of an archaeological and historical nature found in the Area shall be preserved or disposed of for the benefit of mankind as a whole, particular regard being paid to the preferential rights of the State or country of origin, or the State of cultural origin, or the State of historical and archaeological origin.

It is a provision which does not fit easily with others in the same context i.e. those dealing with what has become known as the 'Area'.

Application of this Article is limited to the 'Area' which, as indicated above, 'means the seabed and ocean floor and subsoil thereof, beyond the limits of national jurisdiction'. There are significant problems of interpretation. The phrase 'disposed of' as an alternative to 'preserved' is puzzling. The latter would normally indicate placing of the object in a suitable institution but the use of 'or' suggests something other than preservation. The large number of States with preferential rights could also create problems, particularly as the concept of the State itself is of relatively recent origin. Does it require that modern States be identified with ancient cultures originating within their current territory but having no other connection? Is it intended that the use of the word 'country' is somehow to take care of this eventuality? There is also an argument as to whether Article 149 preserves existing rights or creates new ones. The first approach suffers from the defect that what these rights are is not known; the second from the words 'particular regard being paid to' which is peculiar language for creation of rights. Neither argument is persuasive.

Underwater cultural heritage on the continental shelf or in the exclusive economic zone of States received no attention in the negotiations until 1979. Even then, only a handful of States were interested and the resulting negotiations pitted them against the United States of America and the United Kingdom. The result was Article 303 which embodied many concessions by those who wanted an article on the underwater cultural heritage.

Article 303 of UNCLOS is headed 'Archaeological and historical objects found at sea'. It begins by casting a general duty on States:

> 1. States have the duty to protect objects of an archaeological and historical nature found at sea and shall co-operate for this purpose.

To have any practical effect the duty must be given specific content but any attempt to do this can only be based on the perceptions of the person concerned. Scholarly comment is far from uniform in its conclusions on this duty.[60] For example, Strati reads into the provision certain specific duties on the part of States, such as 'the obligation to report the accidental discovery of marine archaeological sites' and 'the need for the *in situ* protection of archaeological objects'.[61] However, there is no indication that, while these duties may be considered desirable by archaeologists, there has been any more recognition of them by States as a result of Article 303.

The objects to be protected must be of an 'archaeological and historical nature'; a phrase which appears also in Article 149. The adjective 'archaeological' really has no meaning because archaeology is a process and not a description. Objects cannot have an archaeological

---

59   Caflisch, L. fn. 50 above, 6.
60   A number are discussed in Forrest, fn. 1 above, 325-326.
61   Strati, A. fn. 53 above, 225.

nature. What the drafters probably meant were objects which might, through the medium of archaeological interpretation, prove to be of value to humankind. An object of an 'historical nature' is obviously one which is associated with the history of humankind but does it cover all of that history or only part of it? In respect of an earlier version of the phrase, 'archaeological objects and objects of historical nature', Oxman, Vice Chairman of the delegation of the United States of America, has said:

> The provision is not intended to apply to modern objects whatever their historical interest. Retention of the adjective 'historical' was insisted upon by Tunisian delegates, who felt that is was necessary to cover Byzantine relics that might be excluded by some interpretation of the word 'archaeological'. Hence, the term historical 'origin', lacking at best in elegance, when used with the term 'archaeological objects' in an article that expressly does not affect the law of salvage, does at least suggest the idea of objects that are many hundreds of years old.[62]

Oxman goes on to suggest 1453 (the fall of Constantinople) as a suitable date (with the possible application of dates of 1492, 1521 or 1533 in the Americas) for the limit of 'historical'. Caflisch rejected such an interpretation at the time.[63] Today it would be remote from current archaeological and historical scholarship and from legislative practice. It should certainly not be regarded as the correct interpretation of this provision.

Article 303(2) causes greater problems of interpretation. It reads:

> In order to control traffic in such objects [i.e. those of an archaeological and historical nature], the coastal State may, in applying Article 33, presume that their removal from the seabed in the zone referred to in that article without its approval would result in an infringement within its territory or territorial sea of the laws and regulations referred to in that article.

This is said to incorporate a legal fiction. Even as such, it is clumsy. States are not given control over the zone referred to (the contiguous zone) but may make a presumption which gives them the right to take action regarding removals. It is clumsy in that the four matters which States may control in the zone – customs, fiscal, immigration and sanitary – have no relationship to removal of archaeological material and any attempt to say that they do is stretching even a fiction.

Article 303(2) gives very limited protection even within the zone. It refers only to removal of objects. It would not give States the right to control damage which does not extend to removal. This could involve many activities e.g. deliberate or unintentional destruction in the search for items to remove; deposit of rubbish on a site; use of bottom trawling nets in a sensitive area.

There is some evidence that Article 303(2) was based on a misconception. Oxman has written:

> …the vast seaward reaches of the economic zone and continental shelf are not really relevant to the problem. The main issue was the policing of the area immediately beyond the territorial sea.[64]

There is evidence that this view was not correct at the time and, as the discussion on technology above shows, it is certainly not correct today. Once again, it probably flowed from the lack of archaeological expertise at the meetings on the law of the sea.

Article 303(3) disclaims any effect of that Article on certain other specified areas of law.

> Nothing in this article affects the rights of identifiable owners, the law of salvage and other rules of admiralty, or laws and practices with respect to cultural exchanges.

This cannot be read as a prohibition against affecting these rights and laws in other legal

---

62   Oxman, B.H. 'The Third United Nations Conference on the Law of the Sea: The Ninth Session (1980)' (1981) 75 *American Journal of International Law* 211, 241.
63   Caflisch, L. fn. 50 above, 8.
64   Oxman, B.H. fn. 62 above, 240.

instruments. It does not, for example, enshrine the law on salvage as immutable or immune from being abolished. It merely states that nothing in Article 303 affects the laws mentioned in sub-Article 3. It does no more than ensure that the limited provisions of paragraphs 1 and 2 of Article 303 cannot be interpreted so as to bring about such an effect. This interpretation is supported by the provisions of the later International Convention on Salvage 1989. Under that, States may reserve the right not to apply that Convention to maritime cultural property of prehistoric, archaeological or historic interest situated on the seabed. By allowing such a reservation, the Salvage Convention specifically recognizes that Article 303(3) of UNCLOS does not prevent exclusion of salvage law.

Article 303(4) recognizes that there will be later, more specific agreements among States:

> This Article is without prejudice to other international agreements and rules of international law regarding the protection of objects of an archaeological and historical nature.

Paragraph 4 says nothing about the general relationship between such agreements and UNCLOS. It relates solely to the effect of Article 303 itself.

The creation of UNCLOS, the code of universal sea-law in 1982, was one of the great achievements of States in international law-making in the twentieth century, but it gives little protection to underwater cultural heritage. The material covered is unclear. The rights and duties are limited and apply really only in the Area and the contiguous zone. Even in these zones it would be difficult to say what would be required. The general duty in Article 303(1) has no agreed or specified content. The authors of a major commentary on UNCLOS prophesied:

> Presumably, in the course of time, this incipient new branch of law will be completed by the competent international organization, above all UNESCO, and by State practice.[65]

5. The International Law Association Draft

The International Law Association, founded in 1873, conducts its major intellectual activities through committees which have been responsible for a substantial number of instruments in many areas of international law. In 1988 the author was appointed Chairman, and Professor James Nafziger of Willamette University in the United States of America, the Rapporteur of the just founded Cultural Heritage Law Committee. In consultation with the then Director of Studies of the ILA – Professor Ian Brownlie of Oxford University – we decided that the first task of the Committee should be the preparation of a draft convention on the protection of the underwater cultural heritage. The Committee as eventually constituted was composed of lawyers – private practitioners, government officials, academics – with experience in both heritage and law of the sea matters. They came from Algeria, Australia, Canada, China, Denmark, Ecuador, France, Germany, Greece, Hungary, India, Japan, Mexico, Netherlands, United Kingdom, and the United States of America.

Some comment has been made that the Committee did not consult sufficiently during the preparation of the Convention. However, it must be remembered that conditions were very different in the late 1980s compared to those in the period 1998-2001 when the Underwater Convention was being drafted. The Internet was in its infancy, so collecting and disseminating material was much more complicated. There were no organizations of salvors specializing in historic wrecks. The Committee maintained contact with such bodies as the Comité Maritime International which kept a very loose watching brief and the International Maritime Organization, although the latter indicated that it was only interested in wrecks hazardous to navigation. The Law of the Sea Office of the United Nations Organization was approached for comments in 1991 but did not reply.

Contact with the International Council on Monuments and Sites was of particular importance.

---

65   Rosenne, S. and Sohn, L.B. (eds) *United Nations Convention on the Law of the Sae 1982: A Commentary: Volume V* (Martinus Nijhoff, Dordrecht, 1989) 162.

The Committee realized early in its work that States would need objective standards by which to judge the appropriateness of actions in respect of the underwater cultural heritage. In 1991 the author approached Dr Graeme Henderson, Chairman of the newly established ICOMOS International Committee on the Underwater Cultural Heritage and asked if his Committee would assist in the preparation of a set of principles which could be attached to the Draft Convention in a document called the 'Charter'. Henderson took it to his Committee which agreed to proceed. The relevant principles were developed at meetings in Paris, 1994, and London, 1995, and forwarded to UNESCO. The ICOMOS Committee then went further and, from this set of principles, developed its International Charter on the Protection and Management of Underwater Cultural Heritage ratified by the 11th ICOMOS General Assembly in Sofia, Bulgaria, October 1996.

The work of the ILA Committee was publicized to the greatest extent possible taking into account its nature as an unfunded body of persons for whom this was a public service. Open sessions of the Committee were held during the ILA Conferences at Broadbeach, Australia, 1990, and Cairo, 1992, and two reports were published in the respective conference proceedings. The author discussed the proposals with archaeologists and parliamentarians from Belgium, France and Italy during a meeting at Ravello in May 1993.[66] A number of individuals outside the Committee made important comments on the various drafts as they were produced. A former Chairman of the Council of Europe *ad hoc* Committee accepted an invitation to participate in a two day drafting session of the ILA Committee in 1993.

The ILA Draft was prepared with the full knowledge of the existence and contents of the various versions of the Council of Europe Draft. In fact, the author and Professor Lyndel V. Prott, also a member of the ILA Committee, had prepared two[67] of the three reports on which the Parliamentary Assembly Recommendation leading to the Council of Europe activity was based. The debt that the ILA Draft owed to the Council of Europe Draft is apparent if one studies the two documents closely. For example, the Preamble to the latter was taken verbatim and, modified in the light of experience, was attached to the former. Many provisions of the ILA Draft had the same effect as that of the Council of Europe even if the wording and emphasis were not the same. Nevertheless, there was a fundamental difference in purpose of the two drafts. The Council of Europe Draft was intended to cover archaeological sites in internal waters, the territorial sea and an area adjacent to that. But its scope was never envisaged as extending further than the continental shelf or 200 miles (the latter proposal would have given virtually complete coverage of the Mediterranean Sea). On the other hand, the ILA Draft was specifically intended to deal only with the seaward jurisdiction asserted by States but also the seabed beneath the high seas. This was a fundamental difference which bore heavily on the content of the two drafts. Briefly, the ILA Draft was prepared for another context and in the light of some ten years further experience and technological development.

The ILA Draft was not intended to create a structure for the administration of underwater cultural heritage. It envisaged a system whereby anyone would be able to search for and excavate such heritage provided this was done in accordance with the standards set out in the Charter. If the standards were ignored, objects were to be seized on being brought into a Member State and sanctions imposed on the offender. States party were to require their nationals and ships flying their flag to observe the standards; offending persons and vessels were to be denied the use of ports in Member States. A 200-mile cultural protection zone was to be established off the coast of Member States and, within this, the coastal State would be responsible for protection. The Draft did not

---

66   O'Keefe, P.J. 'The International Law Association Draft Convention on the Protection of the Underwater Cultural Heritage' in Vedovato, G. & Borelli, L.V. (eds.) *La tutela del patrimonio archeologico subacqueo* (Instituo Poligrafico e Zecca dello Sato, Rome, 1995) 39.

67   O'Keefe, P.J. & Prott, L.V. 'Final Report on Legal Protection of the Underwater Cultural Heritage' Annex II in *The Underwater Cultural Heritage: Report of the Committee on Culture and Education, Parliamentary Assembly, Council of Europe* Doc. 4200 (Strasbourg, 1978) 45; 'Analysis of Legislation in Individual Countries of the Council of Europe' Annex III in *The Underwater Cultural Heritage: Report of the Committee on Culture and Education, Parliamentary Assembly, Council of Europe* Doc. 4200 (Strasbourg, 1978) 91. The third report on 'Archaeological Aspects' was by David Blackman.

apply to material less than 100 years old; to the wrecks of non-abandoned vessels nor to warships or other government vessels which were specifically excluded.

Following its adoption by the ILA Biennial Conference in 1994, a number of papers were published commenting on the ILA Draft.[68] At the same time, the Draft was subject to a critical but somewhat hysterical reaction.

> The ILA Draft would have sounded the death knell for the international community of sports and treasure divers, and consequently, whatever gains it would have achieved would only have been pyrrhic.[69]
>
> A blueprint has been drawn up by the archaeological community to put sports divers, treasure hunters, and salvors off wrecks permanently. It is entitled the 'Buenos Aires Draft Convention on the Protection of the Underwater Cultural Heritage'.[70]

In spite of reactions such as this, the ILA Draft did indeed act as a blueprint for the development of the UNESCO Convention on the Protection of the Underwater Cultural Heritage.

6. ACTION BY UNESCO

In 1993 the Executive Board of UNESCO invited the Organization's Director-General 'to consider the feasibility of drafting a new instrument for the protection of the underwater cultural heritage'.[71] A study[72] was made and presented to the Executive Board in 1995. It made frequent reference to the ILA Draft and stated that the Draft 'is a useful basis for the development of a UNESCO instrument on the subject'. Having considered the study, the Executive Board decided that States needed to further examine the implications of the jurisdictional aspects. The views of States were sought and, together with the feasibility study, these were put before the UNESCO General Conference in late 1995.[73] The Conference reacted favourably to the proposal for a convention but decided that more discussion was needed. In accordance with its wishes, a meeting of experts representing expertise in archaeology, salvage and jurisdictional regimes was held in Paris, 22nd-24th May 1996. The ILA Draft was a focal point for discussions at this meeting and it became clear that those present considered the Draft, subject to certain modifications, should be used as a basis for the UNESCO instrument. The views of the May meeting were sent to all Member States of UNESCO and to those with observer status – at that time the United Kingdom and the United States of America.

The UNESCO Executive Board, having examined the feasibility study, the report of the May meeting of experts and the comments of States on that report, recommended at its session in May 1997 that the General Conference request the Director-General of UNESCO to prepare a Draft Convention. The General Conference on 12th November 1997 adopted Resolution 29C/3 to the effect that "the protection of the underwater cultural heritage should be regulated at the international level and that the method adopted should be an international convention". The Director-General was invited to prepare a first draft convention; circulate this to States for comments and observations and then convene a group of governmental experts 'representing all regions together with representatives of the competent international organizations in order to consider this draft convention for submission to the General Conference at its thirtieth session' in 1999.[74] Drawing on the ILA Draft, UNESCO and the United Nations Division of Ocean Affairs

---

68 For example, O'Keefe, P.J. & Nafziger, J.A.R. 'The Draft Convention on the Protection of the Underwater Cultural Heritage' (1994) 25 *Ocean Development and International Law* 391; O'Keefe, P.J. 'Protecting the Underwater Cultural Heritage: The International Law Association Draft Convention' (1996) 20 *Marine Policy* 297.

69 Bederman, D. 'Historic Salvage and the Law of the Sea' (1998) 30 *Inter-American Law Review* 99, 113.

70 Reprinted on the Web from Compuserve Scuba Forum 15/3/1995.

71 Paragraph 15, Item 5.5.1, UNESCO Doc. 141EX/18, 28 May 1993.

72 UNESCO Doc. 146 EX/27, 23 March 1995.

73 UNESCO Doc. 28 C/39, 4 Oct. 1995.

74 See UNESCO Doc. 29 C/22. 5 Aug. 1997.

and Law of the Sea (DOALOS)[75] prepared a new draft convention and circulated it to States. It was discussed at a meeting of governmental experts in Paris in June/July 1998 and adopted as the basis for negotiations. Further discussion and negotiations took place at meetings in April 1999 and July 2000. A fourth and final meeting was held 26th March to 6th April 2001 with a week's prolongation during 3rd to 7th July that year. The Draft was adopted at 0h35 on the morning of Sunday 8th July by a vote of 49 in favour, 4 against and 8 abstentions.

The work of the expert meetings was supported by financial contributions from States such as Canada, Japan, Spain and the United States of America. That of Spain enabled a Spanish interpretation service to be available. The Nautical Archaeology Society in the United Kingdom supported the publication of documents on the subject in 1998[76] and France contributed to the production of a second set of documents in 2000.[77]

6.1 Negotiations

These comments are not intended to be critical of any particular State but to indicate to outsiders the pressures at work in shaping the Underwater Convention. They may also give insiders a view of how their work was seen by an observer. It will become obvious that protection of underwater cultural heritage was but one of many forces at work in shaping the negotiating position of States. It will also be obvious that UNCLOS is understood in different ways by different States.

The first meeting of governmental experts elected Carsten Lund of Denmark as its Chairman – a position to which he was re-elected unopposed in all subsequent meetings. He performed this task with dignity and tact. Lund had long been associated with international efforts to protect the underwater cultural heritage, particularly in the context of the Council of Europe.

Negotiation of the UNESCO Convention on the Protection of the Underwater Cultural Heritage was never going to be easy. Many States had what they considered to be vital interests at stake. For example, the self-nominated 'major maritime powers'[78] – France, Germany, Japan, Netherlands, Norway, Russia, United Kingdom, United States of America – did not want to see any coastal State have control over underwater cultural heritage on the continental shelf. These States regarded any move in this direction as an example of what they called 'creeping jurisdiction', that is, the first step in a gradual process by which States claim greater and greater control over the continental shelf thus upsetting the 'delicate balance' to be found in UNCLOS. That this would occur if States had control over the underwater cultural heritage on their continental shelves is no more than a supposition and is not borne out in reality.[79] A number of States have taken control over this area for this purpose without leading to wider claims. Nevertheless, it is an argument strongly supported by the States listed above. They took the view that, as protection of the underwater cultural heritage was raised and discussed in the law of the sea negotiations resulting in Articles 149 and 303, it could not be raised again in the UNESCO negotiations. This is plainly a political position and is not required by international law. Other States were of the opinion that the matter had not been decided at the law of the sea negotiations and could be raised again. This approach was supported by authors such as Caflisch who, writing before UNCLOS had even been concluded, said:

> The third United Nations Conference on the Law of the Sea afforded the international community an excellent opportunity to do this [devise 'an effective

---

75   Advice was given by the International Maritime Organization.
76   Prott, L.V. and Strong, I. (eds) *Background Materials on the Underwater Cultural Heritage* (texts in English and French) (UNESCO/Nautical Archaeology Society, Paris/Portsmouth) 1998.
77   Prott, L.V. and Planche, E. (eds) *Background Materials on the Underwater Cultural Heritage Vol. II* (texts in English, French and Spanish) (French National Commission for UNESCO, Paris) 2000.
78   Greece, a State with a high shipping tonnage, objected to this designation and subsequently they called themselves the 'like-minded States'.
79   Perhaps the States concerned expected other States to act as they had done. For example, the whole continental shelf doctrine originated from a claim by the United States of America in 1948 and in 1982 the United Kingdom threw a 200km security cordon – a 'total exclusion zone' – around the Falkland Islands: Churchill, R.R. and Lowe, A.V. fn. 4 above, 424.

legal framework for the protection and preservation of the world's submarine heritage']. Unfortunately, this opportunity has been passed up. The only hope which can be expressed is that the issues examined in this paper will be solved by instruments other than the future Law of the Sea Convention.[80]

The situation had become much more crucial considering that technological developments had opened up vastly greater areas of the seabed to exploitation. Italy made the point that: 'It would be meaningless to simply repeat the provisions of the UNCLOS, including their shortcomings without adding improvements'.[81] Furthermore, Italy stated:

> The Coastal State should be entitled to be informed of, to regulate and to authorize all activities relating to underwater cultural heritage found on its continental shelf (or in its exclusive economic zone). This is the best way to promote the protection of the heritage and to ensure the disposal of it for the public benefit. Rights of this kind are neither specifically allowed, nor prohibited by UNCLOS. It is the filling of an UNCLOS gap, as permitted by UNCLOS itself.[82]

This is particularly noteworthy as Italy had supported the 'maritime powers' until the American underwater explorer, Robert Ballard, found ancient wrecks on the Italian continental shelf and removed some objects for study in the United States of America without consulting Italy.[83]

It was obvious that the 'major maritime powers' had many interests at play in attempting to ensure that their view of UNCLOS prevailed. For the United States of America in particular there were security considerations and a desire to allow nothing which would interfere with the ability of their armed forces to act in the Area or on continental shelves of other States. For the United Kingdom, there appeared to be an unwillingness to take responsibility for all of the underwater cultural heritage on its continental shelf. In spite of its maritime tradition, the United Kingdom had been wary of devoting resources to protection of that heritage. For example, one study indicated that its policy had been to severely limit the number of protected wrecks within its territorial sea.[84] Moreover, the protected areas are small in size and the object is to facilitate recovery of archaeological material rather that preservation of the site.[85] With this background it was unlikely that the United Kingdom would be willing to extend any control over underwater cultural heritage on its continental shelf. Norway spoke often and vociferously against coastal State control over underwater cultural heritage on the continental shelf.[86] Indeed, it was on record as having reserved its position as to whether UNESCO was the appropriate forum for negotiation and adoption of the Underwater Convention.[87] It would have preferred the negotiations to have been removed to the United Nations in New York; presumably on the grounds that there, law of the sea arguments would be more likely to prevail. However, it was difficult to see the real basis for Norway's objections and obdurate stance. Russia, apart from security concerns which it clearly shared with the United States of America, may well have been anxious about the situation in the Black Sea. Since the break-up of the Soviet Union, leaving Russia with a very small sea coast in this area, it may have seen both UNCLOS and the Underwater Convention as permitting activities too close to that coast for comfort.

---

80   Caflisch, L. fn. 50 above, 32.
81   Document presented by the Government of Italy, Third Meeting of Intergovernmental Experts, UNESCO Headquarters, Paris, 3-7 July 2000, 1. Also reproduced in Allotta, G., *Tutela del Patrimonio Archeologico Subacqueo* (Centro Studi Giulio Pastore, Palerno, 2001) 57.
82   Above p. 2.
83   Above, fn. 81, pp.108-110 reproduces various newspaper reports reflecting particularly the Sicilian view: see also *The Times*, 6 Aug. 1997, 10.
84   In 1998 Firth reported that there were 45 protected wrecks (see below) – a small percentage of those off the coast of the United Kingdom. Today the figure is 48 – a very small increase.
85   Firth, A. 'Making Archaeology: The History of the Protection of Wrecks Act 1973 and the Constitution of an Archaeological Resource' (1999) 28 *International Journal of Nautical Archaeology* 1, 10.
86   Lund, C. 'The Making of the 2001 UNESCO Convention' in Prott, L.V. (ed.) *Finishing the Interrupted Voyage* (UNESCO/Institute of Art and Law; Paris/Builth Wells; 2006) 16.
87   Item 38(a) in the United Nations General Assembly debate on Oceans and Law of the Sea, 1998.

Quite apart from questions involving the law of the sea, States had other interests at play. For example, for Spain and the States of South and Central America and the Caribbean, this involved the remains of warships and other vessels on government business during the colonial period. If these were Spanish wrecks, what were the relative rights between Spain and its former colonies? Were issues of State succession involved?

Another matter of particular importance to the United States of America was the freedom of the diving segment of the public to have access to underwater cultural heritage. In part this consists of sport and hobby divers visiting and photographing wrecks. But there are also historic ship salvors, of whom the great majority are to be found in the United States although they may work in waters around the world. In the end it seemed that this latter group did not exert a significant influence on decisions made by the United States which was much more concerned with ensuring general public access.

The organization of the meetings was affected by a number of problems. Firstly, there had to be a strong educational element. As already noted, UNESCO produced two compilations of background material for the use of delegates.[88] Also there was a lack of continuity among the personnel of delegations. A change of personnel and inadequate briefing made for slow progress as delegates had to learn what had happened at previous meetings. Those who tried to use expressions from UNCLOS, seemingly without knowledge of the criticisms made of these over the past twenty years, also constrained progress. Secondly, the composition of delegations often demonstrated little attention to the complexities of the subject matter. In part this was understandable in that expense precluded some States from sending more than one person. Nevertheless, a generalist diplomat or a lawyer experienced solely in law of the sea matters would have trouble appreciating the nature of archaeological problems and *vice versa* for an archaeologist. Here special mention should be made of the International Council for Monuments and Sites which fielded a significant observer delegation that made substantial philosophical and technical contributions to the debate. Another factor for small delegations was their inability to attend multiple working groups set up to examine specific problems simultaneously. This became particularly significant during the final days of the fourth meeting in 2001 when a drafting committee also had to operate alongside informal negotiating groups and plenary sessions. In the end, the drafting committee system failed for lack of a quorum as delegates concentrated on the policy aspects. Contrariwise, large delegations, often reflecting internal interest groups in their own society, may have had an intimidating aspect for States with smaller numbers.[89] Thirdly, there was the position of the United States of America. This country had played a major role in underwater archaeology. It had provided many of the technological developments giving greater access to the seabed. It was home to the major historic ship salvors. But it was not a Member State of UNESCO.[90] During the debates it could participate only with the invitation of the Chairman following permission by the Member States and had to speak after all Member States. At the final moments of the fourth meeting, it could not vote. This position cast an inhibiting pall over the United States' participation and seemed to create a sense of frustration, if not of victimization. On the other hand there were comments in the corridors that the United States wanted the benefits of membership without paying its dues. This was unfortunate but it is noteworthy that shortly after the negotiations concluded the United States rejoined UNESCO.

The first meeting of governmental experts was presented with a draft, based on the ILA Draft, but jointly proposed by the United Nations Division of Ocean Affairs and Law of the Sea (DOALOS). The participation of DOALOS was attacked during the debate by the United States of America on the grounds that this was not authorized and exceeded the authority of that body. In a measured reply, the representative of DOALOS explained that it had reacted to UNESCO's proposal of

---

88   Prott, L.V. and Strong, I. (eds) fn. 76 above; Prott, L.V., Planche E. and Roca-Hachem, R. (eds) fn. 77 above.
89   Cf. Clute, R.E. 'African Negotiations on the Law of the Sea' in Ress, G. & Will, M.R. *Vorträge, Reden und Berichte aus dem Europa-Institut Nr. 44* (Europa-Institut, Universität des Saarlandes, Saarbrücken, 1984) 15.
90   The United States withdrew from UNESCO in 1985 and did not rejoin until 2002. The United Kingdom withdrew in 1986 but rejoined in 1997.

collaboration on the Draft and responded with advice as it was bound to do. DOALOS continued to attend all meetings but, perhaps in response to further political pressure, was notably silent thereafter except when directly addressed. It would seem that the objective had been to separate UNESCO from any formal contact with the major United Nations law of the sea body. At any rate, the experts at the first meeting adopted the joint UNESCO/DOALOS Draft as the basis of their negotiations and the issue of sponsorship became moot although the tactics adopted in this episode annoyed a large number of delegations and laid a foundation of suspicion.

The first meeting of governmental experts in 1988 began with an extensive statement of position by delegations. Then the text of the UNESCO/DOALOS Draft was examined article by article. This was basically an exchange of views. No decisions were taken and there were no negotiations.

At the second meeting in April 1999, three Working Groups were established to discuss:
1. The definitions, scope and general principles;
2. The Annex i.e. the Rules developed by ICOMOS;
3. Jurisdiction.

Important progress was made at this meeting although the results were somewhat chaotic. There appeared to be substantial agreement on the role and content of the Annex. Possibilities for dealing with the issue of jurisdiction were suggested. A Canadian proposal restricting the Draft Convention to activities 'directed at' underwater cultural heritage overcame a number of problems associated with activities such as cable laying although it did restrict the scope of the Convention.[91]

In November 1999, Kiochiro Matsuura of Japan was elected Director-General of UNESCO in place of Federico Mayor of Spain. Unlike Mayor, Matsuura took a direct interest in the Draft Convention and addressed the opening session of the third meeting of experts in July 2000. He stressed that UNESCO had an important normative role in the creation of legal instruments to protect the cultural heritage. However, the meeting began slowly with the first morning being spent on a discussion of the rules of procedure and the role of consensus as opposed to voting. Eventually the Chairman stated that he intended to conduct the meeting in the spirit of Resolution 26 of the 30th session of the General Conference which called for the meeting to make every effort to reach consensus. Three Working Groups were established to cover roughly the same topics as the second meeting of experts. Refinements were made to the text and various proposals advanced for reaching a consensus but this could not be achieved particularly in relation to the issue of jurisdiction.

Invitations to the fourth meeting of governmental experts indicated that the Director-General of UNESCO wished this to be the final meeting with a settled text at its end. In recognition of the work to be done, the meeting extended from 26th March to 6th April. Once again, there was a procedural wrangle on the issue of consensus that occupied most of the first morning. When substantive proceedings began, the meeting concentrated on a Single Negotiating Text produced by the Chairman and contained in a consolidated working paper reproducing also the 1999 draft together with proposed amendments – all set out in tabular form. In the Chairman's view, the Single Negotiating Text reflected positions taken in all three meetings of governmental experts, on amendments proposed in the course of discussion and on suggestions made during informal meetings. Attention concentrated on the Single Negotiating Text. To allow time for informal discussion on the controversial issues of coastal State control of the continental shelf/EEZ, warships and salvage, work proceeded on those articles where there was general agreement. Eventually, through the activities of an informal group, consensus was reached on provisions dealing with the law of salvage and finds. However, by the afternoon of Wednesday 4th April, it was obvious that the issue of coastal State control was coming to a vote. On one side were the 'major maritime powers' and on the other, the Group of 77 together with such States as Australia, Canada, China, Italy and Portugal. The Chairman left the podium to speak to the Director-General. On his return he indicated that the Director-General would like there to be further efforts to find consensus and

---

91   See further O'Keefe, P.J. 'Second Meeting of Governmental Experts to Consider the Draft Convention on the Protection of Underwater Cultural Heritage: Paris, UNESCO Headquarters (April 19-24 1999)' (1999) 8 *International Journal of Cultural Property* 568.

proposed extending the meeting by a week at some later time. There was uproar in diplomatic terms but eventually the meeting acceded to the Director-General's wishes. The remainder of the meeting was something of an anti-climax as discussion on many of the articles could not proceed until there was a decision on the continental shelf/EEZ issue.

The extension of the fourth meeting of governmental experts took place from 2nd to 7th July 2001. In the interval, the Chairman had gathered small groups for informal meetings on the continental shelf/EEZ and warships. During the July meeting, plenary sessions were frequently suspended to allow for further informal sessions on these two topics. As the week progressed, the pressure intensified. Coffee breaks disappeared and dinner was a sandwich brought in during the half-hour break. Many delegates and the Secretariat worked from 8h00 to 24h00. Finally, as noted above, the Draft was approved and recommended to the General Conference of UNESCO for adoption at 0h35 on the morning of Sunday 8th July by a vote of 49 in favour, four against and eight abstentions. Decisions on a number of matters had been taken with the Chairman agreeing to record a State's adverse position.

The Recommendation to the General Conference was considered by Commission IV (dealing with matters of the Culture Sector) of the UNESCO General Conference on 29th October 2001. The debate began with general comments by States, many of which referred to the Draft Convention's conformity to, or compatibility with, UNCLOS. Most States thought that there was no problem; that there was full compatibility. But some indicated that they considered it contained provisions contrary to UNCLOS. Norway expressly reserved its position under Article 311 of the latter.[92] Then there were a number of amendments proposed by Russia and the United Kingdom with the endorsement of the United States of America. These were overwhelmingly rejected without debate. France withdrew further amendments it had proposed. The Draft Underwater Convention was then approved in Commission IV by 94 votes to five with seventeen abstentions and was recommended to the plenary session. As previously noted, it was definitively adopted there by 87 votes to four with fifteen abstentions.[93] It was signed by the Director-General of UNESCO and the president of the General Conference on 6th November after which it became open for ratification, acceptance, approval or accession in accordance with Article 26. It was UNESCO's fifth international convention dealing with cultural heritage.

The path to this point had been long and arduous for delegations and the Secretariat. The Chairman of all the four intergovernmental meetings some years later expressed his misgivings over the route taken:

> … UNESCO is a poor organization in terms of material resources; not in terms of quality but in terms of supporting resources, which means that their plan of action in the field was a plan of one negotiating meeting a year. This, in my experience, is not a very fruitful way of negotiating because you lose momentum between negotiating meetings and you risk replacement of people in different countries, which means that the same problem will be taken up again by new people from the same country as had presented it before and where a solution had already been found. So the infrequency of the meetings was not very productive for the negotiations.[94]

There is much of merit in this argument although a contrary viewpoint is possible. Might the long period between meetings allow for maturation of policy? Probably this would take place only if States were constantly reminded of the issues so that these were not allowed to slip into the bottom of the drawer until it was time for the next meeting. But this requires resources of personnel and finances both of which were, and are, in short supply for the Secretariat and many States with a direct interest in the negotiations. It is difficult to see how the points Lund makes could have been overcome.

---

92   Article 311 relates to treaties 'modifying or suspending' the operation of UNCLOS.
93   It seemed a number of States had already departed by this time as the Conference was scheduled to close at the end of that day.
94   Lund, C. fn. 86 above, 17.

7. Events since Adoption

Much has happened since 2001. UNESCO, in spite of a miniscule budget and lack of personnel, has been particularly active in working to promote and bring about some of the structure that the Convention mandates. In this it has been helped by donations from States such as Norway, a non-party State, and Spain.

7.1 UNESCO

As already stated, the Underwater Convention came into force on 2nd January 2009. This allowed the meeting of States Parties foreseen in Article 23 to be held. It then established a Scientific and Technical Advisory Body which has met yearly since 2010. These two bodies, in conjunction with the UNESCO Secretariat, have been active in promoting the Underwater Convention and engaging in 'capacity-building and awareness-raising issues'.

> These included the organization of training courses, exhibitions, regional meetings and scientific conferences, the creation of the UNITWIN-network, the publication of a training manual and the Manual for Activities directed at Underwater Cultural Heritage, outreach to youths through children books, cartoons and a new website, a photo exhibition at UNESCO and an Exchange Day on Underwater Cultural Heritage …[95]

7.1.1 Operational Guidelines

At its fourth session, May 2013, the Meeting of States Parties adopted *Operational Guidelines for the Convention on the Protection of the Underwater Cultural Heritage*.[96] The role of these Guidelines is set out in Paragraph 22:

> The present Operational Guidelines can neither be understood as a subsequent agreement nor as rewriting, amending or interpreting the Convention. They merely aim to facilitate its implementation by giving practical guidance. In case of doubt, the text of the Convention prevails as interpreted according to the general rules of interpretation codified in the Vienna Convention of [sic] the Law of Treaties of 1969.

This is an accurate summation of the subservient position of Guidelines. Written years after the adoption of the Convention, by a group of people unrepresentative of those who negotiated it, the Guidelines can do no more than make suggestions to States Parties or provide possible explanations for aspects that may seem ambiguous. They can, however, give guidance on procedures to be followed in implementing the Underwater Convention. Unfortunately, in places the Guidelines use the imperative 'shall' with reference to actions by States; for example, in Paragraphs 26 and 27 dealing with notifications and declarations by States. Other words such as 'may' or 'should' would be appropriate.

There is no provision in the Underwater Convention for Operational Guidelines. However, that is not to say that States Parties cannot adopt them if they so desire. Similarly, the Guidelines make provision for an Underwater Cultural Heritage Fund. Once again, States Parties can establish this but cannot compel contributions to be made. These must be voluntary as Paragraph 66 acknowledges.

Reference will be made to the Guidelines in the following pages when they are relevant to specific Articles of the Convention. However, it must be stated that there are some significant deficiencies. Most importantly, there is no guidance on Articles 14, 15 and 17. These are the heart of enforcement procedures in the Convention and yet the Guidelines ignore them. They are aspects on which States could well benefit from having the implications explained. For example, it could usefully be made clear that Article 14 goes beyond preventing entry into a State's territory of underwater cultural heritage excavated contrary to the Underwater Convention. This Article applies also to dealing in or possession of such heritage. States should check their legislation

---

95   UNESCO Doc. UCH/!5/5.MSP/220/3 p.4.
96   Resolution 6/MSP 4. See <http://www.unesco.org/new/en/culture/themes/underwater-cultural-heritage/2001-convention/meeting-of-states-parties/fourth-session-of-the-meeting-of-the-states-parties> accessed 4 July 2013.

to make sure this is possible. Do States have legislation in place to prohibit the use of their ports for activities directed at underwater cultural heritage which are not in conformity with the Convention?[97] What would be appropriate sanctions for failure to comply with the Convention?[98] None of these are mentioned. Moreover, no attempt is made to clarify the meaning of 'commercial exploitation'. The prohibition against this is a crucial aspect of the Convention but what it means for States is really not explained beyond vague words such as 'traded, sold, bought or bartered' which are taken directly from the Convention itself and on which there is no elaboration.

7.1.2 Manual for Activities Directed at Underwater Cultural Heritage

This is intended to explain the Rules contained in the Annex to the Underwater Convention.[99] Drafted by archaeologists, it concentrates on providing guidance on the practical aspects of organizing activities directed at underwater cultural heritage. It will be referred to in the discussion of the Underwater Convention in the following pages.

7.1.3 Training Manual

UNESCO has also produced a Training Manual for the UNESCO Foundation Course in the Protection and Management of Underwater Cultural Heritage in Asia and the Pacific.[100] This contains much useful information on many aspects of underwater cultural heritage. For example, there are units on management of underwater cultural heritage, *in situ* preservation and museology with eighteen units in all. One unit is devoted to a basic introduction to the Underwater Convention as a whole. The course itself is aimed at site managers and national experts nominated by the competent national authorities responsible for protecting underwater cultural heritage. It is expected to generate a widening pool of expertise as those taking the course should share their newly acquired skills with colleagues on their return home.

7.1.4 Code of Ethics

UNESCO has adopted a Code of Ethics for Diving on Underwater Cultural Heritage Sites.[101] This was approved at the first meeting of the Scientific and Technical Advisory Body in 2010 and adopted by the meeting of States Parties in the following year. It is being promoted in conjunction with the World Underwater Federation.

The Code urges support for the Underwater Convention. More specifically, it advises divers not to touch wrecks and submerged ruins; not to take souvenirs; to report discoveries and be careful when taking photographs. Divers are told that 'objects coming from a submerged archaeological site should not be commercially traded' and 'dispersing this heritage robs us of our past'.

7.2 United Nations

The General Assembly of the United Nations has regularly passed resolutions mentioning the Underwater Convention.[102] What is interesting is the gradual change in these Resolutions and the way they are currently phrased. For example, Resolution A/RES/53/32 of 6th January 1999 reads:

> 20. *Notes with interest* the ongoing work of the United Nations Educational, Scientific and Cultural Organization towards a convention for the implementation of the provisions of the Convention, relating to the protection of the underwater cultural heritage, and stresses the importance of ensuring that the instrument to be elaborated is in full conformity with the relevant provisions of the Convention.

The emphasis on full conformity with the United Nations Convention on the Law of the Sea reflects specifically the attitude of the 'major maritime powers' in negotiations for the Underwater Convention. A similar Resolution was adopted in 2000 and 2001.

---

97 Below page 82.
98 Below page 84.
99 <http://www.unesco.org/culture/en/underwater/pdf/UCH-Manual.pdf>.
100 <http://unesdoc.unesco.org/images/0021/002172/217234e.pdf>.
101 <http://www.unesco.org/new/en/culture/themes/underwater-cultural-heritage/divers/code-of-ethics/>.
102 <http://www.un.org/depts/los/general_assembly/general_assembly_resolutions.htm#1991>.

The issue does not appear again in General Assembly Resolutions in any substantive way until 2006 when it was covered in two paragraphs in Resolution A/RES/60/30:

> 7. *Urges* all States to cooperate, directly or through competent international bodies, in taking measures to protect and preserve objects of an archaeological and historical nature found at sea, in conformity with the Convention, and calls upon States to work together on such diverse challenges and opportunities as the appropriate relationship between salvage law and scientific management and conservation of underwater cultural heritage, increasing technological abilities to discover and reach underwater sites, looting and growing underwater tourism;

> 8. *Notes* the effort made by the United Nations Educational, Scientific and Cultural Organization with respect to the preservation of underwater cultural heritage, and notes in particular the rules annexed to the 2001 Convention on the Protection of the Underwater Cultural Heritage that address the relationship between salvage law and scientific principles of management, conservation and protection of underwater cultural heritage among parties, their nationals and vessels flying their flag.

This Resolution was repeated in the same terms in 2007 and 2008. Paragraph 7 is basically a statement of the content of Articles 149 and 303 of UNCLOS. Paragraph 8 barely acknowledges the work done in UNESCO. The words 'the effort made' seem to suggest that this work was barely successful. Its reference to the Rules of the Annex to the Underwater Convention does not make sense. There is no provision on salvage law in the Annex and certainly nothing that would indicate a relationship between it and scientific principles of management. Rule 2 of the Annex does deal with 'commercial exploitation' but the purpose behind this is to remove any financial incentive from the decision to work on a wrecked vessel. It removes the underlying basis of salvage. This sentence appears to be more a political compromise among States with differing views on the value of the Convention and does not reflect the real text of the Annex.

Resolution A/RES/63/111 in 2009 is the same except that it notes the Underwater Convention would be coming into force. Similarly, Resolution A/RES/65/37 of 2011, while continuing the same theme regarding salvage, notes 'the recent deposit of instruments of ratification and acceptance' of the Underwater Convention. With Resolution A/RES/66/231 of 2012 there is a notable change when it "calls upon States that have not yet done so to consider becoming parties" to the Underwater Convention. This is followed in Resolution A/RES/67/68 of 2013 which:

> *Acknowledges* the tenth anniversary, in November 2011, of the 2001 Convention on the Protection of the Underwater Cultural Heritage, calls upon States that have not yet done so to consider becoming party to that Convention …

The remainder of those two Resolutions dealing with this issue reiterate the statements on salvage. The United Nations Resolutions also had a general clause in the Preamble. That in the 2013 Resolution reads:

> *Emphasizing* that underwater archaeological, cultural and historical heritage, including shipwrecks and watercraft, holds essential information on the history of humankind and that such heritage is a resource that needs to be protected and preserved.

This also has changed over the years. For example, in 2000 it consisted of only a brief reference to Article 303 of UNCLOS. It is telling that the clause does not now use the terminology of UNCLOS although this still appears in the body of the Resolutions e.g. 'objects of an archaeological and historical nature'.

These Resolutions have been set out in considerable detail because they illustrate a changing attitude at the United Nations towards the Underwater Convention. As previously noted, in 1998 Norway was on record as having reserved its position as to whether UNESCO was the appropriate forum for negotiation and adoption of the Underwater Convention.[103] It would have

---

103   Item 38(a) in the United Nations General Assembly debate on Oceans and Law of the Sea, 1998.

preferred the negotiations to have been removed to the United Nations in New York; presumably on the grounds that there, law of the sea arguments would be more likely to prevail. Other States had a similar attitude. The dislike of the Underwater Convention these States held is still evident in the emphasis on salvage even though that emphasis makes no sense. But the call on States to consider becoming a Party to the Convention marks a significant departure from previous attitudes and a welcome move to supporting it.

INTERPRETING THE UNDERWATER CONVENTION

1. Introduction to Treaty Interpretation

The eminent Australian jurist, Daniel O'Connell, once wrote that the problem of treaty interpretation:

> ... is one of ascertaining the logic inherent in the treaty, and pretending that this is what the parties desired. In so far as this logic can be discovered by reference to the terms of the treaty itself, it is impermissible to depart from those terms. In so far as it cannot, it is permissible. These two propositions underlie the so-called 'canons of treaty interpretation', which are no more than logical devices for ascertaining the real area of treaty operation. Writers are divided into those who believe it is possible to formulate definite rules for interpretation and those who believe that this is a delusion. In several decided cases the courts have prefaced their remarks by laying down rules for interpretation and have immediately departed from them because it was found that the text required it.[1]

This suggests that treaty interpretation is more an art than a science but there must be some guides to ascertain the logic, if any, underlying what States have agreed.

Primary guidance for interpreting the Underwater Convention, as indeed all international conventions, is given by the *Vienna Convention on the Law of Treaties* 1969.[2] There, a general rule is stated that:

> A treaty shall be interpreted in good faith in accordance with the ordinary meaning to be given to the terms of the treaty in their context and in the light of its object and purpose.[3]

This indicates that the text, its context and the object and purpose of the treaty have each to be considered.

> By 'context' is meant material related to the conclusion of the treaty .... One naturally begins with the text, followed by the context, and then other matters, in particular subsequent material. ... Interpretation involves an elucidation of the meaning of the text, not a fresh investigation as to the supposed intentions of the parties.[4]

Under Article 32 of the 1969 Vienna Convention, resort may be had to supplementary means of interpretation "in order to confirm the meaning resulting from the application of article 31, or to determine the meaning when the interpretation according to article 31: (a) leaves the meaning ambiguous or obscure; or (b) leads to a result which is manifestly absurd or unreasonable". Among the supplementary means of interpretation is the preparatory work, commonly known as the *travaux préparatoires*, for the convention. What exactly comprises the *travaux* is not definitively established. In the case of the Underwater Convention, it would comprise the successive drafts, the tapes of the debate and position papers presented by States. But all of these are only part of the process by which positions were reached as there were also unrecorded informal sessions and private negotiations. In all, these *travaux* are unlikely to provide significant assistance to

---

1   *International Law* (Stevens, London, 2nd edn, 1970) 253.
2   1155 U.N.T.S. 331.
3   Article 31. This Article is regarded by the International Court of Justice as reflecting customary international law: *Kasikili/Sedudu Island (Botswana/Namibia), Judgment,* I.C.J. Reports 1999, p.1059, para. 19.
4   Aust, A. *Modern Treaty Law and Practice* (Cambridge University Press, 2000) 187.

interpretation. No minutes were kept of the drafting committee's work. There is only a summary record of the proceedings of the meetings of experts. The memories of individual participants carry little weight. As Caflisch notes: "The recollections of negotiators, however accurate, can hardly be considered as conclusive".[5]

Drawing on all of the above it can be said with elementary accuracy that there are two prime considerations to guide interpretation. Firstly, the underwater cultural heritage must be protected. This means it and its context are not to be wantonly destroyed or damaged. If scientific research is to be conducted it can only be on the basis that complete records are kept and available to the public as well as experts. Secondly, the Underwater Convention is based on co-operation. This is to take place at different levels: between States; between States and individuals and among individuals. Only if all those involved co-operate can the Convention reach its full potential to protect the underwater cultural heritage.

RETROACTIVITY

A retroactive convention is one which applies to events which took place before it entered into force for a State. There is no provision for retroactivity in the Underwater Convention. The normal rule of international law as represented by custom and Article 28 of the *Vienna Convention on the Law of Treaties* is indeed that international conventions are not retroactive.

However, a treaty can, of course, apply to a pre-existing act, fact or situation which continues after its entry into force.[6] States, on becoming party, have to take care that existing rights, such as those of salvors, are not affected so as to bring any applicable human rights provisions on property into play.[7]

---

5   Caflisch, L. 'Submarine Antiquities and the International Law of the Sea' (1982) 13 *Netherlands Yearbook of International Law* 3.
6   Aust, A. fn. 4 above.
7   Some of these are discussed in relation to the UNESCO/DOALOS Draft in Fletcher-Tomenius, P. & Williams, M. 'The Draft UNESCO/DOALOS Convention on the Protection of Underwater Cultural Heritage and Conflict with the European Convention on Human Rights' (1999) 28 *International Journal of Nautical Archaeology* 145.

Analysis of Individual Articles

Preamble

The General Conference of the United Nations Educational, Scientific and Cultural Organization, meeting in Paris from 15 October to 3 November 2001, at its 31st session,

Acknowledging the importance of underwater cultural heritage as an integral part of the cultural heritage of humanity and a particularly important element in the history of peoples, nations, and their relations with each other concerning their common heritage,

Realizing the importance of protecting and preserving the underwater cultural heritage and that responsibility therefor rests with all States,

Noting growing public interest in and public appreciation of underwater cultural heritage,

Convinced of the importance of research, information and education to the protection and preservation of underwater cultural heritage,

Convinced of the public's right to enjoy the educational and recreational benefits of responsible non-intrusive access to in situ underwater cultural heritage, and of the value of public education to contribute to awareness, appreciation and protection of that heritage,

Aware of the fact that underwater cultural heritage is threatened by unauthorized activities directed at it, and of the need for stronger measures to prevent such activities,

Conscious of the need to respond appropriately to the possible negative impact on underwater cultural heritage of legitimate activities that may incidentally affect it,

Deeply concerned by the increasing commercial exploitation of underwater cultural heritage, and in particular by certain activities aimed at the sale, acquisition or barter of underwater cultural heritage,

Aware of the availability of advanced technology that enhances discovery of and access to underwater cultural heritage,

Believing that cooperation among States, international organizations, scientific institutions, professional organizations, archaeologists, divers, other interested parties and the public at large is essential for the protection of underwater cultural heritage,

Considering that survey, excavation and protection of underwater cultural heritage necessitate the availability and application of special scientific methods and the use of suitable techniques and equipment as well as a high degree of professional specialization, all of which indicate a need for uniform governing criteria,

Realizing the need to codify and progressively develop rules relating to the protection and preservation of underwater cultural heritage in conformity with international law and practice, including the UNESCO Convention on the Means of Prohibiting and Preventing the Illicit Import, Export and Transfer of Ownership of Cultural Property of 14 November 1970, the UNESCO Convention for the Protection of the World Cultural and Natural Heritage of 16 November 1972 and the United Nations Convention on the Law of the Sea of 10 December 1982,

Committed to improving the effectiveness of measures at international, regional and national levels for the preservation in situ or, if necessary for scientific or protective purposes, the careful recovery of underwater cultural heritage,

Having decided at its twenty-ninth session that this question should be made the subject of an international convention,

Adopts this second day of November 2001 this Convention.

Preamble

The Preamble to an international convention is significant. The *Vienna Convention on the Law of Treaties* states that this is part of the context in terms of which treaties are to be interpreted (Article 31(2)). Thus, the Preamble should be seen as establishing general principles to guide interpretation.

In becoming party to the Underwater Convention, States acknowledge the importance of underwater cultural heritage as stated in the Preamble. Their actions and those of their administrators must be guided by this consideration. For example, States are to impose adequate sanctions for violation of measures taken to implement the Underwater Convention (Article 17). Judges, in imposing sentences, must consider the harm done to the heritage and not be swayed by romantic notions of treasure so heavily emphasized by the popular press. For example, one of the events surrounding the excavation of gold from the *Central America* involved a visit to the home of the judge:

> Robol thought that Judge Kellam should view some of what they had found … and the judge invited the group to his home. … The judge offered them some refreshments, then led them the back way into his home to a study. Bob carried a cosmetics case, and when they reached the judge's study, he placed it on the judge's desk. Robol thanked the judge for agreeing to meet with them on the weekend and spoke for a minute about why he had requested the meeting. Then Bob opened the cosmetics case and pulled out a towel, inside of which was a layer of felt, and inside that was the gold bar they had showed to the investors. Bob peeled back the felt, and the judge examined the bar and its markings. "Lordy, lordy" said the judge, and everyone, including the judge, laughed. The meeting lasted ten minutes.[8]

This is not to say that Judge Kellam was swayed by the sight of the gold but is shows the impression that treasure can make.

The importance of underwater cultural heritage, as the Preamble notes, may well need to be part of a programme of education, both for the general public and specialized groups such as judges. The importance of the archaeological heritage on land has been broadly acknowledged for many years but that underwater has only recently been recognized.

The public's right to 'responsible non-intrusive access to *in situ* underwater cultural heritage' is emphasized in the Preamble. States should not seek to protect this heritage by making it completely off-limits to all but authorized archaeologists. Access may need to be regulated but it must be recognized that it is the public's heritage, not that of some bureaucrat or specialist group. Underwater reserves can be created where the interest of the general public is whetted and education in awareness carried out. For those who want greater involvement, there should be programmes allowing amateurs to learn how underwater archaeology is done and to participate in activities such as surveys and excavations run by archaeologists.

The Preamble refers twice to underwater cultural heritage *in situ*. The second occurrence deals with preservation – preservation *in situ* is seen as the general principle both here and in the Annex. But there must be an exception when – for 'scientific or protective purposes' – recovery is permitted. Unfortunately, the underwater cultural heritage is subject to a number of threats which may necessitate that recovery; threats arising from legitimate activities taking place in or above the seabed with no deliberate intention of harming the heritage, occasionally from natural causes, but frequently from human activities.

The Preamble talks of the 'possible negative impact … of legitimate activities'. For political reasons, these were not specified. However, the UNESCO/DOALOS Draft had referred to 'exploitation of natural resources of various maritime zones, construction, including construction of artificial islands, installation and structures, laying of cables and pipelines'. This was attacked by the cable laying industry which claimed that its activities in no way damaged underwater cultural heritage although it seems inevitable that there is a 'possible negative impact'. Of all legitimate activities, the use of bottom trawl nets in fishing causes the greatest damage by dragging

---

8   Kinder, G. *Ship of Gold in the Deep Blue Sea* (Little Brown and Company, London, 1998) 472.

away that portion of a wreck which lies above the seabed. But any attempt to regulate this and similar activities would lie outside the competence of UNESCO and involve complex political and financial issues. The Preamble to the Underwater Convention thus indicates to States Parties that these threats are something they should consider in adopting policies in relation to such activities. This is made more explicit in Article 5.

The threat the Convention is basically concerned with is looting – the intentional ripping from a wreck or site of commercially valuable material without regard to any information it may have in context and without regard to material of little or no commercial value. Speaking of sites underwater, McManamon finds a contrast in attitude to those on land:

> This is a strikingly different historical perspective than the one we have regarding terrestrial archaeological sites. Even the early historic exploration and archaeological excavation of terrestrial sites aimed to recover works of art and curiosities for aesthetic and educational goals. The intent of these initial efforts was not strictly to amass money or objects for sale, although the recovered objects that were kept often also had inherent monetary value. ... The continuing strong association of shipwrecks with treasure shows the difficulty of changing public perceptions and orientation.[9]

Once again we are brought back to the necessity for 'research, information and education' that the Preamble emphasizes.

Part of the way forward lies in co-operation, as stressed by the Preamble. Basically, the introduction of advanced technology means that underwater cultural heritage is now accessible to those with the funds to exploit it. Their activities could be controlled by the power of the State but much better in the long run is true co-operation when economic power is joined with scholarly objectives. The web of co-operation must be cast wider. For example, that of recreational divers is also needed for they are often a fund of information about what lies on the seabed. Archaeologists should see themselves as part of this sphere of co-operation, both providing specialized knowledge and also learning from others. All of this requires an acknowledged framework providing the guidelines for co-operation or, as the Preamble puts it, 'uniform governing criteria'.

A new international Convention comes into being among a web of duties and obligations created by general international law and other international conventions of greater or lesser relevance. In relation to the Underwater Convention, UNCLOS has already been mentioned. The Preamble also specifically refers to two UNESCO Conventions: the *Convention on the Means of Prohibiting and Preventing the Illicit Import, Export and Transfer of Ownership of Cultural Property* 1970 and the *Convention concerning the Protection of the World Cultural and Natural Heritage* 1972. The 1970 Convention will become relevant when underwater cultural heritage is found within the jurisdiction of a State Party thereto or is brought within that jurisdiction from its resting place. Export from that State will then be governed by the rules of the 1970 Convention as well as the Underwater Convention. If such an object is unlawfully exported, it may be possible to claim it back from another Member State where it is found.[10] The *Convention concerning the Protection of the World Cultural and Natural Heritage* provides for the creation of a List of cultural and natural heritage of outstanding universal value located in the territory of a State Party. 'Territory' is undefined but would include internal waters and the territorial sea of States. The Operational Guidelines adopted by the World Heritage Committee for implementation of that Convention state in paragraph 48 that: "Nominations of immovable heritage which are likely to become movable will not be considered". However, these are merely guidelines and are not binding as part of the Convention. Henry Cleere observes:

> Successful raising operations such as those of the *Vasa* and the *Mary Rose* would therefore appear to be ruled out *ipso facto*. It remains to be tested whether designated

---

9 McManamon, F.P. 'Cultural Resources and Protection Under United States Laws' (2001) 16 *Connecticut Journal of International Law* 247, 269.
10 O'Keefe, P.J. *Commentary on the UNESCO 1970 Convention on Illicit Traffic* (Institute of Art and Law, Builth Wells, 2nd edn, 2007).

wrecks in the territorial waters of a State Party that has a legislatively binding policy not to move sunken wrecks would be considered for inclusion on the List.[11]

There is as yet no State with such a legislative policy but paragraph 48 of the Guidelines does emphasize the preference of the Underwater Convention for *in situ* protection. Nevertheless, there are certain sites on the World Heritage List which are there because of their connection to the sea and, in particular, the underwater cultural heritage. Three of these are Angra do Heroismo in the Azores; Isla de Mozambique and Carthagena in Columbia. One that would be particularly significant is Chuuk Lagoon in the Federated States of Micronesia where there are over 50 Japanese ships and aircraft lying on the sea floor where they sank in the Second World War. It has been called 'one of the great undersea wonders of the world' but Jeffery concludes that there is no adequate management plan in force - an essential ingredient for world heritage listing.[12]

---

[11] Cleere, H. 'The Underwater Heritage and the World Heritage Convention' (1993) 17 *Bulletin of the Australian Institute for Maritime Archaeology* 25.

[12] Jeffery, B. 'World War II Underwater Cultural Heritage Sites in Truk Lagoon: Considering a Case for World Heritage Listing' (2004) 33 *International Journal of Nautical Archaeology* 106.

Article 1 – Definitions

For the purposes of this Convention:

1. (a) "Underwater cultural heritage" means all traces of human existence having a cultural, historical or archaeological character which have been partially or totally under water, periodically or continuously, for at least 100 years such as:
> (i) sites, structures, buildings, artefacts and human remains, together with their archaeological and natural context;
> (ii) vessels, aircraft, other vehicles or any part thereof, their cargo or other contents, together with their archaeological and natural context; and
> (iii) objects of prehistoric character.

(b) Pipelines and cables placed on the seabed shall not be considered as underwater cultural heritage.

(c) Installations other than pipelines and cables, placed on the seabed and still in use, shall not be considered as underwater cultural heritage.

2. (a) "States Parties" means States which have consented to be bound by this Convention and for which this Convention is in force.

(b) This Convention applies mutatis mutandis to those territories referred to in Article 26, paragraph 2(b), which become Parties to this Convention in accordance with the conditions set out in that paragraph, and to that extent "States Parties" refers to those territories.

3. "UNESCO" means the United Nations Educational, Scientific and Cultural Organization.

4. "Director-General" means the Director-General of UNESCO.

5. "Area" means the seabed and ocean floor and subsoil thereof, beyond the limits of national jurisdiction.

6. "Activities directed at underwater cultural heritage" means activities having underwater cultural heritage as their primary object and which may, directly or indirectly, physically disturb or otherwise damage underwater cultural heritage.

7. "Activities incidentally affecting underwater cultural heritage" means activities which, despite not having underwater cultural heritage as their primary object or one of their objects, may physically disturb or otherwise damage underwater cultural heritage.

8. "State vessels and aircraft" means warships, and other vessels or aircraft that were owned or operated by a State and used, at the time of sinking, only for government non-commercial purposes, that are identified as such and that meet the definition of underwater cultural heritage.

9. "Rules" means the Rules concerning activities directed at underwater cultural heritage, as referred to in Article 33 of this Convention.

In many ways the definition article is one of the most important provisions in an international convention for it is this which sets its scope. Paragraph 1 defines 'underwater cultural heritage' essentially as 'all traces of human existence'. This would apply to many things and the remainder of the paragraph either attempts to reduce its coverage or is illustrative of particular categories.

Article 1 of the Underwater Convention contains some provisions which would seem to have been inserted in an excess of caution. For example, the other five UNESCO Conventions dealing with aspects of cultural heritage seem to have worked quite well without definitions of 'States Parties', 'UNESCO' and 'Director-General' all of which are self-evident. The concept of the 'Area' is defined by taking that used in UNCLOS.[13] Paragraph 9 is not really a definition but merely directs attention to the existence of the Rules which are referred to in Article 33 and form the content of the Annex. The significant definitions are analysed below.

---

13   Article 1.

Paragraph 1

The words 'traces of human existence' come from Article 1 of the *European Convention on the Protection of the Archaeological Heritage* 1969[14] and were used in the ILA Draft. The trace must somehow be connected to humanity. But, as Paragraph 1 states, it must also have been underwater for at least 100 years. On land there are traces of humanity which often require expert determination to establish their existence e.g. soil discolouration where post holes have been. Because of the nature of the environment, traces like these are very unlikely to be found underwater unless close to the shoreline. In shallow waters the remains of habitation sites dating from a time when sea levels were lower may be found far from shore. But these are relatively rare finds. Artefacts created by humans will be the main subject of the Underwater Convention. The 100-year qualification further refines the concept of 'trace'. There is no scientific reason for using a cut-off figure. It is purely a device for excluding material of more recent origin for purposes of administration. It is also useful for the salvage industry to be able to know if work can be done on a wreck without any need to comply with the Rules in the Annex. The figure of 100 years is found in much national legislation dealing with cultural heritage and has been adopted in the Underwater Convention to be consistent with that legislation.[15] At the moment, it does exclude, for example, wrecks from the period of the Second World War that some may consider important for historical reasons. These can still be protected by national legislation if a State so desires. An example is the UK *Protection of Military Remains Act* 1986.[16]

'Underwater' is usually a straightforward concept although Paragraph 1 makes clear that certain marginal possibilities are included such as partial or periodic submersion. Apart from an object close to the shoreline, this could occur in respect of something on, or buried in, a reef.

Finally, there is the qualifying phrase 'having a cultural, historical or archaeological character'. Inclusion of this phrase was hotly debated and it was admitted only following what seemed to be a misreading by the Chairman of the nature of the consensus. During the expert meetings in 1999 and 2000, there had been proposals by the United Kingdom and the United States of America to add a requirement that the underwater cultural heritage be 'significant' before it came within the scope of the Underwater Convention. In 2001 the United Kingdom proposed that the phrase 'having a cultural, historical or archaeological character' be inserted. That State has a requirement in its *Protection of Wrecks Act* 1973 that wrecks have to be of 'historical, archaeological or artistic importance' to qualify for protection. It may be easier to establish a 'character' of this nature than whether it is of 'importance' but the issues are similar. Many other jurisdictions have moved beyond this notion to what is called 'blanket protection', that is, everything over a certain age is protected. One administrator with long experience of both systems sums up the advantages of blanket protection thus:

> ... the administrators are not called upon for repetitious significance assessment decisions, the archaeologists can concentrate on programmes with more significant outcomes such as publications and museum exhibits, the general public gets better value for money in the form of new knowledge products rather than endless significance assessments, and developers have a clearer sense of compliance requirements.[17]

Whether the phrase 'having a cultural, historical or archaeological character' actually adds anything to the definition is doubtful. First, as already noted, the word 'archaeological' in this context is meaningless – something may be of archaeological interest or significance but nothing is of archaeological character. This was pointed out by the representative of ICOMOS and

---

14 European Treaty Series No. 66.
15 At one point in the negotiations, a period of 50 years was inserted but this was later withdrawn in a return to 100 years.
16 Dromgoole, S. 'Military Remains on and Around the Coast of the United Kingdom: Statutory Mechanisms of Protection' (1996) 11 *International Journal of Marine and Coastal Law* 23.
17 Henderson, G. 'Significance Assessment or Blanket Protection' in Prott, L.V., Planche, E. and Roca-Hachem, R. (eds) *Background Materials on the Protection of the Underwater Cultural Heritage* (UNESCO & Ministère de la Communication (France), Paris, 2000) 350, 352.

was clearly supported by many experts but unfortunately the word found its way into the text. Whether something is of a cultural or historical character cannot be objectively determined. There cannot be any trace of human existence which does not have a cultural element or an historical character. Even human remains qualify. Indeed, anything over 100 years of age may be said to have an 'historical character' by its very nature. Much of the opposition to this phrase centred on an argument that, often, the cultural or historical importance of an object cannot be determined in advance of excavation. But the importance of something is very different to its character and the latter is the word used in the definition.[18] The phrase 'cultural, historical or archaeological character' thus neither adds to nor detracts from the already established scope of the definition. It mirrors the wording of UNCLOS in Articles 149 and 303 and is an unfortunate revival of a phrase which the ILA and UNESCO/DOALOS drafts carefully avoided.

The remainder of Paragraph 1(a) consists of examples of underwater cultural heritage intended to guide interpretation of the definition. These cannot be used to cut down the overall concept of traces of human existence over 100 years old. This is quite clear from the use of the words 'such as'.

The examples given are those most likely to be encountered in activities affecting the underwater cultural heritage – sites, structures, buildings and artefacts. Human remains are specifically mentioned because of the significance these have in the eyes of the general public and the importance of the scientific information they may carry in respect of life at the time a ship sank, for example. The phrase 'archaeological and natural context' is intended to include in the zone of protection the surroundings of a trace of human existence to the extent necessary to enable all the information held to be preserved. The object may have aesthetic value or be of interest to the general public because of historical associations but the crucial aspect is the information it can give about the times when it was used.

The specific reference to 'vessels, aircraft, other vehicles' may be an excess of caution because they are artefacts which have already been mentioned. However, specific inclusion directs the attention of persons affected by the Underwater Convention to vessels and aircraft which are probably the most often encountered of all aspects of underwater cultural heritage. The inclusion of aircraft is only now becoming significant as humanity enters into the period when the more frequent use of aircraft occurred more than 100 years ago.

The phrase 'their cargo or other contents' makes clear that these are also part of the underwater heritage. For example, in Norway the wreck of the *Akerendam* – a Dutch East Indiaman – was found in 1972. In the wreck were large quantities of gold and silver coins from chests aboard the vessel at the time it was wrecked. The Norwegian *Protection of Antiquities Act* 1951 at that time provided rules relating to 'vessels, ships' hulls, and objects pertaining thereto or parts of such objects…'. It was argued that:

> … the coins were part of the *Akerendam's* cargo and thus did not fall within the scope of the rules of the Antiquities Act … The only debatable point was whether the *Akerendam's* treasure chests were cargo or whether they were to be classed as ship's appurtenances, because, for example, they constituted the master's funds for the voyage.[19]

The Norwegian Act was subsequently changed to make clear that cargo was covered. In the context of the Underwater Convention, cargo would certainly be a trace of human existence but Paragraph 1(a)(ii) puts its inclusion beyond doubt.

The final example of 'traces of human existence' is that of 'objects of prehistoric character'. There was considerable argument as to whether paleontological material should be included in the definition of underwater cultural heritage. Such objects are included in the definition of

---

18   Mention was often made during the experts' meeting of the finding of a Coca Cola can as illustrating the absurdity of considering this to be an important trace of human existence, quite overlooking the importance that a 100-year-old can would have, considering such things did not exist 100 years ago!

19   Braekhus, S. 'Salvage of Wrecks and Wreckage: Legal Issues Arising from the Runde Find' (1976) 20 *Scandinavian Studies in Law* 39, 63.

'cultural property' in the UNESCO *Convention on the Means of Prohibiting and Preventing the Illicit Import, Export and Transfer of Ownership of Cultural Property* 1970 and are often covered by national legislation. However, such paleontological material has no relationship to humanity as such. In the end, a compromise was to include 'objects of prehistoric character'. These must be related to traces of human existence. They would certainly include tools that prehistoric humanity worked, their settlements and other artefacts. Bones showing butchering, for example, have been found in the Taiwan Strait.[20]

Paragraph 1(b) deals with pipelines and cables. The first undersea telegraph cable was laid between England and France in 1850 and another between Ireland and Newfoundland in 1858. Today the world is crossed by such cables. It is obvious that the early ones would qualify as underwater cultural heritage. However, both cables and pipelines are specifically excluded under the definition. The reason for this is unclear and was never specifically mentioned in the negotiations. Certainly the cable industry in particular protested against any possibility that its activities might be affected by the Underwater Convention – referring to the privileged position it was given under UNCLOS. It seems that members of the industry want to pick up and remove old cables themselves. One problem is that while this is the current position, there is no guarantee that it will continue and, if it does not, those cables would be without protection.

Cables and pipelines are only two of many types of installations placed on the seabed. There are many other constructions – some for purposes of military security. Rather than attempt to separate out military and industrial installations – and in some cases this may be very difficult – the definition in Paragraph 1(c) excludes from cultural heritage those still in use. Once decommissioned and left *in situ*, such installations become subject to the regime of the Underwater Convention.

Paragraphs 6 and 7

As noted above, underwater cultural heritage may be affected by a variety of activities, the authors of which do not intend to affect it in any way or are oblivious to the consequences of their actions. Thus, fisherman using bottom trawl nets may be concerned to maximize their haul without realizing they are obliterating evidence of underwater cultural heritage. For example, exploration by Ballard in 1988/89 of an underwater plateau at the west end of the Strait of Sicily found that much of the deep seabed had been scoured by such nets.[21] Regulating these activities to remove their effects on the heritage is beyond the power of UNESCO acting alone. It would raise complex financial, political and practical issues involving a number of United Nations bodies as well as large numbers of commercial companies. Moreover, it was never intended that a primary objective of the Underwater Convention would be to deal with these issues.

Canada took the lead in seeking to define the scope of the Underwater Convention with the result that Paragraphs 6 and 7 draw a distinction between activities directed at underwater cultural heritage and those incidentally affecting such heritage. Both are limited to physical disturbance or damage to the heritage. Activities which do not have this effect are not caught by the definition. An example could be visits by tourists to a site which involve only viewing of the wreck. The distinction between the two types of activities depends on whether the primary objective of the person undertaking the activity is disturbance of, or damage to, the heritage. The phrasing of the clause indicates that the test of whether something is a primary objective is itself objective i.e. the actual intention of the person undertaking the activity is irrelevant. If it would appear to the normal person considering the matter that the intention is to disturb or damage the heritage that is sufficient.

Paragraph 8

The definition of 'State vessels and aircraft' commences by referring to 'warships'. Unfortunately, this term itself is undefined and there is no general definition in international law. However, Article 3 states that the Underwater Convention is to be interpreted in a manner consistent

---

20 Chuan-Kun Ho 'Prehistoric Landbridge Mammalian and Human Fossils Discovered Under Taiwan Strait' in CCA *Proceedings of International Roundtable Meeting on the Protection of Underwater Cultural Heritage* (Taipei, Taiwan, 2010) 84.

21 Gibbins, D. 'Archaeology in Deep Water – A Preliminary View' (1991) 20 *International Journal of Nautical Archaeology* 163, 167.

with UNCLOS which contains a definition of 'warship' in Article 29. There would seem to be no alternative to using that definition even though the concept of the warship that it adopts is really only intended for modern navies. It has three criteria: the vessel must bear external marks showing its nationality; the commanding officer must be duly commissioned with his or her name appearing in the appropriate service list; the vessel must be manned by a crew under regular armed forces discipline. This definition would begin to apply to different navies at different times. For example, as far as the British Navy is concerned, it would go back to 1780 when David Steel published privately his first *List of the Royal Navy* followed in 1814 by the first official *Admiralty Navy List*. Certainly, this concept of the warship would exclude vessels such as the privateer – 'a privately owned and armed ship commissioned by a government to make reprisals, to gain reparation for specified offences in time of peace, or to prey upon the enemy in time of war'.[22]

But warships are only one part of the category of 'State vessels and aircraft'. It also includes 'other vessels or aircraft that were owned or operated by a State and used, at the time of sinking, only for government non-commercial purposes'. This will be a question of fact to be ascertained from all the circumstances of a particular situation. The further one goes back in time, the more difficult will it be to establish the circumstances. The concept of the 'State' and 'non-commercial purposes' may depend on both the time of the sinking and in what part of the world it occurred. For example, *La Juliana* was a Catalonian merchant ship pressed into service by Phillip II of Spain for the Spanish Armada and wrecked at Streeda Strand, County Sligo, Ireland, in 1588. Under the laws of the time, was the vessel operated by the Spanish State and was it being used for non-commercial purposes?

Paragraph 8 stresses that 'State vessels and aircraft' must meet the definition of underwater cultural heritage. In other words, they must have been underwater for at least 100 years in addition to fulfilling the other criteria.

---

22   *Encyclopaedia Britannica* (Chicago, 15th edn, 1986) Vol. 9, 464.

ARTICLE 2 – OBJECTIVES AND GENERAL PRINCIPLES

1. This Convention aims to ensure and strengthen the protection of underwater cultural heritage.

2. States Parties shall cooperate in the protection of underwater cultural heritage.

3. States Parties shall preserve underwater cultural heritage for the benefit of humanity in conformity with the provisions of this Convention.

4. States Parties shall, individually or jointly as appropriate, take all appropriate measures in conformity with this Convention and with international law that are necessary to protect underwater cultural heritage, using for this purpose the best practicable means at their disposal and in accordance with their capabilities.

5. The preservation in situ of underwater cultural heritage shall be considered as the first option before allowing or engaging in any activities directed at this heritage.

6. Recovered underwater cultural heritage shall be deposited, conserved and managed in a manner that ensures its long-term preservation.

7. Underwater cultural heritage shall not be commercially exploited.

8. Consistent with State practice and international law, including the United Nations Convention on the Law of the Sea, nothing in this Convention shall be interpreted as modifying the rules of international law and State practice pertaining to sovereign immunities, nor any State's rights with respect to its State vessels and aircraft.

9. States Parties shall ensure that proper respect is given to all human remains located in maritime waters.

10. Responsible non-intrusive access to observe or document in situ underwater cultural heritage shall be encouraged to create public awareness, appreciation, and protection of the heritage except where such access is incompatible with its protection and management.

11. No act or activity undertaken on the basis of this Convention shall constitute grounds for claiming, contending or disputing any claim to national sovereignty or jurisdiction

Article 2 is one of the most important in the entire Underwater Convention. It sets out the general principles guiding interpretation of the remainder. Other provisions may have a clear meaning on their face but, if not, resort is to be made to Article 2 to establish how the provision should be treated.

PARAGRAPHS 1-5

These first five paragraphs will be discussed as a whole. They are all closely related and the overall approach inherent in Article 2 can best be seen from looking at them as a unity.

Paragraph 1 sets out the basic purpose of the Underwater Convention – protection of underwater cultural heritage. Use of the word 'protection' as opposed to 'recovery', 'commercialization' or exploitation is significant. Such words as these could have been added but were not. The only aim of the Underwater Convention is 'protection'. While this may seem clear on its face, it does beg the question of what is meant by protection. In broad terms this would be encapsulated in the notion of keeping safe from damage or destruction whether it be intentional or fortuitous, natural or caused by humans. Underwater cultural heritage has often reached a state of equilibrium with its surroundings and any interference disturbs this. Even if the object is left in place it still has to continue to adjust, since additional deterioration does occur, though it may be very slow. Consequently, Paragraph 5 requires consideration of *in situ* preservation as the first option before allowing or engaging in any activities directed at underwater cultural heritage. Much will depend on the nature of the site and the degree of stability achieved.[23]

---

23 This should be read in conjunction with comments on Rule 1 of the Annex: p.121 below.

But even leaving an object undisturbed on or in the seabed may not sufficiently fulfil the obligation to protect set out in Paragraph 4. There is no territorial limitation on this duty provided what is done is in conformity with the Underwater Convention and international law. The former lays down the minimum rules for protection and the latter does not prevent the emergence of new obligations. Consequently, steps may have to be taken to prevent change in the surroundings of the site that may have adverse effects. For example, discharge of chemicals from an installation on the continental shelf, the dropping overboard of rubbish, the testing of weapons are some of the activities that may need to be reassessed if they affect the site of underwater cultural heritage. Unfortunately, there are often strong economic, political and military interests involved in these activities. Paragraph 4 recognizes the limitations of States by qualifying their obligation to protect. They have to use the best practicable means at their disposal and in accordance with their capabilities. If better means are available but a State cannot afford them, it has not breached its duty (although this may of course raise the question of allocation of resources). Perhaps one way out of this problem would be for a State, in reliance on Paragraph 2, to seek co-operation from other Member States. This Paragraph is in the imperative – 'shall co-operate' – and forms the second major aim of the Underwater Convention. States, on becoming party to the Convention, agree to help each other in carrying out their obligations and duties and, in particular, protecting the underwater cultural heritage.

A State, in taking measures to protect underwater cultural heritage, shall preserve underwater cultural heritage for humanity (Paragraph 3). This means that a State is not to make decisions based on the importance of that heritage to it alone. For example, the heritage may be related to a religion that the State does not favour or to another State with which it is at odds. All underwater heritage is of value to humanity and must be protected. It must also be remembered that all possible information must be extracted from that heritage and be preserved.

PARAGRAPH 6

Once underwater cultural heritage is recovered there is immediately the need for conservation. This is not the same for all materials. Gold will not be affected but things made of iron and wood will disintegrate rapidly if not treated. Once conserved, objects need appropriate storage facilities. Underwater cultural heritage in particular may need a controlled environment where temperature, humidity and light provide conditions for the continued existence of the object. All these considerations are reflected in Paragraph 6 where States undertake to deposit, conserve and manage recovered cultural heritage so as to ensure its long-term preservation. This will be costly, particularly as storage is an open-ended commitment. These obligations must be considered by States when deciding to permit excavation rather than requiring preservation *in situ*. Once again, some of the problems found may be solved by co-operation with other States Parties.

PARAGRAPH 7

This is one of two provisions in the Underwater Convention dealing with commercial exploitation: the other being Rule 2 of the Annex. Paragraph 7 was inserted because States considered the prohibition against commercial exploitation was a very important principle which needed to be specifically stated as an aim of the Convention. There are also ties to Article 4 dealing with the law on salvage and finds.

Although Paragraph 7 forbids the commercial exploitation of underwater cultural heritage, there is nothing in the Underwater Convention which establishes precisely what is meant by this. The matter is discussed more extensively in relation to Rule 2.

Apart from exhibition of excavated material, there are other ways of making money from wreck sites. Films can be profitable whether these are intended for public television or, as in the 1997 film 'Titanic' produced by James Cameron, incorporation in a feature movie. Tourism is another source and this can range from guided dives in shallow waters to submersibles visiting the site of the actual *Titanic*. In essence these are no different to guided tours to archaeological sites on land. All such activities involve the payment of money to those organizing the visits or making the film. They are thus commercial, but are they prohibited?

On its face, the prohibition in Paragraph 7 is not restricted to commercial gain solely from activities directed at underwater cultural heritage within the terms of the definition. However, all the provisions for authorization in the Underwater Convention are tied to activities of this nature. There is simply no provision for activities that do not physically disturb or otherwise damage underwater cultural heritage. To say that these activities are prohibited if they are commercially motivated is to adopt an ideological position beyond the scope of the Underwater Convention. In respect of such activities States are free to make their own rules within the jurisdiction allowed them under international law. They should be guided by the principle of restricting controls to activities directed at underwater cultural heritage and the encouragement given for public access in Paragraph 10 and in the Preamble.

What is the connection between commercial exploitation and 'looting'? The word 'looting' appears in only two provisions of the Convention – Articles 9(4) and 12(3) – and yet looting is a widely used term. It appears as much in academic works as it does in popular literature and media reports. Where it appears in the Convention, it does so in relation to situations of danger to the underwater cultural heritage where it is given as the only specific instance of danger arising from human activities. Elsewhere the Underwater Convention refers to actions 'contrary to the Convention' or similar. There is no definition of 'looting' in the Convention. In relation to the underwater cultural heritage, 'looting' would commonly be seen as removal of material from a site without regard to the scientific value of that site and for personal benefit.

Looting is common in many parts of the world. Fisherman snag wrecks with their nets, raise objects and sell them. This was the reason that *in situ* preservation was not adopted for the 'No. 1 Nanhai' wreck some 20 kilometres off the coast of Guangdong Province, China. The wreck was located in a traditional fishing area which 'posed a serious security threat to the wreck' with stealing of underwater cultural heritage.[24]

Then there are the commercial historic ship salvors. They wish to place themselves in a special category far removed from fishermen and even their own past. Kingsley, referring to Sinclair, says:

> The days of the uncritical extraction of 'booty' from shipwrecks has passed and modern professional salvage and commercial archaeology companies impose sets of scientific objectives on sites, in which the contextual recovery of high-value material is just one.[25]

However, to what extent does the rhetoric match their activities? Kingsley's paper was published in a collection of papers and reports detailing the activities of Odyssey Marine Exploration, a major treasure salvaging company. Odyssey has a chequered past. For example, it raised 17 tons of coins from a wreck off Portugal; took them to Gibraltar and then flew them to Florida. Spain began legal proceedings in the American courts on the basis the vessel was entitled to sovereign immunity. There was argument over the identity of the wreck but the court determined it was the *Nuestra Señora de las Mercedes*. After fruitless appeals, Odyssey was ordered to return the coins to Spain and did so.

Odyssey has also been accused of failure to comply with the requirements of the Annex to the Underwater Convention in its past and possible future work on HMS *Victory*.[26] Both of these activities create a perception that Odyssey is no different from earlier treasure hunters. That perception is reinforced by talk of gold and other treasure aboard the *Victory*. Dobson and Kingsley speculate as to the value of the bullion HMS *Victory* may have been carrying, including

---

24   Wei Jun 'Innovative Thoughts on the Preservation of Underwater Cultural Heritage in China: No.1 Nanhai as a Project Example' in International Meeting on the Protection, Presentation and Valorisation of Underwater Cultural Heritage – Chongqing, China (23 to 27 Nov. 2010): <http://www.unesco.org/culture/underwater/pdf/uch_publication_chine_en.pdf>.
25   Kingsley, S. 'Underwater Cultural Heritage & UNESCO in New Orleans: An Introduction' in Stemm, G. & Kingsley, S. (eds) *Oceans Odyssey 2: Underwater Heritage Management & Deep-Sea Shipwrecks in the English Channel & Atlantic Ocean* (Oxbow Books, Oxford, 2011) 1, 5.
26   Page 126 below.

possibly four tons of gold coins.[27] While this may inspire investors and be newsworthy, it too creates a perception of obsession with treasure. Proof of this is the references to Odyssey as a 'treasure hunter' in newspapers and on the Internet.[28]

The prohibition of commercial exploitation in the Underwater Convention is sometimes portrayed as Eurocentric and elitist; that it is a standard which only wealthy and highly organized countries can reach and is not appropriate for other parts of the world. Flecker takes this approach in his article on maritime archaeology in South East Asia. After saying that the Underwater Convention primarily aims to 'exclude commercial salvage operators from working on historic wreck-sites' he goes on to state:

> This is a perfectionist policy for shipwrecks full of unique artefacts lost in the waters of developed countries that are willing to commit public funds to carry out archaeological excavations, inclusive of the time-consuming and costly tasks of conservation and long-term storage of large numbers of artefacts, documentation, dissemination, and display.[29]

Flecker argues that archaeologists must be more tolerant and accept that commercial exploitation should be allowed until 'cultural awareness gains the upper hand over profits and politics'. In the meantime the salvors must be made aware of the value of good documentation as the 'cargo from a properly documented wreck-site is worth more financially than the cargo from a looted site'.[30] The problem with this argument is that it in effect preserves the existing situation. There is very little incentive for improvement as salvors will still only be concerned with high value objects and not those with little or no commercial interest. Flecker himself has been engaged in activities where that was the case. He was archaeologist on site during the second season of excavation of the Belitung wreck when the cargo was sought but the stern of the vessel left behind.[31]

Jeremy Green paints a different picture of what could be:

> … until substantial archaeological excavations are undertaken in the Southeast Asian region, which can demonstrate a real alternative, with real benefits to the country, and to underwater cultural heritage in general, the Belitung wreck is what we are going to get. Countries like Indonesia need to wake up to the reality of what they could have – they could have the material in their country and call it: 'Tang Shipwreck Treasure: Indonesia's Maritime Collection'. They could have done it themselves – they do have maritime archaeologists after all. The wealthy sponsors could have funded a proper archaeological excavation, and while Indonesia would not have got half, or whatever its percentage of the sale was, it would benefit from having a permanent exhibition collection that would generate recurring income, with added long-term benefits for the public in knowledge and understanding, ….[32]

States, wherever they may be, must have a goal to work towards. European States themselves have a way to go to meet the standards of the Underwater Convention. Matters cannot be left to

---

27 Dobson, N.C. and Kingsley, S. 'HMS Victory, a First-Rate Royal Navy Warship Lost in the English Channel, 1744, Preliminary Survey & Identification' in Stemm, G. & Kingsley, S. (eds.) *Oceans Odyssey: Deep-sea Shipwrecks in the English Channel, Straits of Gibraltar & Atlantic Ocean* (Oxbow Books, Oxford, 2010) 235, 273.

28 Part of this paragraph is taken from a review of Stemm, G. and Kingsley, S. (eds) *Oceans Odyssey 2: Underwater Heritage Management & Deep-Sea Shipwrecks in the English Channel & Atlantic Ocean* (Oxbow Books, Oxford, 2011) by P.J. O'Keefe in (2013) 42 *International Journal of Nautical Archaeology* 239, 240.

29 Flecker, M. 'The Ethics, Politics, and Realities of Maritime Archaeology in Southeast Asia' (2002) 31 *International Journal of Nautical Archaeology* 12, 13.

30 Above 23.

31 This episode and its aftermath are discussed in some detail under commercial exploitation in Rule 2 of the Annex at page 129.

32 Green, J. review of Krahl, R. *et al.* (eds) *Shipwrecked: Tang Treasures and Monsoon Winds* (Smithsonian Institution, Washington, 2010) in (2011) 40 *International Journal of Nautical Archaeology* 449, 452.

the vagaries of public opinion and the self-interest of salvors in the hope that these will eventually lead to protection of some of the underwater cultural heritage.

Paragraph 8

There was a tendency during the negotiations to refer to the rules of international law even where those rules were insufficient. Such references avoided a difference of opinion which could not be solved in the negotiations and put the resolution of such issues back in the field of general international law. Paragraph 8 is one such case. It states that nothing in the Underwater Convention shall be interpreted as modifying the rules of international law and State practice pertaining to sovereign immunities. What those rules and practice are is unclear. Sovereign immunity in this context means that certain ships of one State are not subject to the jurisdiction of any other State. But when such a ship sinks, a different regime may apply. Strati argues that a sunken vessel, including a warship, lying on the seabed cannot qualify as a ship since it cannot navigate.[33] The United States of America appears to take a different view. Under its *Sunken Military Craft Act*,[34] it is prohibited to do anything 'directed at sunken military craft that disturbs, removes, or injures any' such craft without authorization.[35]

Paragraph 8 goes on to state that nothing in the Underwater Convention shall be interpreted as modifying any State's right with respect to its State vessels or aircraft. This comes after the reference to 'sovereign immunities' and thus must be intended to mean something different as otherwise it is pure repetition. The UNESCO/DOALOS Draft included a definition of when a vessel should be considered to be 'abandoned' by its owner. The First Meeting of Governmental Experts decided to omit that definition and not deal with questions of title.[36] However, the reference in Paragraph 8 can refer only to State ownership of such vessels: an issue which must be distinguished from that of immunity.

The significance of this can be seen from the *Sunken Military Craft Act* of the United States which states that the only way United States ownership of such craft can be extinguished is by 'express divestiture' by the United States and not by passage of time, regardless of when the craft sank. The law of finds is expressly excluded by this law from applying to these craft and no salvage rights or awards are to be made in respect of any American sunken military craft without the express permission of the United States government. Under this law, the same applies to foreign sunken military craft located in United States waters where the express permission of the foreign State must be obtained before any action may be taken in respect of such craft.

Paragraph 9

Inclusion of this provision emphasizing the giving of proper respect to human remains received almost universal support during the negotiations. Such remains are sometimes found during excavation of a site. Proper respect means that the remains are to be treated reverently as befitting a fellow human. Inappropriate treatment is abhorred by the general public as evidenced by the uproar over the alleged (later proved false) placement of a light inside a skull during the excavation of gold from HMS *Edinburgh*.[37] However, the treatment of human remains is culturally conditioned and proper respect will depend very much on the background of those who find them.

The remains of military personnel who died in battle are a particularly sensitive issue. During negotiation of the Underwater Convention, various States had made proposals to specifically mention 'war graves'. The general thrust of the proposals was encapsulated in the report of an informal subgroup of the working group on warships. After requiring that proper respect be given to all human remains located underwater, the report went on to say: 'and in particular

---

33   Strati, A. *The Protection of the Underwater Cultural Heritage: An Emerging Objective of the Contemporary Law of the Sea* (Martinus Nijhoff, The Hague, 1995) 221.
34   <http://www.history.navy.mil/branches/org12-12a.htm>.
35   S. 1402.
36   UNESCO *Final Report of the First Meeting of Governmental Experts on the Draft Convention on the Protection of the Underwater Cultural Heritage* UNESCO Doc. CLT-98/CONF.202.7, p.2.
37   Williams, M. 'War Graves' and Salvage: Murky Waters' (2000) 5 *International Maritime Law* 151, 152.

[States] shall consult and coordinate with respect to the protection of military maritime graves, irrespective of when the State vessel or aircraft was sunk.' However, in the final discussion in plenary session, the reference was deleted. For example, Viet Nam spoke strongly about the inclusion of anything in the Underwater Convention that would reopen wounds brought about by armed conflict. Others considered that if the military were to receive special mention, then all those who died in conflict should similarly be included.[38] These States strongly opposed any specific reference to military remains and their opposition was such that the text refers only to human remains in general.

Treating human remains with respect does not, however, indicate what is actually to be done with them. They may, of course, be left in place if this does not hinder whatever work is being done. That is what Rule 5 of the Annex suggests. However, this may expose them to the depredations of later unscrupulous divers. In some cases they are reburied after examination. For example, the remains of a sailor found on the wreck of the *Mary Rose* (which sank in 1545 and was raised in 1982) were reburied with full military honours after a dual Catholic and Protestant service, thus bridging dissent as to the appropriate form of religious ceremony. Other remains were studied and stored with a view to later reburial. So far the remains of three sailors have been found on the wreck of HMS *Pandora* which sank in 1791 with the loss of 31 persons 110 kilometres east of Cape York on the edge of the Great Barrier Reef off Australia. One has been re-interred in an obelisk placed on the seabed at the site of the wreck. This was done during a special burial service conducted by a Royal Australian Navy chaplain. It is intended that the other two will be similarly reburied. But often such remains are kept as part of the excavation archive on the basis that they should be available for future examination e.g. if any question should arise requiring an osteological examination. The Museum of Tropical Queensland is storing the two sets of skeletal remains in a secure, environmentally controlled room. Recent work at Bond University on DNA sequencing has provided a little more detail of their lineage.

How far retention in collections should be taken raises complex issues beyond the scope of the Underwater Convention. For example, the Western Australian Maritime Museum had on exhibition a skeleton from the wreck site of the *Batavia*. The skull of the skeleton exhibited a slash from a sword. It was argued that the exhibition was necessary to illustrate what happened on the site and the brutality involved: otherwise the story would have to rely on the written text and European illustrations from that time.[39]

Paragraph 10

This Paragraph reinforces the interpretation of Paragraph 7 given above. Underwater cultural heritage ultimately is the heritage of the public. It is not that of the State, politicians, administrators or specialists. Consequently, Paragraph 10 encourages non-intrusive access to *in situ* underwater cultural heritage. There is an element of paternalism present in that access is to be encouraged for the purpose of creating public awareness, appreciation, and protection of the heritage. The Preamble speaks of the *public's* right to access and also emphasizes the notion of public enjoyment to be had from the educational and recreational benefits of non-intrusive access. Certainly, private guided tours of underwater cultural heritage and films made for profit should be seen as part of the public's right to access provided they can take place without disturbance of the site.

According to Paragraph 10, access is not allowed when it is incompatible with protection and management of the underwater cultural heritage. This should not be seen by heritage specialists as justification for excluding the public in order to make their management tasks easier. Public

---

38 Dromgoole refers to controversy in the United Kingdom over including the remains of armed merchant vessels sunk during war under the *Protection of Military Remains Act* 1986: Dromgoole, S. 'United Kingdom' in Dromgoole, S. (ed.) *The Protection of the Underwater Cultural Heritage: National Perspectives in Light of the UNESCO Convention 2001* (Martinus Nijhoff, Leiden, 2006) 313, 333.

39 The *Batavia*, a Dutch East Indiaman, was on its maiden voyage to the Dutch East Indies when, in 1629, it struck a reef off Western Australia. Pelsaert, the senior officer, set off with some others to try and reach what is now Jakarta. He succeeded and returned with a rescue ship. However, while he was absent there was a mutiny and over 100 of the survivors were massacred.

access may need to be controlled but only in exceptional cases should it be denied. Those who find underwater cultural heritage and those appointed by States to manage it need to consider the implications of their action in denying access to a site. This encompasses not only physical access but also access to the results of activities directed at underwater cultural heritage. Failure to publish the details of an excavation and the conclusion to be drawn from these is also a denial of access.

PARAGRAPH 11

This provision was inserted between the final approved version of the Underwater Convention dated 23rd July and the official UNESCO document of 3rd August. It was not discussed during the negotiations. One delegation pointed out during the revision of the six linguistic versions that, because of the lack of a second reading, the provision had apparently been omitted. The Chairman concurred and a *corrigendum* was issued. However, because it had not passed through the drafting committee, it is clumsily worded and could give rise to misunderstanding: 'claiming … any claim' does not make sense. The motivation behind the clause on which it was based, originally proposed by Argentina, was to ensure that nothing authorized by the Convention would affect existing territorial claims. Accordingly, at the session of Commission IV of the UNESCO General Conference adopting the Draft Convention, Australia made the following declaration of understanding:

> It is the understanding of Australia that in relation to Article 2(11), the phrase 'shall constitute grounds for claiming, contending or disputing any claim to national sovereignty or jurisdiction' is intended only to be a reference to territorial disputes.

The Chairman of the Meetings of Governmental Experts, Lund, was called upon for his views which coincided with the declaration made by Australia.

> Art. 2, 11 was introduced as a text that had been proposed at an earlier meeting and had not received any negative reactions. It was felt necessary by the chair in order to deal with seabed areas on which there were disputes of jurisdiction between different Sovereign States in accordance with the reasons that had been given by the sponsor of the proposal at the time it was presented to the meeting of Governmental Experts.

It should of course be interpreted in this limited fashion.

ARTICLE 3 – RELATIONSHIP BETWEEN THIS CONVENTION AND THE UNITED NATIONS CONVENTION ON THE LAW OF THE SEA

> Nothing in this Convention shall prejudice the rights, jurisdiction and duties of States under international law, including the United Nations Convention on the Law of the Sea. This Convention shall be interpreted and applied in the context of and in a manner consistent with international law, including the United Nations Convention on the Law of the Sea.

This Article was inserted in response to those who claim UNCLOS represents a 'delicate balance' which the Underwater Convention might disturb. UNCLOS enshrines, for example, the principle of freedom of navigation and has rules concerning the exploitation of natural resources and the laying of cables and pipelines. It regulates the way international fishing is conducted. But it has only minimal provisions on underwater cultural heritage[40] which are given flesh by the Underwater Convention. If there is any overlap, then the latter has to be interpreted and applied in a manner consistent with UNCLOS. This obviously indicates that the supporters of the Underwater Convention regarded it as compatible with UNCLOS.

Consider, for example, the situation where underwater cultural heritage is recovered contrary to the Underwater Convention. Under Article 14 a Member State is obliged to take measures to prevent the entry into its territory of such material. Suppose the material is aboard a vessel, flying a foreign flag, simply passing through the territorial sea of that Member State with no intention of calling at any port in that State. Under Article 17 of UNCLOS, ships of all States enjoy a right of innocent passage through the territorial sea. The passage posited above would be innocent within the terms of Article 19 of that Convention. Moreover, under Article 27 of UNCLOS, the coastal State would have no criminal jurisdiction over the vessel. But, in these circumstances, Article 14 of the Underwater Convention should be read as requiring a State to take action to prevent passage by the vessel through its territorial sea.

However, Article 3 is the negotiated answer to different interpretations. On the one hand, there are those who consider UNCLOS as the only international instrument which should guide all developments concerning underwater cultural heritage. Other States see it as a significant guide but only one among many relevant rules of international law. Both positions have been accommodated in Article 3.

The Underwater Convention provides that it will not prejudice the rights, jurisdiction and duties of States under international law. Moreover, it is to be interpreted and applied in the context of and consistent with international law. UNCLOS is part of international law. This wording allows for future developments in the interpretation of UNCLOS and in international law through custom or other international instruments.

One area where this could take place is in relation to underwater cultural heritage on the continental shelf. Some have argued that there is little evidence of States exercising control over sites on their continental shelf. For example, Symmons argued that "the Irish claim is virtually unique among maritime States"[41] and that Ireland was out of step with European legislation and international law on the matter. But a number of States presently exercise control over underwater cultural heritage outside their territorial seas. For example, courts in the United States of America, in the exercise of their admiralty jurisdiction, have granted salvage rights to American corporations in respect of the *Titanic* – 640 kilometres off the coast of Newfoundland and on the Canadian continental shelf – and the SS *Central America* – 256 kilometres off the coast of South Carolina. In connection with this, injunctions have been issued closing off substantial areas of the high seas to other would-be salvors. The effectiveness of these orders depends on a defendant coming within the jurisdiction of the American court or the orders being enforced through foreign courts.

---

40 See p. 12 above.
41 Symmons, C.R. *Ireland and the Law of the Sea* (Round Hall Sweet & Maxwell, Dublin, 2000) 133.

The United States of America has also used its *National Marine Sanctuary Act* to create protected areas on its continental shelf. For example, the first vessel to be designated under this legislation was the USS *Monitor* which, in 1975, lay outside the then territorial sea and contiguous zone of the United States of America. The United States *Sunken Military Craft Act* applies to such foreign craft located in United States waters which, without explanation and by definition, extend to cover the contiguous zone in spite of the varying interpretations placed on Article 303(2) of UNCLOS.[42] Internationally, a growing number of States are making claims over the continental shelf. Australia[43] and Ireland[44] control shipwrecks on their continental shelves. Albania, Cyprus, Jamaica and the Seychelles also exercise jurisdiction over antiquities on their continental shelves. Legislation in Morocco provides that every archaeological excavation undertaken by a foreign State or individual within its EEZ must be approved by the administration.[45]

The Underwater Convention should not be seen as affecting this exercise of jurisdiction. Article 3 states that nothing in the Underwater Convention shall prejudice the rights, jurisdiction and duties of States under international law, including UNCLOS. This is a clear indication that the Underwater Convention is to be seen as establishing a minimum international standard from which further developments can be made by custom and other agreements among States. Those who already claim a control over the continental shelf, for example, can continue to exercise this while others are not prevented from claiming such control when the need arises.

The General Assembly of the United Nations passed a number of Resolutions which, among other things, called for the Underwater Convention to be in 'full conformity with the relevant provisions of the Convention [UNCLOS]'.[46] The meetings of experts had discussed how this issue should be treated at each of its four sessions. Nevertheless, at the meeting of Commission IV on 29th October 2001, one of the amendments proposed by the Russian Federation and the United Kingdom, with the endorsement of the United States of America, was to delete the words 'international law, including'. That group of amendments was defeated, without debate, by 77 votes to eight with 21 abstentions. Clearly the great majority of States saw it as necessary to emphasize the primacy of international law in general – particularly as there are so many States with significant underwater cultural heritage that are not party to UNCLOS.[47]

As already noted,[48] many of the States – for example, Argentina, Australia, China, Finland, Ireland, Italy, Japan – in the general debate during Commission IV said that they regarded the Underwater Convention as in full conformity with UNCLOS. Some – France, Israel, Netherlands, Russia, United States of America – disagreed. Norway, as it had done on previous occasions, referred darkly to Article 311 of UNCLOS.

Paragraph 3 of that Article reads:

> Two or more States Parties may conclude agreements modifying or suspending the operation of provisions of this Convention, applicable solely to the relations between them, provided that such agreements do not relate to a provision derogation from which is incompatible with the effective execution of the object and purpose of this Convention, and provided further that such agreements shall not affect the application of the basic principles embodied herein, and that the

---

42   Forrest, C. *International Law and the Protection of Cultural Heritage* (Routledge, Abingdon, 2010) 326-327.
43   *Historic Shipwrecks Act* 1976. Symmons' statement is based on a table produced in Churchill, R.R. and Lowe, A.V. *The Law of the Sea* (Manchester University Press, Manchester, 3rd edn 1999) 472. This is obviously an error as the text of that book itself states that 'several States' have unilaterally asserted this jurisdiction.
44   S.3(1) of the *National Monuments (Amendment) Act* 1987.
45   *Article 5, Dahir of 8 April 1981 instituting a 200 nautical mile exclusive economic zone off the Moroccan Coast.*
46   Para. 36 of Resolution A/RES/55/7 of 2 May 2001; also Para. 30 of A/RES/54/31 of 18 Jan. 2000, and Para 20 of A/RES/53/32 of 6 Jan. 1999 – see above p. 23.
47   Page 2 .
48   Page 21.

provisions of such agreements do not affect the enjoyment by other States Parties of their rights or the performance of their obligations under this Convention.

It is obvious that Article 311(3) can only apply where the other agreement modifies or suspends provisions of UNCLOS. Those who support recourse to Article 311 would most likely seek to apply it to the provisions in the Underwater Convention on the continental shelf and EEZ. But here it can be argued that UNCLOS simply does not deal with the issue of jurisdiction over underwater cultural heritage in these areas. There is no mention of it in UNCLOS. On the primary rules of interpretation already discussed,[49] there can be no argument that just because a matter was raised during negotiation of a treaty and dealt with in a limited manner, it cannot be raised years later when conditions have changed and it can be dealt with more extensively.[50] It is true that the relationship of the coastal State to limited categories of underwater cultural heritage on the continental shelf was discussed during negotiation of UNCLOS and the narrow provisions of Article 303 incorporated. But under the international law rules on interpretation, and here we are discussing such law in the context of interpreting Article 311, that does not prevent it being raised again and new provisions being incorporated in another treaty.

---

49 Page 27.
50 '… the 'sanctification' of the relevant provisions of UNCLOS, the discussion of which took place in the early 1970s when the general awareness of the question and the relevant technology were in their infancy should be seriously reconsidered': Lee, K-G., 'An Inquiry into the Compatibility of the UNESCO Convention 2001 with UNCLOS 1982' in Prott, L.V. (ed.) *Finishing the Interrupted Voyage* (UNESCO, Institute of Art and Law; Paris, Builth Wells; 2006) 20, 26.

ARTICLE 4 – RELATIONSHIP TO LAW OF SALVAGE AND LAW OF FINDS

> Any activity relating to underwater cultural heritage to which this Convention applies shall not be subject to the law of salvage or law of finds, unless it:
> (a) is authorized by the competent authorities, and
> (b) is in full conformity with this Convention, and
> (c) ensures that any recovery of the underwater cultural heritage achieves its maximum protection.

The nature of salvage has been briefly discussed.[51] To reiterate, the salvage reward is the compensation allowed to persons (salvors) by whose voluntary assistance a ship or cargo is saved from danger or loss at sea. A person who salves a ship or cargo does not automatically become its owner. He or she is entitled to an award based on the nature of the work done as a percentage of the value of what is saved. For example, if saving a cargo has been particularly difficult or involved great risk the salvor will be awarded a high percentage of its value which has to be paid by the owner or taken from the value of the cargo. The law of salvage determines when salvage occurs and how the award is to be calculated.

When a ship has been lost at sea, the owner may abandon it. The implications of this depend on the applicable legal system. For example, under the law in England, when ownership is abandoned in this way the ship becomes the property of the Crown. On the other hand, law in the United States of America considers that the ship becomes the property of the person who finds it and reduces it to possession. Once again, these are highly technical rules determining how the law operates.

During negotiation of the Underwater Convention, many delegates were mystified as to the need for a provision excluding salvage law and the law of finds. In the law of their countries, once a ship sinks, it is no longer subject to the rules of salvage. Moreover, after a short period of time, it becomes State property. For States with legal systems having such effect, it seemed that laws on salvage and finds were irrelevant. However, this was only true within those national legal systems. There could be situations where the rules of salvage or finds applying in one State are sought to be exercised over underwater cultural heritage in the territory of another State.

For example, courts in the United States of America in the exercise of their admiralty jurisdiction have granted an American company salvage rights to RMS *Titanic*, lying on the seabed some 480 kilometres from Newfoundland at a depth of approximately four kilometres. In one decision, the court attempted to exclude persons wanting to visit the wreck and photograph it from a 168-square mile area of the North Atlantic, saying 'restricting freedom of navigation over a few square miles of the vast North Atlantic Ocean is hardly a significant intrusion'.[52] In *Bemis v. RMS Lusitania*[53] the United States court purported to grant salvage rights over the wreck of the *Lusitania* which lies within the territorial sea of Ireland. Consequently, although a particular national law may not recognize any application of salvage to wrecks lying on the seabed, salvage law may be applied by a court in another State acting extraterritorially. This could well lead to a conflict of jurisdiction and perhaps an actual conflict if one side decides to ignore the other.

Another problem with salvage is that it was never designed to preserve the surviving structure and contents of historic wrecks and the information they contain. For example, the Underwater Convention emphasizes that the first option for protection of a wreck should be *in situ* preservation. This conflicts with the freedom to initiate salvage. Moreover, the whole notion of salvage is based on the award made to the salvor in light of the value of what has been rescued. There is little point in salvaging material of no commercial value such as ship's timbers. In addition, the salvage award is calculated when the work is done – too late for protection if the

---

51 Page 6.
52 *RMS Titanic v. Wrecked and Abandoned Vessel* 9 F.Supp. 2d (1998) 624, 634. This was reversed on appeal: *RMS Titanic v. Haver* (1999) AMC 1330.
53 884 F.Supp. 1042 (1995).

work has not met archaeological standards. As already noted,[54] courts in the United States of America have attempted to require salvors working on historic wrecks to adopt such standards. A study of this phenomenon concludes that "in doing this the courts have applied their own notions of what these principles mean, notions that reflect only partially the requirements of the archaeological profession."[55]

Faced with these considerations, the ILA Draft had stated: 'Underwater cultural heritage to which this Convention applies shall not be subject to the law of salvage'. This was subjected to some criticism and the UNESCO/DOALOS Draft substituted the following:

> States Parties shall provide for the non-application of any internal law or regulation having the effect of providing commercial incentives for the excavation and removal of underwater cultural heritage.

There was some debate on this provision during the expert meetings with a number of States indicating their wish that salvage law be excluded. The Single Negotiating Text produced by the Chairman at the Fourth Expert Meeting was the same as the ILA Draft but added exclusion of the law of finds. Following inconclusive debate the matter was referred to a small sub-committee which eventually came up with the text in Article 4. This was adopted unanimously – the first of the crucial issues in the Underwater Convention to be resolved.

Article 4 begins by referring to any 'activity relating to underwater cultural heritage'. This is a departure from the terminology set out in Article 1 which refers to activities directed at underwater cultural heritage and activities incidentally affecting such heritage. 'Relating to' would appear to be wider than 'directed at' but narrower than 'incidentally affecting'. It would seem necessary to have a causal connection between the activity and the heritage for 'relating to' to apply. There is a further linguistic problem in that it is unclear what ensures that any recovery of the underwater cultural heritage achieves its maximum protection as required by sub-paragraph (c). 'It' at the end of the second line refers to this seemingly in the context of 'activity' but, although this would make sense in in the context of (a) and (b), an activity cannot ensure anything. The Article has to be read as requiring that the authorization issued by the competent authorities contain conditions ensuring that any recovery of the underwater cultural heritage achieves its maximum protection.

Subject to the specified conditions, the law of salvage and the law of finds do not apply to underwater cultural heritage to which the Underwater Convention applies. The justification for not applying the former has been given. Exclusion of the law of finds is more complex. The main reason is that this law, particularly as developed in the United States of America, treats the finder as owner with complete control over what has been found. This was seen as incompatible with protection of the heritage values inherent in an underwater site. On the other hand, if the law of finds is excluded, it means that an ancient wreck found on the deep seabed, for example, and brought ashore, has no owner unless the State where it comes ashore provides for this, as does England.[56] The Underwater Convention provides no guidance on the basis that it is not a Convention dealing with ownership issues.

The effect of the conditions set out in Article 4 is to bring the situation applying beyond national jurisdiction into line with that already existing in many national legal systems. Most systems require a permit for any activity in relation to their concept of underwater cultural heritage. The permit will specify how the activity is to be conducted and, in many cases, what happens to the objects excavated. In effect, these are the three conditions set out in Article 4.[57] The authorization will be given by the responsible authorities as set out in Articles 7, 8, 10 and 12. The activity in

---

54 Page 7.
55 Fletcher-Tomenius, P., O'Keefe, P.J. and Williams, M. 'Salvor in Possession: Friend or Foe to Marine Archaeology?' (2000) 9 *International Journal of Cultural Property* 263, 298.
56 See further discussion below under Article 18 page 86.
57 The three conditions are cumulative i.e. all must be satisfied: Carducci, G. 'The UNESCO Convention 2001: A Crucial Compromise on Salvage Law and the Law of Finds' in Prott, L.V. (ed.) *Finishing the Interrupted Voyage* (UNESCO/Institute of Art and Law; Paris/Builth Wells; 2006) 27, 29.

question will have to conform to the Underwater Convention which in practice will mean that it is carried out in accordance with the Rules of the Annex. To achieve maximum protection of the underwater cultural heritage recovered, provision will have to be made both for conservation and long term storage and exhibition. Guidance is given in Articles 18 and 19 and the Rules of the Annex. In sum, the effect of the conditions set out in Article 4 is to validate existing national practice and extend it beyond current State jurisdiction to activity relating to underwater cultural heritage on the continental shelf and deep seabed.

Although Article 4 is worded such that the law of salvage and the law of finds can apply in specified circumstances, if those circumstances are indeed satisfied, there will be little left of the original concepts underlying these two fields of law. For example, originally, if the law of finds applied, the finder could excavate or not as he or she wished. Apart from the attempts described above by courts in the United States of America to apply archaeological principles to salvage operations, salvors and finders were free to perform the work as they saw fit although the salvage award would reflect what the court thought of their efforts. Finders could do what they wished with anything raised. That brought up by salvors often ended up for sale in the hands of the salvors although its precise distribution depended on the rules of salvage. It will be thus obvious that the preconditions in Article 4 will undercut much of the traditional content of salvage and finders' law even if those laws continue to apply. We do not agree with Forrest that Article 4 undermines the Annex and allows "States to interpret these rules so as to allow the continuation of the application of a modified salvage law to underwater cultural heritage".[58]

In implementing the provisions of Article 4, States will have to be careful not to contravene the property rights aspects of human rights law. Apart from provisions in the *European Convention on Human Rights*, these property rights are little developed.[59] For those States party to it, the *First Protocol to the European Convention on Human Rights* would apply to salvage rights existing at the time the regime provided for by the Underwater Convention is implemented.[60] The future regime would not be affected by human rights considerations as no proprietary interest would have been acquired. Potential salvors could not argue that they had been deprived of anything when all they have is the potential of gaining an interest when a wreck is discovered and reduced to possession. Expectations do not have the degree of concreteness to bring them within the idea of possessions which is what the *First Protocol* refers to.

---

58 Forrest, C. fn. 42, above.
59 O'Keefe, P.J. 'Archaeology and Human Rights' (2000) 1 *Public Archaeology* 181.
60 Fletcher-Tomenius, P. and Williams, M. 'The Protection of Wrecks Act 1973: A Breach of Human Rights' (1998) 13 *International Journal of Marine and Coastal Law* 623.

ARTICLE 5 – ACTIVITIES INCIDENTALLY AFFECTING UNDERWATER CULTURAL HERITAGE

> Each State Party shall use the best practicable means at its disposal to prevent or mitigate any adverse effects that might arise from activities under its jurisdiction incidentally affecting underwater cultural heritage.

The concept of 'activities incidentally affecting underwater cultural heritage' was discussed under Article 1. Although certain activities are not directed at that heritage, they can disturb or damage it. Article 5 draws the attention of States to this possibility and establishes certain obligations in that regard. States Party do not have any option in taking action. The duty is imperative – they 'shall' prevent or mitigate adverse effects.

The activities in question may be of great economic (fishing, mining, oil drilling) or national security (weapons testing) importance. A balance has to be struck between continuation of these activities and protection of the underwater cultural heritage which, as we have seen, is the primary purpose of the Underwater Convention. Consequently, Article 5 requires a State to use only the 'best practicable means at its disposal'. This reflects Article 2(4) which sets out the nature of the duty to protect as the aim of the Convention. It means that States are not bound to pursue the most extreme means of preventing or mitigating adverse effects. 'Practicable means' would be those most appropriate taking into account the physical situation, the science involved and the cost of taking action. States cannot sit back and do nothing. They have to consider the problem and take positive action within the practical limitations on their power. But it is sufficient merely to mitigate adverse effects. This means to reduce the severity of those effects. The disturbance or damage will continue. That could be seen as a defect in the provision. Forrest, for example, takes the view that 'the Article provides too weak an obligation on States to provide for an effective protection regime'.[61] However, politically it is probably as much as could be gained in the context of the Underwater Convention. There may be an extensive and expensive project underway which is suddenly faced with a shipwreck and no way of avoiding it. Underwater cultural heritage may well have to be excavated in order to mitigate damage to it: *in situ* protection is the first option but that may have to be discarded if it is in serious danger. This conforms to the UNESCO *Recommendation concerning the Preservation of Cultural Property Endangered by Public or Private Works* 1968, particularly Paragraph 9:

> Member States should give due priority to measures required for the preservation *in situ* of cultural property endangered by public or private works in order to preserve historical associations and continuity. When overriding economic or social conditions require the cultural property be transferred, abandoned or destroyed, the salvage or rescue operations should always include careful study of the cultural property involved and the preparations of detailed records.

The activities giving rise to adverse effects have to be under the jurisdiction of the State Party. This obligation is not limited to the territory of the State. Consequently, activities on the continental shelf or in the EEZ allowed by UNCLOS would still fall under the purview of Article 5. For example, oil drilling or the operation of a chemical process could create adverse effects which would need to be prevented or mitigated. Underwater cultural heritage in the Area might be affected by the activities of vessels flying the flag of a State Party which would bring it within the scope of Article 5.

In practical terms, active and effective management is the key to preventing or mitigating adverse effects on the underwater cultural heritage. All those who have an interest affecting the heritage must be involved. The State should provide a means of bringing these groups together so that each knows what the other is doing but, more importantly, how their actions are likely to affect the heritage.

> At the end of the day, once a site is damaged and destroyed it is gone for good. Managed effectively it could provide a cultural and economic benefit for many years to come.[62]

---

61   Forrest, C. fn. 42 above, 339.
62   Jeffery, B. "' Activities Incidentally Affecting Underwater Cultural Heritage " in the 2001

Article 6 – Bilateral, Regional or Other Multilateral Agreements

> 1. States Parties are encouraged to enter into bilateral, regional or other multilateral agreements or develop existing agreements, for the preservation of underwater cultural heritage. All such agreements shall be in full conformity with the provisions of this Convention and shall not dilute its universal character. States may, in such agreements, adopt rules and regulations which would ensure better protection of underwater cultural heritage than those adopted in this Convention.
>
> 2. The Parties to such bilateral, regional or other multilateral agreements may invite States with a verifiable link, especially a cultural, historical or archaeological link, to the underwater cultural heritage concerned to join such agreements.
>
> 3. This Convention shall not alter the rights and obligations of States Parties regarding the protection of sunken vessels, arising from other bilateral, regional or other multilateral agreements concluded before its adoption, and, in particular, those that are in conformity with the purposes of this Convention.

The Underwater Convention is to apply world-wide. As such it must accommodate a variety of views as to what measures should be taken for the protection of underwater cultural heritage. Sometimes States may find it desirable to take a stricter approach to a particular matter or it may be necessary to deal with something omitted from the general international convention. Here the bilateral treaty or regional agreement may fulfil a need.

Paragraph 1

There were already a number of international arrangements applying to underwater cultural heritage before the Underwater Convention was adopted. At the bilateral level there was the *Agreement between The Netherlands and Australia Concerning Old Dutch Shipwrecks* 1972;[63] the 1989 *Exchange of Notes between the Government of the United Kingdom of Great Britain and Northern Ireland and the Government of the Republic of South Africa Concerning the Regulation of the Terms of Settlement of the Salvaging of the Wreck of HMS Birkenhead*[64] and also in 1989 the *Arrangement entre le Gouvernement de la République française et le Gouvernement des Etats-Unis d'Amérique au sujet de l'épave du CSS Alabama.*[65] A bilateral agreement entered into since the Underwater Convention was adopted is the *Agreement between the Government of the United States of America and the Government of the French Republic Regarding the Wreck of La Belle* which was signed in March 2003.[66] This was an auxiliary vessel of the French Navy sent by the King of France to establish a colony at the mouth of the Mississippi River. It sank in 1686 in what is now Matagorda Bay in Texas and was found in 1995. Under the treaty, ownership of the wreck was to remain with the French Government but the Texas Historical Commission would hold the wreck and its artefacts for a renewable term of 99 years.

The *Protocol concerning Specially Protected Areas and Biological Diversity in the Mediterranean* 1995[67] is an example of a regional agreement. It entered into force in 1999. Article 4(d) states that the objective of a specially protected area as defined in the Protocol is to safeguard *inter alia* 'sites of particular importance because of their scientific, aesthetic, cultural or educational interest'.

In 2003 an agreement was negotiated to protect RMS *Titanic.*[68] The parties involved were Canada, France, United Kingdom and United States of America. The Agreement is subject to

---

UNESCO Convention' in Prott, L.V. (ed.) *Finishing the Interrupted Voyage* fn. ?? above, 96, 99.
63   1972 Australian Treaty Series No. 8.
64   CM 906 (1990).
65   (1989) 93 *Revue générale de Droit International Public* 975.
66   <http://www.gc.noaa.gov/documents/gcil_la_belle_agmt.pdf>.
67   <http://ec.europa.eu/world/agreements/prepareCreateTreatiesWorkspace/treatiesGeneralData.do?step=0&redirect=true&treatyId=598>.
68   *Agreement Concerning the Shipwrecked Vessel RMS Titanic* 2003: <http://www.gc.noaa.gov/documents/titanic-agreement.pdf>.

ratification. Two States have to ratify for it to come into force but to date (June 2013) only the United Kingdom has done so and its implementing legislation will not come into force until the Agreement itself is in force. The United States signed the Agreement on 18th June 2004 subject to passage of necessary implementing domestic legislation which has not yet eventuated. Attached to the Agreement is a set of 'Rules Concerning Activities Aimed at the RMS *Titanic* and/or Its Artifacts'. These are based on those contained in the Annex to the Underwater Convention.[69]

It is obvious that States have not rushed to enter into bilateral or regional agreements concerning underwater cultural heritage. In encouraging States to do this, Article 6 recognizes that the Underwater Convention is a framework convention which may well need to be supplemented by other agreements to meet the needs of a specific situation. For example, the problems that arose in the late 1960s between the Netherlands and Australia illustrate one such type of situation. A number of vessels of the *Vereenigde Oostindische Compagnie* (V.O.C. that is, the Dutch East India Company) were wrecked off the coast of Western Australia some 400 years ago. The Netherlands claimed that it was successor in title to the V.O.C. and owner of those vessels. Australia took the view that, since the Netherlands had done nothing to find them for hundreds of years, they were abandoned. In the *Agreement between The Netherlands and Australia Concerning Old Dutch Shipwrecks* 1972, the Netherlands transferred 'all its right, title and interest in and to the wrecked vessels of the V.O.C. lying on or off the coast of the State of Western Australia and in and to any articles thereof to Australia'. The Agreement did not state that the Netherlands had title to the wrecks and thus does not constitute an acknowledgement of this claim by the Australian Government. Rather, whatever title the Netherlands did in fact have under its law and/or any other system of law, was transferred to Australia. For its part, Australia recognized the 'continuing interest' of the Netherlands in articles recovered from the vessels.

A Committee was established under the Agreement 'to determine the disposition and subsequent ownership of the recovered articles between the Netherlands, Australia and the state of Western Australia'. To guide the Committee in its work, an 'Arrangement' was attached to the Agreement. This sets out both general and operating principles. For example, among the latter is a provision:

> In its deliberations the Committee will have, as its general aim, the purpose of ensuring that representative series of statistical samples and sufficient examples of the rarer objects will be deposited in the museums of the Netherlands and Australia to convey the variety and contents of each wreck to both the public and to scholars while, at the same time, ensuring that major projects of scholarly research will not be impeded by overfragmentation of the collection. Dispersal in this way, among separate repositories will also help to ensure the permanent safety of representative material in the event of the destruction of any one repository.

The Agreement between Australia and the Netherlands has been described in some detail because it deals with matters not covered by the Underwater Convention (for example, abandonment and ownership) or dealt with only in very general terms (such as disposition of material raised). It resolved a number of problems that were threatening to cause difficulties in the relations between the two countries. The Agreement thus ensured better protection of underwater cultural heritage than would have been the case if the Convention had then existed and been the only international agreement applying. The Committee set up by the Agreement worked very well. Collections were established in the Western Australian Maritime Museum at Fremantle and Geraldton, the Australian National Maritime Museum in Sydney and at the Scheepsvart Museum in the Netherlands. However, in 2012 the Scheepsvart Museum sent back to Australia its representative sample of artefacts, reflecting the growing philosophy of keeping collections together.

The Council of Europe Draft Convention on Protection of the Underwater Cultural Heritage[70] was an attempt to ensure better protection in the European region. It failed to achieve acceptance because of differing views on jurisdiction between Greece and Turkey. Such regional agreements

---

69   For a detailed discussion of the Agreement and its possible role in protection of the *Titanic*: Aznar, M.J. and Varmer, O. 'The *Titanic* as Underwater Cultural Heritage: Challenges to its Legal International Protection' (2013) 44 *Ocean Development and International Law* 96.
70   Page 11.

offer great scope for enhanced protection if the States concerned have a common attitude to this heritage. Geographic proximity may well be insufficient to provide that common attitude. Shared cultures and history are better glue that will unite particular groups of States to protect their underwater cultural heritage. This may be found in such areas as the Mediterranean, the Baltic and the Caribbean.

There are no existing examples of general multilateral agreements other than the Underwater Convention. There would not seem to be any point in attempting to negotiate another such general agreement in the near future. A more strict and specific convention would be possible, for it would not dilute the universal character of the Underwater Convention which, under Paragraph 1, States are required to maintain. Nevertheless, politically, such work could not be foreseen for many years. On the other hand, multilateral agreements with narrower objects could be envisaged, such as the protection of wrecks from certain countries which had far flung mercantile and military interests. Spain might find it useful to enter into a multilateral agreement to protect the remains of Spanish vessels found in the Caribbean, United States of America, Asia and Northern Europe. China might find advantages in the same approach for its vessels in Asia.

Paragraph 2

There will be cases where a State has part of its cultural heritage lying in far off waters. Such examples abound: English warships in the Baltic or the Mediterranean; Spanish vessels in the Caribbean; Dutch merchantmen in Asian waters. In many cases the link between these shipwrecks and the country from which the vessels originally came can be made relatively easily. But much depends on the period of time elapsed. The older the wreck the less the chance of establishing a link, particularly when one gets back to a time when States as currently constituted did not exist.

Paragraph 2 refers to a 'verifiable link' but qualifies it by addition of the words 'especially a cultural, historical or archaeological link'. The purpose of the addition is unclear as it adds very little to the meaning. 'Archaeological' is inappropriate in this context as already explained.[71] Cultural and historical aspects of a link would always have been an essential component of any attempt to establish a 'verifiable link' but why have these been singled out at the expense of other criteria? There may be a scientific link such as scientific expeditions with researchers from various countries (Arctic explorations, botanical collecting) or artistic links (such as paintings of famous shipwrecks or writings related to them). The 'verifiable link' is the sum total of all the possible connecting factors. The most that can be said is that the criteria of cultural and historical links simply direct attention to something which is already obvious. Of much greater complexity is the situation where the link is to a site which is now part of a modern State. For example, suppose the remains of a Phoenician cargo vessel are found in the Western Mediterranean. Is there a cultural or historical link to Lebanon or other Levantine State?

Should the verifiable link be affected by legal concepts such as abandonment? If an owner abandons a vessel (i.e. relinquishes all claims to it) does this destroy any verifiable link between the State of that vessel and the wreck? The better view would be that the link should not be affected by the actions of a private party.

Presumably, a regional agreement would deal with all underwater cultural heritage in the region. A State from outside the region would normally be interested in only that for which there is a verifiable link. Care would have to be taken when drafting such agreements to make provision for restricting the activities of any State which it is envisaged might be invited to join; it would have to limit its rights to only that underwater cultural heritage with which it has a verifiable link. Finally, it must be noted that becoming a party to such an agreement is by invitation only. States cannot demand that status.

Paragraph 3

This is a provision saving the position of States party to agreements existing before the Underwater Convention was adopted. The wording is in the imperative and so leaves no room for argument that rights existing before the Underwater Convention was adopted may somehow

---

71   Page 34.

be affected because of a possible contrary provision. An example could be the *Agreement between The Netherlands and Australia Concerning Old Dutch Shipwrecks* 1972 which, as already explained, applies to wrecked vessels of the V.O.C. 'lying on or off the coast of Western Australia'. This Agreement is implemented in Australia by the *Historic Shipwrecks Act* 1976. Neither the Agreement nor the Act specifies what is meant by 'lying on or off the coast', but the general tenor of both documents indicates that Dutch wrecks on the continental shelf off Western Australia would be covered, and the Australian Act referred to above applies to the continental shelf. The Act requires reporting of such wrecks found on the continental shelf. But both the Agreement and the Act predate UNCLOS and the Underwater Convention. It illustrates Australia's interpretation of the Agreement which would allow extension of control over wrecks on the continental shelf.

There are some peculiar features to Paragraph 3. Why should the date of adoption of the Underwater Convention be the benchmark as opposed to the date when the Convention came into force? The argument in support of the former would be that after the Underwater Convention is adopted, States have knowledge of its contents and should not act so as to defeat its object and purpose in terms analogous to those of Article 18 of the *Vienna Convention on the Law of Treaties* which reads:

> A State is obliged to refrain from acts which would defeat the object and purpose of a treaty when:
>
>> It has signed the treaty or has exchanged instruments constituting the treaty subject to ratification, acceptance or approval, until it shall have made its intention clear not to become party to the treaty;
>>
>> It has expressed its consent to be bound by the treaty, pending the entry into force of the treaty and provided that such entry into force is not unduly delayed.

The wording of Article 18 of the Vienna Convention is not directly applicable to the adoption of a multilateral convention by the UNESCO General Conference. Article 18 refers to the process of a State signifying agreement with the terms of a treaty by means of signature which does not take place for a UNESCO Convention. However, official UNESCO advice is that "adoption of a recommendation by the General Conference in fact gives rise, for the Member States as a body – and thus even for those which did not vote for its adoption – to specific obligations under the Constitution and Rules of Procedure".[72] The provisions relied on refer to international conventions as well as recommendations so the same arguments would be applicable. After that date, States have obligations as set out in the UNESCO Constitution and cannot enter into agreements in terms contrary to the Underwater Convention.

Quite apart from Paragraph 3, the scope for the Underwater Convention to alter rights and obligations under existing bilateral, regional and multilateral agreements is limited. There are certain circumstances set out in the *Vienna Convention on the Law of Treaties* – for example, termination or suspension of the operation of a treaty implied by conclusion of a later treaty[73] – but these are of limited application.

The concluding words of Paragraph 3 – 'and, in particular, those that are in conformity with the purposes of this Convention' – do not add anything to the substance of the provision. As already noted, Paragraph 3 is in the imperative and all pre-existing treaties are protected.

---

[72] UNESCO/CUA/68, 9 Aug. 1955, pp. 3-4; reproduced in O'Keefe, P.J. & Prott, L.V. (eds) *Cultural Heritage Conventions and Other Instruments: A Compendium with Commentaries* (Institute of Art and Law, Builth Wells, 2011) 205.

[73] Article 59.

Article 7 – Underwater Cultural Heritage in Internal Waters, Archipelagic Waters and Territorial Sea

> 1. States Parties, in the exercise of their sovereignty, have the exclusive right to regulate and authorize activities directed at underwater cultural heritage in their internal waters, archipelagic waters and territorial sea.
>
> 2. Without prejudice to other international agreements and rules of international law regarding the protection of underwater cultural heritage, States Parties shall require that the Rules be applied to activities directed at underwater cultural heritage in their internal waters, archipelagic waters and territorial sea.
>
> 3. Within their archipelagic waters and territorial sea, in the exercise of their sovereignty and in recognition of general practice among States, States Parties, with a view to cooperating on the best methods of protecting State vessels and aircraft, should inform the flag State Party to this Convention and, if applicable, other States with a verifiable link, especially a cultural, historical or archaeological link, with respect to the discovery of such identifiable State vessels and aircraft.

With Article 7 the Underwater Convention ventures into a very complex and sensitive area. States are normally very conscious of their sovereign status and proposals for applying internationally adopted standards are subject to intense scrutiny. It is a testament to their recognized expression of widely acceptable standards that States saw fit to require application of the Rules in internal waters, archipelagic waters and the territorial sea.

Paragraph 1

This Paragraph is a restatement of the basic rule of international law that a State has sovereignty in its internal waters, archipelagic waters, and territorial sea. Internal waters are those lying on the landward side of the baseline[74] from which the territorial sea is measured. In the words of UNCLOS, an archipelago is a "group of islands, including parts of islands, interconnecting waters and other natural features which are so closely interrelated that such islands, waters and other natural features form an intrinsic, geographical, economic and political entity, or which historically have been regarded as such".[75] UNCLOS lays down detailed rules for the drawing of baselines around an archipelago. In practical terms it means that these may be drawn around the outer edges of a group of islands. The territorial sea is measured from these baselines and in terms of UNCLOS should not be more than twelve nautical miles in breadth[76] although some States claim more.

In archipelagic waters, territorial seas and some internal waters, another State may have rights such as those of innocent passage for vessels flying its flag. But activities directed at underwater cultural heritage are subject to the exclusive right of the coastal State to regulate and authorize them although the remains of warships may be in a special category.[77] This is usually done through national legislation.

Paragraph 2

Under Article 7(2) of the Underwater Convention, States Parties are required to apply the Rules contained in the Annex to activities directed at underwater cultural heritage in their internal waters, archipelagic waters and territorial sea. But no study has been done showing how this will impact on the very complex system of existing State controls.

Currently, there is little uniformity in national legislation used to regulate activities directed at underwater cultural heritage. What does exist comes from common reactions to similar problems. The methods adopted vary widely. For example, some States have legislation applying

---

74   Page 2.
75   Article 46(b).
76   Article 3.
77   Page 57.

specifically to underwater cultural heritage – usually shipwrecks. The *Abandoned Shipwreck Act* 1987 of the United States of America applies only to abandoned wrecks embedded in submerged lands of a state or those eligible for inclusion in the National Register. Under the United Kingdom *Protection of Wrecks Act* 1973 a wreck may be protected when it is designated by the relevant Minister whereas in Australia, under the *Historic Shipwrecks Act* 1976, the remains of ships underwater for at least 75 years are automatically protected. Other States have legislation of general application to all heritage whether on land or underwater. For example, the Swedish *Act Concerning Ancient Monuments and Finds* 1988 covers such things as graves, remains of homes, ruins and 'wrecked ships, if at least 100 years have presumably elapsed since the ship was wrecked'. Under the consolidated *Antiquities Law* of Cyprus, 'antiquity' is defined *inter alia* as meaning any object 'recovered from the sea within the territorial waters of Cyprus'. While shipwrecks are often the subject of this legislation, there are variations as to which ones are covered. For example, the *Abandoned Shipwreck Act* of the United States of America mentioned above applies only to wrecks where the owner has either expressly or by conduct indicated that he or she no longer regards the wreck as their property. Thus, the issue of abandonment can become an important threshold question.[78] The 2002 *Law of the People's Republic of China on the Protection of Cultural Relics* states quite simply that all cultural relics in the inland waters or territorial sea of China are owned by the State.

The degree to which States on becoming party to the Underwater Convention will find it necessary to amend their laws will depend not only on the existing situation but also on what can be done administratively. For example, many of the Rules in the Annex could be implemented as conditions in a permit allowing activities directed at underwater cultural heritage. However, some, such as that stating that this heritage shall not be traded, sold, bought or bartered as commercial goods (Rule 2), would appear to need legislative implementation.

According to Paragraph 2, application of the Rules by the coastal State shall not prejudice other international agreements and rules of international law regarding the protection of underwater cultural heritage. This means that if there is any difference between the Rules and another international agreement, the latter prevails. The only agreement of significance would be the *European Convention on Protection of the Archaeological Heritage (Revised)* 1992 which extends to all areas within the jurisdiction of the Parties.[79] The Convention[80] contains a number of provisions dealing with the same topics as the Rules although there does not appear to be any clash. For example, Article 4(ii) of the European Convention requires States party to make provision 'for the conservation and maintenance of the archaeological heritage, preferably *in situ*'. Rule 1 of the Annex to the Underwater Convention, states that 'the protection of underwater cultural heritage preferably through *in situ* preservation shall be considered as the first option'. Both instruments contain provisions on funding, reporting, conservation etc.

Paragraph 3

This is the first of three Articles dealing with 'State vessels and aircraft'.[81] The treatment to be accorded them was highly controversial. The ILA Draft had specifically excluded them from the scope of the Convention. However, they do comprise a significant portion of the underwater cultural heritage and many experts thought that the Underwater Convention should cover them. Some wanted to exclude any reference to these vessels in the Convention thus leaving the issue of control over the wrecks to the general rules of public international law. In the end it was decided to specifically include 'State vessels and aircraft' with the method of treating them to be decided according to whether they lay in archipelagic waters or the territorial sea; on the continental shelf or in the EEZ; or in the Area.

Thus Paragraph 3 is of importance to a number of States. It emphasizes the basic need for co-

---

78 Walker, J.E. 'A Contemporary Standard for Determining Title to Sunken Warships: A Tale of Two Vessels and Two Nations' (1999-2000) 12 U.S.F. *Maritime Law Journal* 311.
79 Page 11.
80 See generally O'Keefe, P.J. 'The European Convention on the Protection of the Archaeological Heritage' (1993) 67 *Antiquity* 406.
81 The others are Articles 10 and 12.

operation among the States concerned when the remains of a warship of one State are found within the archipelagic waters or territorial sea of another State. Unlike Paragraphs 1 and 2 of Article 7, Paragraph 3 does not refer to internal waters. Moreover, in light of the fact that the Article deals with areas over which the coastal State has sovereignty, the requirement to inform the flag State of the discovery of one of its vessels is not made an imperative; rather it is something that a State should do in the desire to co-operate.[82]

When a State vessel sinks in the territorial sea or archipelagic waters of another State, there comes about a possible clash between the sovereignty of the coastal State and that of the flag State. The sovereignty of the latter in the vessel must survive the sinking and the vessel must not be abandoned for such a clash to be possible.[83] But if it does, there can be serious political and diplomatic problems regarding any activities directed at the wreck.

An example of this concerned the remains of the C.S.S. *Alabama*, a Confederate warship that raided Union shipping during the American Civil War. She was sunk by the U.S.S. *Kearsarge* on 19th June 1864 in French territorial waters off Cherbourg. The remains were located by a French Navy mine hunter in 1984.[84] The French authorities appeared to take the view that they were entitled to investigate the wreck irrespective of American interests. In 1987, the State Department of the United States of America wrote to the French Government 'to claim ownership and to reserve the right to approve anyone who can dive on the ship'. The State Department actively advised against officials from other United States agencies having any contact with French officials on the matter and discouraged financial contributions from United States citizens for the funding of work on the site. Bills were introduced in the United States Senate and House of Representatives.

> ... a variety [of] highly vocal individuals created considerable confusion and political pressure. Demand for return of *Alabama*, claims for material from the site, and charges that the French were stealing America's history created a highly antagonistic atmosphere.[85]

Negotiations between the two States began in 1988 and concluded in 1989 with the *Arrangement entre le Gouvernement de la Rèpublique française et le Gouvernement des Etats-Unis d'Amérique au sujet de l'*èpave du CSS Alabama referred to above.[86] The two States agreed to establish a joint scientific committee with two representatives each. Under the Agreement all proposed work on the site was to be reviewed by the Committee and submitted to the French Minister of Culture who had authority to authorize research in accordance with French law. The French zone of protection around the site was to remain in place.

The episode surrounding the *Alabama* has been discussed at some length to illustrate the emotional, political and legal problems that such a discovery can cause, particularly where there is no guidance for policy makers. The Agreement concerning the *Alabama* sets out possible ways in which this could be achieved although much will depend on the circumstances. For example, the *Exchange of Notes between the Government of the United Kingdom of Great Britain and*

---

82 The amendments (UNESCO Doc. 31 C/COM.IV/DR.4) proposed by the Russian Federation and the United Kingdom during the meeting of Commission IV would have changed the wording to 'shall consult' which would have increased the burden on the State Party concerned and given the Flag State a larger role. It was also proposed to extend the provision to internal waters. The amendments were not adopted (see page 21).
83 Page 42.
84 The bell of the Alabama had been found in about 1936 by a diver who, it seems, traded it at a local bar in Guernsey for drinks. In 1979 it was bought at a gun show in London by an American dealer who was later sued by the United States Government to recover its possession: *U.S. v. Steinmetz* 763 F.Supp. 1293 (1991) 1297.
85 Watts, G.P. 'C.S.S *Alabama*: Controversial as Always, Yet Offering Opportunities for International Co-operation' (1987) *Underwater Archaeology: Proceedings from the Society for Historical Archaeology Conference, 1990, Tucson, Arizona* 75, 77.
86 Page 52. Further details on the background to the negotiations can be found in Dudley, W.S. 'C.S.S. *Alabama*: The Evolution of a Policy' (1991) *Underwater Archaeology: Proceedings from the Society for Historical Archaeology Conference, 1991, Richmond, Virginia*, 47.

Northern Ireland and the Government of the Republic of South Africa Concerning the Regulation of the Terms of Settlement of the Salvaging of the Wreck of HMS Birkenhead 1989[87] did result in co-operation between the United Kingdom and South Africa although it would now conflict with the Rules in the Annex to the Underwater Convention. The *Birkenhead* – a British warship – sank in 1852 in South African territorial waters. The Exchange of Notes outlined the terms on which salvage was to be conducted by salvors licensed by the South African authorities. Regimental badges and personal effects of soldiers and crew were raised, some of which went to the South African Cultural History Museum while the remainder were auctioned by Sotheby's in 1994.

It is not necessary that co-operation be formalized by an agreement between the States concerned. For example, in 1998 a US District Court granted an American company – Sea Hunt, Inc. – salvage rights over two wrecks believed to be the Spanish frigates *Juno* and *La Galga*. The United States filed a motion to intervene and a claim on behalf of Spain asserting ownership of the two vessels. Thereafter, the United States tried by a variety of means to promote the Spanish claim. It tried to act as counsel for Spain in the proceedings but the court held that it lacked authority to do so.[88] It later submitted an Amicus Curiae Brief supporting the Spanish position which stated in part that the United States:

> .. is the owner of military vessels, thousands of which have been lost at sea, along with their crews. In supporting Spain, the United States seeks to ensure that its sunken vessels and lost crews are treated as sovereign ships and honoured graves, and are not subject to exploration, or exploitation, by private parties seeking treasures of the sea.[89]

Eventually, Spain had to appear and be represented by counsel. The Court of Appeal found that Spain retained its ownership of the two vessels. The Sea Hunt case illustrates another means of co-operation between States: one of many possibilities.

The necessity to notify States with a verifiable link to the discovery of a State vessel in addition to notification to the flag State arises from the fact that there could be situations where parts of the flag State may have become independent States since the vessel sank. Nevertheless, for many reasons, including the listed cultural and historical reasons, the latter State may well wish to be informed of the discovery and possibly take part in the co-operative process.

There are two possible problems with this procedure of notifying other States. The first is the need to identify the wreck. This is often very difficult and may take considerable time. An example is that of HMS *Fowey* which sank in 1748 in what is now the Biscayne National Park off the coast of Florida. The wreck site was found in 1978 but experts differed as to which wreck it was. Some thought Spanish and others British. It only in the late 1990s when opinion confirmed that the site was indeed that of HMS *Fowey*. The second problem is whether the local authorities realize the necessity to notify the flag State. In the case of the Fowey it was not until 2000 that contact was made with the British Government and then through a person not directly concerned with the excavation and identification of the wreck. The historian of the Upper Keys, a Major Trelewicz, wrote to the British Ministry of Defence for an opinion regarding ownership of the vessel. At the conclusion of an exchange of correspondence, the Ministry advised "we would expect to be consulted about any proposal for further recoveries from the Wreck of HMS *Fowey* or major preservation works thereon".[90] Of course, one would hope that administrators today would be more aware of the rights of the flag State and the requirement to notify it of discoveries of State vessels and aircraft.

---

87   Page 52.
88   *Sea Hunt, Inc. v. Unidentified, Shipwrecked Vessel or Vessels* 22 F.Supp. 2d 521 (1998).
89   Quoted in the judgment of the Fourth Circuit Court of Appeal, *Sea Hunt, Inc. v. Unidentified, Shipwrecked Vessel or Vessels* 2000 A.M.C. 2113, 2127.
90   Quoted in Skowronek, R.K. and Fischer, G.R. *HMS Fowey Lost and Found* (University Press of Florida, Gainesville, 2009) 183. On 15 Aug. 2013 the Governments of the United States of America and the United Kingdom signed a Memorandum of Understanding acknowledging that the wreck belongs to the British Government and that the two States would co-operate in its preservation and protection.

Once again, the States with a verifiable link may be far flung. For example, HMS *Roebuck* was a British warship captained by the 'pirate and hydrographer' William Dampier which sank off Ascension Island in 1701. Among other States with a verifiable link to this ship is Australia arising from the explorations of Dampier along the west coast of the continent. A team under the auspices of the Western Australian Maritime Museum made a search for the wreck site working under an agreement with the British Government and local authorities.[91]

---

91   McCarthy, M. 'HM Ship *Roebuck* (1690-1701): Global Maritime Heritage' (2004) *33 International Journal of Nautical Archaeology* 54.

ARTICLE 8 – UNDERWATER CULTURAL HERITAGE IN THE CONTIGUOUS ZONE

> Without prejudice to and in addition to Articles 9 and 10, and in accordance with Article 303, paragraph 2, of the United Nations Convention on the Law of the Sea, States Parties may regulate and authorize activities directed at underwater cultural heritage within their contiguous zone. In so doing, they shall require that the Rules be applied.

The contiguous zone extends 24 nautical miles from the baselines from which the territorial sea is measured. As the latter is twelve miles wide, the contiguous zone thus covers an additional twelve miles. Here the coastal State may exercise control to 'prevent infringement of its customs, fiscal, immigration or sanitary law and regulations within its territory or territorial sea'.[92] Claiming a contiguous zone is not mandatory.

The opening words of Article 8 indicate that in their contiguous zone States may act in ways giving greater protection to the underwater cultural heritage provided there is no conflict with Articles 9 and 10 of the Underwater Convention and Article 303(2) of UNCLOS. As already noted,[93] the latter gives States certain powers in respect of archaeological and historical objects in the contiguous zone but the triggering effect for bringing these into effect is 'removal from the seabed'. This accords with the opening words of Article 303(2) – 'In order to control traffic in such objects …'. Consequently, under Article 8, the regulation and authorization of activities directed at underwater cultural heritage in the contiguous zone must be directed at those resulting or likely to result in removal of the heritage concerned.

If a State does claim a contiguous zone and takes action to regulate or authorize activities directed at underwater cultural heritage within that zone, it must apply the Rules set out in the Annex to the activities interdicted.

---

92   Article 33(1)(a) UNCLOS.
93   Page 13.

ARTICLE 9 – REPORTING AND NOTIFICATION IN THE EXCLUSIVE ECONOMIC ZONE AND ON THE CONTINENTAL SHELF

1. All States Parties have a responsibility to protect underwater cultural heritage in the exclusive economic zone and on the continental shelf in conformity with this Convention. Accordingly:

(a) a State Party shall require that when its national, or a vessel flying its flag, discovers or intends to engage in activities directed at underwater cultural heritage located in its exclusive economic zone or on its continental shelf, the national or the master of the vessel shall report such discovery or activity to it;
(b) in the exclusive economic zone or on the continental shelf of another State Party:
(i) States Parties shall require the national or the master of the vessel to report such discovery or activity to them and to that other State Party;
(ii) alternatively, a State Party shall require the national or master of the vessel to report such discovery or activity to it and shall ensure the rapid and effective transmission of such reports to all other States Parties.

2. On depositing its instrument of ratification, acceptance, approval or accession, a State Party shall declare the manner in which reports will be transmitted under paragraph 1(b) of this Article.

3. A State Party shall notify the Director-General of discoveries or activities reported to it under paragraph 1 of this Article.

4. The Director-General shall promptly make available to all States Parties any information notified to him under paragraph 3 of this Article.

5. Any State Party may declare to the State Party in whose exclusive economic zone or on whose continental shelf the underwater cultural heritage is located its interest in being consulted on how to ensure the effective protection of that underwater cultural heritage. Such declaration shall be based on a verifiable link, especially a cultural, historical or archaeological link, to the underwater cultural heritage concerned.

This was one of the most controversial provisions to be negotiated during the experts' meetings. The problem lies in the relationship between the coastal State and discoveries of underwater cultural heritage on its continental shelf. Article 9 goes to the question of to whom reports of such discoveries shall be made. For years a number of States required persons searching for oil and minerals on their continental shelves to report any finds of underwater cultural heritage even though they were not nationals of that State. For example, in 1978 Norway included in oil exploration permits over parts of its continental shelf a requirement that the licensee report objects of cultural, historic or archaeological importance discovered during the course of exploration.[94] But the situation envisaged here goes much further. Reports are to be made by any person who makes such finds, including those with no relationship to the coastal State. An example would be the discovery by an US citizen of ancient wrecks on the Italian continental shelf.[95]

Although it is not expressly stated, Article 9 can be seen as fleshing out the requirement in Article 303(1) of UNCLOS that: 'States have the duty to protect objects of an archaeological and historical nature found at sea and shall co-operate for this purpose'. UNCLOS does not indicate the content of that duty but left it for a later international agreement which is now represented by the Underwater Convention. Reporting and notification of finds are obviously the first steps in the process of protection.

---

94   O'Keefe, P.J. and Prott, L.V. 'Final Report on Legal Protection of the Underwater Cultural Heritage' Annex II in *The Underwater Cultural Heritage: Report of the Committee on Culture and Education, Parliamentary Assembly, Council of Europe* Doc.4200 (Strasbourg, 1978) 45, 56.
95   Page 18.

Paragraph 1

In line with the statement of objectives in Article 2(1), Paragraph 1 is careful to impose a responsibility on all States Parties to protect underwater cultural heritage on the continental shelf and in the exclusive economic zone. This is an over-riding requirement and the most practical solution to a difficult problem. It does not matter where the discovery is made provided it is within such a zone or on a continental shelf somewhere in the world. But some States will be more directly concerned than others. Coastal States have specific rights on their adjacent continental shelf and in their EEZ which they have the exclusive right to protect as against all other States. They are also the nearest and therefore the most likely to be aware of activities in these areas. Some such States considered that they were authorized to control these areas, even before the advent of UNCLOS in 1982, which made no change to that situation, but passed over it in silence. Others regard the provisions of Article 303(1) as authorizing such action. However, certain other States regard this as excluded by UNCLOS because there was no specific mention of it and they had political interests in not agreeing to such action by the coastal State. To reach a compromise between these two groups of States, a complex scheme was devised based on nationality and the flag of the vessel involved.

This operates in two ways. The first, in Paragraph 1(a), involves the coastal State imposing reporting obligations on its national or the master of a vessel flying its flag. There is nothing untoward with this. Apart from possible considerations of human rights, States are quite free under international law to impose duties on their nationals and ships flying their flag, even though they are outside the territorial jurisdiction of the State. There may be problems of enforcement but that is another issue. The national or the master is to report to the coastal State any discovery of underwater cultural heritage or any intention he or she may have to engage in activities directed at such heritage on the State's continental shelf or in its EEZ.

But what of the situation where a national or the flag vessel of one State discovers underwater cultural heritage on, or intends to engage in activities directed at it, in the exclusive economic zone or on the continental shelf of another State? In other words, there is no link of nationality or flag between the coastal State and the individual or the vessel concerned. Paragraph 1(b) is intended to deal with this.

A State, let us say for ease of description, Xanadu, has a continental shelf on which a vessel flying the flag of Lilliput makes a discovery of underwater cultural heritage. The expedition is led by a person from Shangri-la. Under one interpretation of Paragraph 1(b)(i), Xanadu is regarded as one of the States Parties referred to in the paragraph. Consequently, Xanadu would require the national of Lilliput or the master of the Shangri-la vessel to report the discovery to it i.e. Xanadu, and Lilliput and Shangri-la would likewise require reporting to themselves. 'States Parties', since in the plural, would thus be interpreted as requiring each individual State Party to act regarding discoveries on its own continental shelf or in its EEZ, as well as requiring the State of the flag of the vessel and of the nationality of the team leader to report to each of these States respectively.

Another interpretation would require reference back to (1)(a) and from that reading into (b) the qualifications made by 'its'. Under this interpretation, Lilliput and Shangri-la, on becoming party to the Underwater Convention, would require their nationals and the masters of vessels flying their flag to report discoveries of and activities directed at underwater cultural heritage to them and to Xanadu. The latter would be nothing more than the recipient of the report. No jurisdiction or control would be exercised by Xanadu.

Paragraph 1(b) was drafted by the United States of America. During the Fourth Meeting of Governmental Experts, Norway tried to insert an amendment, also desired by the United States of America, of the provision which was defeated. A similar amendment was proposed by the Russian Federation and the United Kingdom and endorsed by the United States of America during the session of Commission IV. This was defeated. It would have changed 'States Parties' to 'a State Party'; qualified 'national' by 'its' and added after vessel the words 'flying its flag'. The provision would then have read:

> When the discovery or activity is located in the exclusive economic zone or on the continental shelf of another State Party:

A State Party shall require its national or the master of a vessel flying its flag to report its discovery or activity to it and to that other State Party;

Alternatively, a State Party shall require its national or master of a vessel flying its flag to report such discovery or activity to it and shall ensure the rapid and effective transmission of such reports to all other States Parties.

The overwhelming rejection of the proposed amendment[96] indicates that the great majority of States wanted Paragraph 1(b)(i) in its current form.

Paragraph 1(b)(i) has been called a 'constructive ambiguity'. 'Ambiguous' because it is capable of two interpretations. 'Constructive' in that it represents a compromise which would make the Underwater Convention acceptable to more countries. It was clearly the furthest that the majority of States were prepared to go in seeking such a compromise. Rejection of the proposed amendment is a clear indication that the majority wished to retain both interpretations given above within the ambiguity.

Paragraph 1(b)(ii) is an alternative to 1(b)(i). Under this provision, on receiving a report from its national or a ship flying its flag, Lilliput would rapidly and effectively transmit it to all other States Parties; thus including Xanadu provided that State is party to the Underwater Convention. This would have had the somewhat peculiar consequence that many States may be notified of a discovery or of an intention to engage in activities directed at underwater cultural heritage but not Xanadu if the latter was not a Party. The provision would also rely heavily on efficient communication between a number of different entities. There would be communication from the Master to the Lilliput administration; from that to all other States Parties and then distribution within the bureaucracy of those States. It is difficult to envisage this process as acting quickly and efficiently.

There are a number of practical problems in imposing obligations on the State of the national or the flag State requiring that national or the master of the vessel to make a report. Firstly, the discovery or the activities envisaged may occur at a place far removed from either of the States concerned – for, of course, the State of the national may well not be the flag State of the vessel. Enforcing the requirement to report may be very difficult if not impossible.

Secondly, it must be realized that activities directed at underwater cultural heritage often involve many different nationalities. It would be unworkable if Paragraph 1 required every person on the vessel to report to their own State. It could also put a person in a very difficult position if he or she had signed a non-disclosure contract. There was discussion of this issue during the Plenary Session of the Fourth Meeting of Experts and general agreement was reached that the reference to 'national' should be considered as confined to the leader of the expedition or other operation. That agreement has not been recorded in the Underwater Convention itself. However, States could interpret their obligations in this way and implement it through their law and administrative practice.

Thirdly, the flag State is seen as playing a significant role. Experience shows that this may be unrealistic. Many vessels are registered in flag of convenience States. This occurs when a vessel is registered in a State which is different from that of the ship's owners. There is often very little connection between the ship's operators and the flag State. Often the major reason for using a flag of convenience State is to avoid what the operators consider to be onerous regulation. Little attention is paid to enforcement of such regulations as exist. Such States may be unlikely to become party to the Underwater Convention if this means that they will have to require reporting of discoveries of underwater cultural heritage or the intent to engage in activities directed at it. If they do will the requirements of Article 9 be observed by or enforced on masters of vessels registered in that State? To what extent are the authorities concerned with underwater cultural heritage able to influence those who are administering ship registration and management? There is debate about the States that fall into this category although Panama, Liberia and the Marshall Islands are usually listed as the most significant.[97]

---

96 Page 21.
97 <https://www.bimco.org/en/Education/Seascapes/Questions_of_shipping/What_are_flags_of_convenience.aspx> (consulted 18 July 2013).

If the coastal State is a Party, it may be faced with a situation where no report has been made or circulated but there is a vessel which appears to be about to do something in its exclusive economic zone or on its continental shelf. The coastal State could approach the State of the national or the flag State to see whether or not any report had been lodged. Normally the identity of the flag State will be easily ascertained. But if the flag State is not party to the Convention, the coastal State would have to establish the State of the 'national' concerned, something which may be impossible. It would then be necessary to wait until something is done or threatened which brings the jurisdiction under Article 10(2) into operation.

While Paragraph 1 refers to a requirement that there be a report of an intention to engage in activities directed at underwater cultural heritage, 1(b) only refers to 'activity'. Nevertheless, the phrasing 'such activity' obviously refers to the activity set out in Paragraph 1(a). But does it include the intention to engage in such activities? The point is not clear but very significant. The obligation to report on behalf of a national arises the moment the intention is formed which in many cases will be well in advance of the vessel putting to sea. Reasons of consistency with Paragraph 1(a) and the logic of cross-referencing as adopted in that paragraph require that the 'intention to engage' applies equally to Paragraph 1(b). In practical terms, the intention should be determined objectively as, for example, evidenced by the national commencing the planning process set out in the Annex to the Underwater Convention or otherwise preparing equipment, engaging workers, hiring a vessel etc.

Paragraph 1 seems to assume that the procedures set out in (b) will be part of a standing requirement for all vessels and nationals of a State Party. This would be imposed either by law or administrative decree. The alternative would be instructions issued for each individual case which, in practical terms, would be unworkable. The proposed interpretation would require States, on becoming party to the Underwater Convention, to put in place an effective system of reporting and to ensure that its nationals and ships flying its flag are aware of this. Merely putting the system in place is insufficient. It would have to be widely publicized and should be included in all standing instructions.

As part of this process, States would find it necessary to specify the nature of the information required. In the case of a discovery there may not be much information available before further work is done on the site. Where information is available, it should be distributed in such a way that other States are able to make informed decisions in implementing their rights under the Underwater Convention.

Paragraph 2

This Paragraph requires a State, at the time of becoming party, to indicate how reports will be transmitted in the procedure set out in Paragraph 1(b). This is only part of the process involved in distributing reports. The whole of the reporting requirement needs careful implementation by States when they become party. For example, to whom does the master of the vessel send the report – the maritime or the cultural authorities? Who distributes the report – the authorities who receive it or the diplomatic authorities? Similar issues arise for recipient States. At all stages there are possibilities for delay and mistakes, particularly where there are language and cultural differences. Under Paragraphs 3 and 4, UNESCO is to play a role in the distribution of information. The Operational Guidelines, relying on Article 22, provide for the establishment of component authorities for, *inter alia*, 'management of underwater cultural heritage'. The names and addresses of these authorities are to be communicated to the Director-General who is to make them available to all States Parties.[98]

Paragraphs 3 and 4

Paragraph 3 of the Convention requires a State Party to notify the Director-General of UNESCO of discoveries or activities reported to it under Paragraph 1. The Operational Guidelines include a provision dealing with this. The notification is to be made through diplomatic channels using forms included in the Guidelines: Form 1 for notifying a discovery and Form 2 for notifying an activity.[99]

---

98 Paragraphs 13 and 14, Operational Guidelines.
99 Paragraphs 16 and 26, Operational Guidelines.

Paragraph 3 of the Convention does not require the use of diplomatic channels for notifications although it has been written into the Guidelines. There would seem no good reason for stipulating this. Electronic communications would be more efficient using secure systems. There must be a focal point within UNESCO for reception of notifications and distribution of information to States. By default this seems to be the section in the Secretariat handling general matters of underwater cultural heritage. To date (August 2013) the only notification has been by Italy. As more States join the Convention and they become more accustomed to making notifications, UNESCO will find it necessary to formalize the procedures and provide more staff and other resources.

There has been some discussion in the Scientific and Technical Advisory Body and the Meeting of States Parties[100] about the nature of the information that should be provided particularly where the information is sensitive. It should be borne in mind that such information must be sufficient and of such a nature to enable the recipient State to decide whether there exists a verifiable link in terms of Paragraph 5.

Paragraph 4 of Article 9 requires the Director-General 'to promptly make available to all States Parties any information notified to him'. What is the precise role of the Secretariat in this? It could mean that UNESCO distributes the information it receives to all States party to the Underwater Convention although this is not required by the Convention. Alternatively, UNESCO could keep the information in such a way that it would be accessible to any State Party that wanted to access it but would not take any action itself to distribute it. The former is preferable and should not cost very much if it is in electronic form.

Paragraph 5

This provision is strangely placed since it is not part of the reporting or notification of reports procedures. It is more closely related to Article 10 dealing with protection and indeed that Article refers to Article 9(5) in its Paragraph 3. However, ignoring the issue of position in the Underwater Convention, information about a discovery or intent to engage in activities directed at underwater cultural heritage will normally come to a State Party under one of the procedures set out in the preceding paragraphs of Article 9. However, Paragraph 5 does not apply any restrictions to the source of the information and accordingly it may come from anywhere.

The Operational Guidelines state that a declaration of interest shall be made through diplomatic channels using Form 3 contained in those Guidelines.[101] If it is intended that this should be the exclusive method of notifying a verifiable link, and the use of the word 'shall' indicates this, then it is not in accordance with the Underwater Convention. States may use whatever means they wish to make such notification, although use of Form 3 and diplomatic channels would probably be the least controversial method given that it has been specified in the Guidelines.

> In declaring its interest to be consulted, a State Party shall inform on [sic] its link to the underwater cultural heritage concerned by accompanying its declaration by;
> The results of scientific expertises [sic];
> Historic documentation; or
> Any other adequate documentation.[102]

Under Paragraph 9 a State Party may declare to the coastal State its interest in being consulted on how to ensure effective protection of that underwater cultural heritage. There must be a verifiable link – the nature of which has already been discussed[103] - between that heritage and the State declaring an interest. It is of course highly probable that the verifiable link will not emerge until work, and it could be considerable work, has been done on the site to identify the nature of the underwater cultural heritage found. Another peculiarity of Paragraph 5 of the Convention is the phrase 'interest in being consulted'. This is a mild statement and should be contrasted with Paragraphs 3 and 5 of Article 10. 'Interest' could be taken as merely indicating a concern or it could be related to rights. 'Consultation' implies engaging in discussion, not the making of decisions to be carried into effect. This will be analysed further below.

---

100   Article 23, Operational Guidelines.
101   Paragraph 27, Operational Guidelines.
102   Form 3.
103   Page 54.

ARTICLE 10 – PROTECTION OF UNDERWATER CULTURAL HERITAGE IN THE EXCLUSIVE ECONOMIC ZONE AND ON THE CONTINENTAL SHELF

1. No authorization shall be granted for an activity directed at underwater cultural heritage located in the exclusive economic zone or on the continental shelf except in conformity with the provisions of this Article.

2. A State Party in whose exclusive economic zone or on whose continental shelf underwater cultural heritage is located has the right to prohibit or authorize any activity directed at such heritage to prevent interference with its sovereign rights or jurisdiction as provided for by international law including the United Nations Convention on the Law of the Sea.

3. Where there is a discovery of underwater cultural heritage or it is intended that activity shall be directed at underwater cultural heritage in a State Party's exclusive economic zone or on its continental shelf, that State Party shall:
   (a) consult all other States Parties which have declared an interest under Article 9, paragraph 5, on how best to protect the underwater cultural heritage;
   (b) coordinate such consultations as "Coordinating State", unless it expressly declares that it does not wish to do so, in which case the States Parties which have declared an interest under Article 9, paragraph 5, shall appoint a Coordinating State.

4. Without prejudice to the duty of all States Parties to protect underwater cultural heritage by way of all practicable measures taken in accordance with international law to prevent immediate danger to the underwater cultural heritage, including looting, the Coordinating State may take all practicable measures, and/or issue any necessary authorizations in conformity with this Convention and, if necessary prior to consultations, to prevent any immediate danger to the underwater cultural heritage, whether arising from human activities or any other cause, including looting. In taking such measures assistance may be requested from other States Parties.

5. The Coordinating State:
   (a) shall implement measures of protection which have been agreed by the consulting States, which include the Coordinating State, unless the consulting States, which include the Coordinating State, agree that another State Party shall implement those measures;
   (b) shall issue all necessary authorizations for such agreed measures in conformity with the Rules, unless the consulting States, which include the Coordinating State, agree that another State Party shall issue those authorizations;
   (c) may conduct any necessary preliminary research on the underwater cultural heritage and shall issue all necessary authorizations therefore, and shall promptly inform the Director-General of the results, who in turn will make such information promptly available to other States Parties.

6. In coordinating consultations, taking measures, conducting preliminary research and/or issuing authorizations pursuant to this Article, the Coordinating State shall act on behalf of the States Parties as a whole and not in its own interest. Any such action shall not in itself constitute a basis for the assertion of any preferential or jurisdictional rights not provided for in international law, including the United Nations Convention on the Law of the Sea.

7. Subject to the provisions of paragraphs 2 and 4 of this Article, no activity directed at State vessels and aircraft shall be conducted without the agreement of the flag State and the collaboration of the Coordinating State.

Article 10 deals with what was the most controversial issue in the negotiation of the Underwater Convention; namely, the protection of underwater cultural heritage in the exclusive economic zone and on the continental shelf. As explained above,[104] this was greatly affected by how States viewed the effect of UNCLOS and the proper role of the coastal State. The solution adopted is

---

104   Page 46.

complex and requires goodwill on the part of all States Parties to make it work. The danger is that the underwater cultural heritage may be damaged or destroyed while the various processes are being implemented. Paragraph 4 responds to this only in part.

The role played by the coastal State is crucial. It has rights under Article 10 that give it considerable means for protection of underwater cultural heritage in its exclusive economic zone or on its continental shelf. Under Paragraph 2 it can prohibit or authorize activities directed at the heritage in order to prevent interference with its sovereign rights or jurisdiction. Under Paragraph 4, as co-ordinating State, it can take all practicable measures to prevent immediate danger to the heritage. Also as co-ordinating State it can, under Article 10(5)(c), conduct preliminary research and issue authorizations for these actions. Together these amount to a powerful package of measures available to the coastal State if it wishes to use them. If it does not, then the process of consultation set out in Article 10(3) and (5) may delay the implementation of any protection for the underwater cultural heritage.

On the other hand, Articles 9 and 10 set up a co-operative system spreading duties and obligations from the coastal State to the broader international community. A coastal State may be quite relieved for this to happen if it wishes to use scarce resources for other purposes; for example, if it lacks an administrative structure to handle the work involved; it does not have the requisite technology for the task; or the underwater cultural heritage in question has no particular relationship to its own territory or people.

Paragraph 1

The main problem with this paragraph is to ascertain the scope of its application. The wording itself is quite clear. It is aimed at activities directed at underwater cultural heritage in the exclusive economic zone or on the continental shelf. Any authorization for such activities has to be in conformity with the provisions following in Article 10.

The Paragraph refers solely to authorizations. It does not mention prohibitions so these fall entirely outside the coverage of the Article. Paragraph 1 refers to the exclusive economic zone and continental shelf in general terms. This shows that all such areas are covered provided they are adjacent to States Party. The Underwater Convention does not purport to allow authorization for activities directed at underwater cultural heritage on the continental shelves or in the exclusive economic zones of non-State Parties.

The injunction against the giving of authorization is absolute. On becoming party to the Underwater Convention, a State surrenders any rights it had previously enjoyed under its own legislation to grant such authorizations if this went beyond the provisions in Article 10. On the other hand, prohibitions, as previously mentioned, are not affected.

Paragraph 2

Under this Paragraph, a State can prohibit or authorize an activity directed at underwater cultural heritage located in its exclusive economic zone or on its continental shelf. However, the prohibition or authorization must be aimed at preventing interference with that State's sovereign rights or jurisdiction as provided for in international law including UNCLOS. In Parts V and VI of the latter, there are set out certain rights which are relevant to this depending on the nature of the activity: for example, exploring and exploiting natural resources of the shelf; exploring, exploiting, conserving and managing living marine resources in the exclusive economic zone; control of installations, structures, drilling etc.

Underwater cultural heritage is often intimately associated with natural resources. For example, a ship may be partially embedded in a reef or its remains may be a habitat for fish. Any activity directed at the wreck will inevitably interfere with those natural resources. Under Article 77 of UNCLOS a State 'exercises over the continental shelf rights for the purpose of exploring and exploiting its natural resources'. These are already existing rights and they are exclusive: this means that 'no one may undertake these activities without the express consent of the coastal State'.[105] Consequently, the coastal State is entitled to prohibit or regulate activity in

---

105   Article 77(2), UNCLOS.

relation to those natural resources. Even if such prohibition or regulation has the incidental effect of protecting underwater cultural heritage, there is no issue of 'creeping jurisdiction' or contravention of the provisions of UNCLOS.

The power given to the coastal State under Paragraph 2 is broad and can be used to provide extensive protection to underwater cultural heritage. It would be possible for another State to challenge an exercise of that power on the ground that sovereign rights or jurisdiction are not being interfered with by the activity in question. But this is highly unlikely. A determination by a State that its sovereign rights are suffering is not likely to be put aside. It would be necessary for the other State to prove its allegations – not only the practical aspects but also something approaching misconduct on the part of the coastal State.

Although Paragraph 2 does not specify that an authorization issued by the coastal State should require compliance with the Rules set out in the Annex to the Underwater Convention the whole scheme of the Convention would necessitate this.

Paragraph 3

Paragraph 3 applies in situations where the coastal State cannot, or does not, act under Paragraph 2. The former would occur where there is no interference with the State's sovereign rights or jurisdiction as provided for by international law including UNCLOS. Such an interpretation is not expressly stated in Article 10 but it is the only logical one. Paragraph 2 gives the coastal State the 'right' to prohibit or authorize activities to prevent interference as described above. The procedures set out in Paragraph 3 and following paragraphs would seriously undercut that 'right' which is itself based on sovereign rights guaranteed by UNCLOS. Since this cannot have been the intention of the negotiators, the only logical interpretation is that given above. This means that in practice the procedures set out in Paragraph 3 and following paragraphs may have only a limited application. In many cases it is likely that the coastal State, if it desires to act, will be able to find an interference of the nature specified in Paragraph 2 such that it can proceed without having to consult other States. On the other hand, as noted above, States may prefer to use the co-operative system set up by Article 10.

In the event that Paragraph 3 applies, the coastal State must consult all other States Parties which have declared an interest under Article 9(5) on how best to protect the underwater cultural heritage concerned. There is a question as to when this should take place. It is unlikely that States Parties will all declare their interest at the same time. When they receive the information will depend on the procedure being used for its distribution under Article 9 or otherwise. Then there will be delays depending on the relative efficiency of their own bureaucracy and the need to consult experts in the field. Consequently, declarations of an interest will probably be made over a period.

Paragraph 3 requires the coastal State to 'consult' other States Parties as indicated. This is more than simple consultation which implies only a requirement to take into consideration the views of others. Under Paragraph 5 the consultation required by Paragraph 3 is to result in measures of protection which are to be implemented as set out in Article 10. The coastal State cannot ignore the results of consultation if it disagrees with their proposals.

Consequently, it is essential to avoid the situation where a State declares an interest under Article 9(5) only to find that the consultations have been made and the measures of protection agreed are being implemented. The best way to avoid that situation would be for the coastal State itself, as soon as it learns of a discovery or someone intending to engage in an activity directed at underwater cultural heritage in its exclusive economic zone or on its continental shelf, to pass the information to all those States it thinks might have an interest. It could also indicate that consultations would begin on a specified date. Co-operation and information sharing are required under Article 19 and the suggested procedure is an example of this in practice.

The coastal State is to act as co-ordinator of the consultations unless it declares it does not wish to do so. Although the heritage concerned lies in its exclusive economic zone or on its continental shelf, there may be good reasons for the coastal State to take this approach. For example, it may not wish to devote resources – funding and personnel – to such an exercise, particularly if the underwater cultural heritage has little or no connection with it. If the coastal State makes such a declaration, the States Parties which have declared an interest under Article 9(5) are to appoint a co-ordinating State. This would normally be from among the ranks of States which have declared an interest but there is nothing in the Underwater Convention to restrict their choice; they may even include a State not party to the Convention, if they all agree to this. The coastal State will have to take some part in this process as it is the one to whom other States make declarations of interest under Article 9(5). The coastal States would at least have to register the States doing so and circulate their names within the group otherwise the procedure for their appointing a co-ordinating State would not work.

Paragraph 4

This Paragraph deals with emergency situations. However, the English text is badly drafted and the meaning has to be teased out of a complex sentence. The first part is based on Article 2(4) of the Underwater Convention and Article 303(1) of UNCLOS. It gives substance to those provisions in times of immediate danger to underwater cultural heritage and makes this an integral part of the general duty to protect the heritage. 'Looting' is specifically mentioned as an example of an immediate danger. What is meant by this is not specified. It is defined in the *Oxford Dictionary* as 'plundering' which, in turn, is seen as the dishonest acquisition of property. In the context of Article 10, it should be seen as undertaking activities directed at underwater cultural heritage with the object of removing it without authorization as provided for by that Article and reducing it to a personal possession.

Action 'may' be taken by the co-ordinating State. Exercise of the power is not mandatory. It is entirely at the option of that State. A drawback is that the identity of the co-ordinating State may not be known for some time depending on what decision the coastal State takes under Paragraph 3(b).

Once there is a co-ordinating State, it may take all practicable measures to prevent any immediate danger to the underwater cultural heritage. This gives that State a wide range of options the use of which will depend on the nature of the danger experienced. It may take action before any consultations if that be necessary. The decision to do so would be one for the coordinating State and is not subject to question by other States, even those who declare an interest under Article 9(5). Paragraph 4 specifically mentions the issue of an authorization 'in conformity with this Convention' as one measure that may be taken. This means the authorization must be subject to the Rules of the Annex which, under Article 33, form an integral part of the Underwater Convention. Article 33 further states that 'a reference to this Convention includes a reference to the Rules'. But the provision goes further. The authorization would have to comply with any rule of international law including UNCLOS as provided for in Article 3.

The danger must be immediate before the coordinating State is entitled to act but its nature is very broadly defined. It can arise 'from human activities or any other cause, including looting'. The phrase 'any other cause' was inserted to cover situations which could not be envisaged by the drafters but may arise in practice. Certainly it is not restricted to events analogous to human activity but would cover naturally occurring causes of danger such as currents affecting recently exposed objects.

Paragraph 5

In this Paragraph are set out the procedures to be followed after the consultation has taken place. There is an assumption that the States concerned have managed to agree on measures of protection. If they do not, then resort may be necessary to the provisions on peaceful settlement of disputes set out in Article 25 although this is a complex and may result in a tribunal making decisions with no experience in issues involving underwater cultural heritage. However, if they are agreed, the procedures are to be implemented by the coordinating State unless all the States involved have agreed that another State Party is to undertake the task. There is no requirement that the State chosen should be one of those involved in the consultations. There may be factors such as access to technology that make the choice of a State outside the group logical. The coordinating State or another agreed State is to issue any authorization necessary for implementing the measures of protection agreed provided this is 'in conformity with the Rules'. Since authorizations under

Paragraph 4 have to be 'in conformity with this Convention', should any distinction be drawn? A possible explanation is that under Paragraph 4, the coordinating State is acting alone whereas under Paragraph 5(b) it is acting in concert with all the other consulting States.

The Operational Guidelines recommend that the group of consulting States 'should decide on the common financing of such measures'. In doing this they should consider the capacity of the individual States; the strength of the verifiable link with the heritage involved and the interest in its protection and the location of the heritage. Unless there is immediate danger, no measures should be implemented unless adequate funding is certain.[106]

Paragraph 5(c) is strangely placed in this context. The first two sentences of the Paragraph follow logically from the consultation procedure set up under Paragraph 3. But (c) appears to be divorced from the consultation process. Under this the coordinating State 'may conduct any necessary preliminary research' on its own initiative and 'shall issue all necessary authorizations'. No mention is made of conformity with the Convention. On the other hand, Rules 14 and 15 of the Annex deal with preliminary work and what such work comprehends. At the very least, those Rules would have to be complied with in doing the research and authorizations would have to allow for them.

Under Paragraph 5(c) there does not have to be an immediate danger to the underwater cultural heritage as required by Paragraph 4. The power to make preliminary investigations is certainly a necessary one in order to identify the nature of what has been found and the coordinating State is the one best suited to undertake this task. The results of the research are to be made known to the Director-General of UNESCO, not the consulting States. The Director-General is to make the information promptly available to all other States Parties.

Paragraph 6

This Paragraph is a savings provision. Essentially, it flows from the different points of view on the powers of the coastal State in relation to its exclusive economic zone and its continental shelf. As set out above, Article 10 enumerates a range of activities available to the coastal State although some of them may only be undertaken in a role as coordinating State. Paragraph 6 makes clear that any coordinating State, whether it be the coastal State or not, is acting on behalf of the States Parties and not in its own interest. Moreover, the carrying out of an action as coordinating State is not to form 'a basis for the assertion of any preferential or jurisdictional rights not provided for in international law, including the United Nations Convention on the Law of the Sea'. This means that existing positions regarding interpretation of UNCLOS are preserved. But development of international law cannot be frozen and, as time passes and practice develops under Article 10, a new norm of international law may emerge based on that practice.

Paragraph 7

As already noted, State vessels presented the negotiators of the Underwater Convention with particular problems. The agreed solution was to vary the relative powers of a State depending on where the remains of the vessel lie. Article 7 has already indicated the need for co-operation between the State in whose archipelagic or territorial waters the remains are found and the flag State. Article 10(7) provides another solution for remains found in the exclusive economic zone or on the continental shelf. It prohibits activity directed at State vessels or aircraft 'without the agreement of the flag State and the collaboration of the Coordinating State'. There is no mention that either State has to be a party to the Underwater Convention. The coordinating State need not be although this would be unlikely in practice. However, to be bound by Paragraph 7, both States, under general rules of international law, would have to be party to the Convention.

Paragraph 7 is subject to the provisions of Paragraphs 2 and 4. For example, under Paragraph 2 a State Party may prohibit or authorize activity directed at a State vessel to prevent interference with its sovereign rights or jurisdiction as set out in that Article. Here the rights of the coastal State take precedent to those of the flag State.

---

106   Paras. 61-63, Operational Guidelines.

Article 11 – Reporting and Notification in the Area

> 1. States Parties have a responsibility to protect underwater cultural heritage in the Area in conformity with this Convention and Article 149 of the United Nations Convention on the Law of the Sea. Accordingly when a national, or a vessel flying the flag of a State Party, discovers or intends to engage in activities directed at underwater cultural heritage located in the Area, that State Party shall require its national, or the master of the vessel, to report such discovery or activity to it.
>
> 2. States Parties shall notify the Director-General and the Secretary-General of the International Seabed Authority of such discoveries or activities reported to them.
>
> 3. The Director-General shall promptly make available to all States Parties any such information supplied by States Parties.
>
> 4. Any State Party may declare to the Director-General its interest in being consulted on how to ensure the effective protection of that underwater cultural heritage. Such declaration shall be based on a verifiable link to the underwater cultural heritage concerned, particular regard being paid to the preferential rights of States of cultural, historical or archaeological origin.

The Area is defined both in the Underwater Convention and UNCLOS as the seabed and ocean floor and subsoil thereof, beyond the limits of national jurisdiction. In effect, this means beyond the exclusive economic zone and continental shelf of States. As already mentioned[107], most of the Area is now accessible through advanced technology. Underwater cultural heritage in the Area may be in an excellent state of preservation. Accordingly, its importance has increased greatly over the years and will continue to do so. It needs an effective system of protection.

Paragraph 1

The duty to protect underwater cultural heritage found in the Area is clear. It flows, as the Paragraph notes, both from the Underwater Convention – Article 2 – and UNCLOS – Article 149.[108] The latter is vague and it is difficult to find an effective interpretation but the core duty of protection can be discerned. Flowing from the duty to protect, Paragraph 1 imposes a duty on a State Party to require it's national or the master of a vessel flying its flag to report to it any discovery of underwater cultural heritage in the Area or any intention to engage in activities directed at such heritage. Various aspects of this are similar to those appearing in respect of reporting in the exclusive economic zone and continental shelf (Article 9); for example, the meaning to be given to 'national'; the problem of flag of convenience States; administrative arrangements and the question of when an intention is formed. The same analysis applies here as there.

Paragraphs 2 and 3

The requirements of these Paragraphs are the same as those in Article 9(3) and (4) and the same discussion applies. There is the addition that States Parties have also to notify the Secretary-General of the International Seabed Authority of reports received. That body is established under Article 156 of UNCLOS. The Authority is the organization through which States Party to UNCLOS 'organize and control activities in the Area'. As such it is fitting that it be notified of discoveries of underwater cultural heritage in the Area or of any intent to engage in activities directed at that heritage. The Authority has regulations for exploration and mining operations in the Area which will require prospectors and contractors to notify the Secretary-General of any finds of objects of an archaeological and historical nature. All reasonable measures are to be taken to avoid disturbing such objects. The Secretary-General is to notify the Director-General of UNESCO of such finds. The Operational Guidelines contain Forms 1 and 2 providing assistance in making notifications.[109]

---

107 Page 3.
108 Page 12.
109 Discussed under Article 11(2).

Paragraph 4

If a State finds it has a verifiable link to the underwater cultural heritage concerned, it may, and this is at the option of the State, declare its interest in being consulted to the Director-General of UNESCO. Once again, an attempt is made to somehow explain the concept of a 'verifiable link' through reference to other criteria.[110] Here it is intended to refer to the criteria set out in Article 149 of UNCLOS. However, the wording has been changed to 'particular regard being paid to the preferential rights of States of cultural, historical or archaeological origin'. Obviously this refers to the States which have links of this nature to the heritage concerned although the phrasing suggests it relates to the origin of the State. In practical terms, the additional words add nothing to the concept of a verifiable link. Form 3 in the Operational Guidelines, intended to provide guidance in declaring an interest, has been discussed under Article 9(5).

---

110   See prior discussion at p. 54.

Article 12 – Protection of Underwater Cultural Heritage in the Area

1. No authorization shall be granted for any activity directed at underwater cultural heritage located in the Area except in conformity with the provisions of this Article.

2. The Director-General shall invite all States Parties which have declared an interest under Article 11, paragraph 4, to consult on how best to protect the underwater cultural heritage, and to appoint a State Party to coordinate such consultations as the "Coordinating State". The Director-General shall also invite the International Seabed Authority to participate in such consultations.

3. All States Parties may take all practicable measures in conformity with this Convention, if necessary prior to consultations, to prevent any immediate danger to the underwater cultural heritage, whether arising from human activity or any other cause including looting.

4. The Coordinating State shall:
(a) implement measures of protection which have been agreed by the consulting States, which include the Coordinating State, unless the consulting States, which include the Coordinating State, agree that another State Party shall implement those measures; and
(b) issue all necessary authorizations for such agreed measures, in conformity with this Convention, unless the consulting States, which include the Coordinating State, agree that another State Party shall issue those authorizations.

5. The Coordinating State may conduct any necessary preliminary research on the underwater cultural heritage and shall issue all necessary authorizations therefor, and shall promptly inform the Director-General of the results, who in turn shall make such information available to other States Parties.

6. In coordinating consultations, taking measures, conducting preliminary research, and/or issuing authorizations pursuant to this Article, the Coordinating State shall act for the benefit of humanity as a whole, on behalf of all States Parties. Particular regard shall be paid to the preferential rights of States of cultural, historical or archaeological origin in respect of the underwater cultural heritage concerned.

7. No State Party shall undertake or authorize activities directed at State vessels and aircraft in the Area without the consent of the flag State.

Apart from Article 149 of UNCLOS, there has been little attempt to regulate activities directed at underwater cultural heritage in the Area. The British *Protection of Military Remains Act* 1986 is an example of national action but can be used only against a British controlled ship or British nationals in respect of certain remains. Consequently, Article 12 is very important in the overall scheme for protection of the underwater cultural heritage. As is the case for Article 10, the procedures envisaged in Article 12 are bureaucratic and their effective operation will depend very much on the good-will of States and their desire to co-operate. As many of the same issues arise, the discussion below should be supplemented by that on Article 10.

Paragraph 1

Under Paragraph 1, any authorization granted for activity directed at underwater cultural heritage in the Area has to be in conformity with the provisions of the Article. No mention is made of prohibitions which are therefore unaffected and may be established if a State wishes.

Paragraph 2

The procedure required by this paragraph is straightforward. States Parties which have declared an interest under Article 11(4) are to be invited by the Director-General of UNESCO to consult on how best to protect the underwater cultural heritage concerned. This appears to envisage that UNESCO will have to play a role in bringing the States together for a meeting. The Director-General will have to consider when the invitation is to be issued so that no State is excluded by tardiness in declaring an interest. The invited States are to appoint a State Party – not necessarily one of their number – to act as coordinating State. The International Sea-bed Authority is to be invited to participate. This is worded so as to require an invitation to issue to the Authority for all such consultations. Presumably it would allow the Authority to decide if any of its interests are affected thus requiring its presence. The attendance of the Authority may be useful as it will know where seabed prospectors are operating and their nationality.

Paragraph 3

This Paragraph states quite clearly that all States Parties may take practicable measures to prevent any immediate danger to the underwater cultural heritage. Such measures are entirely optional and their implementation is not confined to State Parties who have declared an interest under Article 11(4). However, the measures must be in conformity with the Convention which means that anything done and any authorizations granted must comply with the Rules in the Annex as well as international law including UNCLOS. There is nothing preventing the making of prohibitions although these would have to be directed at nationals and ships flying the flag of the State concerned in order to satisfy jurisdictional limitations. Measures to prevent immediate danger can be taken at any time.

Paragraph 4

With one exception, this Paragraph is identical to Paragraph 10(5) and the same discussion is applicable. The exception relates to the requirement that authorizations must be 'in conformity with this Convention' under Paragraph 4(b) whereas under Article 10(5)(b) they have to be in conformity with the Rules. There would not seem to be any logical reason to make this distinction. The former phrase would seem to cast a wider net but there is little in international law, including UNCLOS, which would be relevant to the formulation of an authorization. In practical terms there would be little difference between the two Paragraphs.

Paragraph 5

Basically Paragraph 5 is the same as Article 10(5)(c) although the former stands alone and is not set out in the same context as the consultation process. This is a logical improvement in the drafting.

There is a small distinction between the role of the Director-General of UNESCO under Paragraph 5 and that under Article 10(5)(c). The latter says that he or she 'shall make such information available' whereas the former requires it to be made available 'promptly'. Good administrative practice would require the Director-General to act promptly even if this is not specifically required.

Paragraph 6

It seems that this Paragraph was inserted to incorporate in the processes described above the notion of a 'benefit to humanity' flowing from the reference to this phrase in Article 149 of UNCLOS. The idea is that the coordinating State acts 'on behalf of all States Parties' for the 'benefit of humanity as a whole'. This is a very vague concept and any attempt at seeking to achieve this in a practical sense would be hampered by two factors arising from Article 12 itself.

The first is that under Paragraph 2 the Coordinating State has to coordinate consultations with States which have declared an interest under Article 11(4) and under Paragraph 4 it is to implement the measures of protection on which they have agreed. This appears at odds with the notion that it is to act 'on behalf of all States Parties'.

Second, Paragraph 6 states that the coordinating State has to pay particular regard 'to the preferential rights of States of cultural, historical or archaeological origin in respect of the underwater cultural heritage concerned'. Does this mean that a non-State Party which has these 'preferential rights' can join in the process? Under Article 11(4), the States Parties having a verifiable link to the underwater cultural heritage are to declare their interest in being consulted on how to ensure the effective protection of the underwater cultural heritage concerned. They are then invited to consult on this under Article 12(2) and choose a coordinating State which carries the agreed measures of protection into effect. It can hardly be said that Paragraph 6 purports to allow the coordinating State to depart from the agreed measures of protection if it considers that some State which did not act, or could not act because it was not a Party, under Article 11(4) should have a preferential right.

In practice the co-ordinating State will probably proceed to carry out the agreed measures. Paragraph 6 says only that it should pay 'particular regard' to the preferential rights. These are not overriding. Moreover, by acting in accordance with the consulting States' decision, it could be argued that it is acting on behalf of all States for the benefit of humanity as a whole.

Paragraph 7

The prohibition on States Parties under Paragraph 7 is clear. They undertake to refrain from activities directed at State vessels or aircraft in the Area unless the flag State consents. There is no requirement that the flag State concerned be a Party to the Underwater Convention. It would seem that persons acting without authorization are unaffected i.e. there is no provision for prohibiting nationals or ships flying the flag of a State Party from undertaking activities directed at the State vessels of other States. Providing such activities comply with the Rules in the Annex, thus avoiding sanctions and seizure, these persons would appear to have freedom to act as they wish, although the general rules of international law would apply. States may, of course, create such prohibitions but there is nothing in the Convention obliging them to do so.

Article 13 – Sovereign Immunity

> Warships and other government ships or military aircraft with sovereign immunity, operated for non-commercial purposes, undertaking their normal mode of operations, and not engaged in activities directed at underwater cultural heritage, shall not be obliged to report discoveries of underwater cultural heritage under Articles 9, 10, 11 and 12 of this Convention. However States Parties shall ensure, by the adoption of appropriate measures not impairing the operations or operational capabilities of their warships or other government ships or military aircraft with sovereign immunity operated for non-commercial purposes, that they comply, as far as is reasonable and practicable, with Articles 9, 10, 11 and 12 of this Convention.

Article 13 is aimed at the situation where a warship or other government vessel with sovereign immunity engaged in State controlled operations comes across underwater cultural heritage. Disclosure of the discovery might reveal details of the operation which the State concerned would prefer to keep secret. For example, the vessel may have been performing clandestine acts, such as laying listening devices, on the continental shelf of another State. It may have been testing new weapons in the Area or trying out new equipment. One of its submarines may have come across underwater cultural heritage on a voyage. Obviously, this derogation from the requirements of the Underwater Convention is mainly for the benefit of the major naval powers.

The three criteria for excluding the obligation to report are that the vessel: one, must be operating for non-commercial purposes; two, be operating in its normal mode; three, not engaged in activities directed at underwater cultural heritage. The first of these may sometimes be difficult to establish. For example, would a naval vessel appearing in a commercial film with the permission of the authorities and on payment of a nominal sum be operating for a non-commercial purpose, particularly if, in addition, the authorities allowed its use for recruitment and image creation? This may be answered by saying that the vessel was not acting in its normal mode of operation which refers not only to its technical abilities but also the ordinary way in which it is used. Clearly, as a prop in a film the vessel is not being used in its normal way.

The second sentence in Article 13 is a savings provision requiring States, in effect, not to withhold information where there is no need to keep secret what was being done when the discovery was made. For example, it may have been found by naval divers on a routine training exercise. This requirement could be satisfied by the authorities of a State Party requiring all personnel to report discoveries to the master of the vessel who then passes this information to his or her superiors where the decision is made whether or not to make a report in accordance with the Underwater Convention.

ARTICLE 14 – CONTROL OF ENTRY INTO THE TERRITORY, DEALING AND POSSESSION

> States Parties shall take measures to prevent the entry into their territory, the dealing in, or the possession of, underwater cultural heritage illicitly exported and/or recovered, where recovery was contrary to this Convention.

This is one of the most important Articles in the Underwater Convention. It complements two other major international conventions: the UNESCO *Convention on the Means of Prohibiting and Preventing the Illicit Import, Export and Transfer of Ownership of Cultural Property* 1970 and the UNIDROIT *Convention on Stolen or Illegally Exported Cultural Objects* 1995. It provides the most effective sanction against activities directed at underwater cultural heritage contrary to the Underwater Convention.

The language of Article 14 is convoluted by the use of the conjunctive/disjunctive 'and/or'. Taking first the conjunctive, it would read 'underwater cultural heritage illicitly exported and recovered, where recovery was contrary to this Convention'. There would have to be two elements – export and recovery – but this reverses the sequence of events: recovery should come first followed by export. 'Illicit' should be read as referring solely to 'traffic' and not also joined to 'recovered' because the qualifier for that word is the phrase 'where recovery was contrary to this Convention'. In spite of the language, the intent appears clear. The first possibility is one where underwater cultural heritage is recovered contrary to the Convention and then illicitly exported. Applying the disjunctive 'or', there are two further possibilities: where such heritage is illicitly exported and where it is recovered contrary to the Underwater Convention. So it would appear there are three possibilities all told. However, the first is nothing but an amalgam of the other two although it emphasizes the illicit nature of the operation as a whole. On that basis, States Parties are required to take measures in respect of underwater cultural heritage which has been either recovered contrary to the Convention or illicitly exported. Such measures would cover the situation where it falls into both categories.

States will have to consider their existing obligations under the other international conventions mentioned above: the UNESCO *Convention on the Means of Prohibiting and Preventing the Illicit Import, Export and Transfer of Ownership of Cultural Property* 1970 and the UNIDROIT *Convention on Stolen or Illegally Exported Cultural Objects* 1995. All in all, there are a number of issues on which States will have to take policy decisions when implementing Article 14.

'Illicit export' is not defined in the Underwater Convention and, in fact, this is the only time it is mentioned. The phrase does appear in the *Convention on the Means of Prohibiting and Preventing the Illicit Import, Export and Transfer of Ownership of Cultural Property* 1970. This Convention is listed in the Preamble to the Underwater Convention as one to be considered in the progressive development of international law and practice. In relation to the 1970 Convention, it has been suggested that 'illicit' should be considered as meaning 'contrary to law'[111] and the same meaning would be appropriate in the context of Article 14. 'Export' also is not defined but implies that an object is taken out of the territory of a State although the precise moment of export may need to be established by legislation.[112] Although the word 'illicit' is infrequently used in Common Law legislation, it is clear that it reflects the language of the 1970 Convention and is familiar and will be clearly understood. As applied to export, the State is entitled to regulate the traffic of cultural heritage objects from its territory. Most States do this to a greater or less degree. There are variations in the nature of the objects covered, their monetary value and the administrative procedures that have to be observed for export to be lawful. Usually the legislation defines the objects covered which are then said to be prohibited exports. There may be provision for permitting export after an administrative procedure has given a favourable decision

---

111 O'Keefe, P.J. fn. 10, above.
112 This is done in the *Protection of Movable Cultural Heritage Act* 1986 (Australia) where, for the purposes of that Act, export is broadly defined to occur when the object is placed on the means of transport taking it to another country.

and a permit is issued. Consequently, there would be nothing unusual or noteworthy in a State prohibiting or regulating the export of underwater cultural heritage as defined in the Convention. On the other hand, the recovery itself could be authorized but the State may wish to retain whatever is recovered in its territory and do this by way of an export prohibition. In this regard, Article 14 would fit easily into the existing regime.

The second situation covered by the Article is that where underwater cultural heritage is recovered contrary to the Convention. The nature of recovery not in conformity with the Convention is to be deduced from the scope and form of the instrument as a whole. For example, all operations of recovery have to comply with the Rules Concerning Activities Directed at Underwater Cultural Heritage set out in the Annex which is an integral part of the Convention (Article 33). In addition, Articles 10 and 12 allow States Party to implement agreed measures of protection in the exclusive economic zone, on the continental shelf and in the Area. Such measures of protection would have to be in conformity with the Rules but could be more stringent. Objects would be covered by this provision even though there has been no illicit export from any State. Nor does the fact that no State legislation has been breached affect the matter. For example, a State may have given permission for an excavation and approved the methods used but if the whole operation does not comply with the Convention, then it falls under Article 14.

DUTY OF STATES PARTIES

Article 14 makes the recovery of underwater cultural heritage contrary to the Underwater Convention, and particularly that contrary to the Rules in the Annex, unattractive by creating difficulties for those who later handle it. States Parties are to take 'measures' in performance of their duty. There is no mention of what specifically these measures are: nor are States required to take 'all' measures, or 'all practicable' measures. States Parties thus have considerable latitude in how they implement this Article. A State may adopt administrative or legal procedures appropriate to its circumstances. On the other hand, at least some measures have to be taken since the imperative 'shall' is used. The measures taken must have the purpose of preventing the entry into the territory of the State, the dealing in, or the possession of underwater cultural heritage as set out in the Article.

ENTRY INTO THE TERRITORY

Most States have legislation prohibiting the entry of defined categories of cultural heritage. If such an object is imported, it may be subject to seizure and the person responsible liable to a fine and/or imprisonment. For example, the Australian *Protection of Movable Cultural Heritage Act* 1986 applies to 'objects imported after 1st July 1987, but which were previously exported from another country at any time when there was a cultural heritage protection law in force, contrary to the provisions of that law'.[113] If the object is imported into Australia it is liable to forfeiture. In the United Kingdom, the *Dealing in Cultural Objects (Offences) Act* 2003, applies to monuments which include 'any site comprising, or comprising the remains of, any vehicle, vessel, aircraft or other movable structure, or part of any such thing.[114] It is immaterial whether the site is above or below water. Under the Act a person is guilty of an offence if he or she 'dishonestly deals in a cultural object that is tainted, knowing or believing that the object is tainted'. The object is tainted if it is removed or excavated from a monument and that act constitutes an offence.

> It is immaterial whether—
> (a) the removal or excavation was done in the United Kingdom or elsewhere,
> (b) the offence is committed under the law of a part of the United Kingdom or under the law of any other country or territory.

Neither of the States mentioned above is yet party to the Underwater Convention. However, they show that there are States which would return objects unlawfully exported from a State Party under the terms of Article 14.

---

113 Ley, J.F. *Australia's Protection of Movable Cultural Heritage: Report on the Ministerial Review on the Protection of Movable Cultural Heritage Act 1986 and Regulations* (Australian Government Publishing Service, Canberra, 1991) 125.
114 S. 2(5).

Thus, preventing the entry of underwater cultural heritage as required by Article 14 would not be peculiar in international arrangements. It applies to entry of material in transit as well as that with a final destination in the State concerned. Entry into a free port[115] should be regarded as entry into the territory as the wording of Article 14 is not qualified. Moreover, the international trend appears to be to restrict the use of free ports to avoid controls on movement. For example, the Swiss *Loi fédérale sur le transfert international des biens culturels* of 2005 implements the *Convention on the Means of Prohibiting and Preventing the Illicit Import, Export and Transfer of Ownership of Cultural Property* 1970. Article 19(3) contains a specific statement that depositing cultural property in a free port area is the same as importing it in the sense of the legislation. It must be declared to Customs.[116]

States may use a variety of means to prevent entry into their territory as required by Article 14. Physical means include checks by border officials. Various techniques, such as profiling, have been developed to enable authorities to target particular persons and movements of cargo. These can help but they are only an aid.[117] Dutch authorities are using principles of risk analysis to assist in detecting illicit traffic.[118] Legislation prohibiting entry of underwater cultural heritage may dissuade many people from bringing it into a country. It does not have to be seized at the border. It can be declared a prohibited import with the result that it could be seized at a later time when information on its whereabouts is obtained by the authorities.

DEALING OR POSSESSION

On the other hand, preventing the 'dealing in, or the possession of' the underwater cultural heritage covered by Article 14 is a major step in controlling illicit trade. The wording is very broad. "Dealing in" covers all those who buy and sell the objects concerned. Persons who do it regularly as a business are obviously affected as are those who buy and sell from time to time although this is a question of degree. Once again, many States already regulate dealing in items of the cultural heritage, particularly that which has been illegally imported.

Article 14 requires Member States to prevent the 'possession' of underwater cultural heritage. Possession is of course different from ownership. A person can possess an object but not own it and *vice versa*. Possession was chosen as the criterion for a State Party taking action because the idea is to seize the object and this can be done more effectively from the person in possession. Also, there is the consideration of who should have the burden of proof in a particular case. From an enforcement perspective, it can be difficult for a government to prove the ownership of an object entering its territory and even more difficult to prove that the one in possession does not own the artefact that is in their possession. It is relatively easier for the government to prove that someone was in possession of an artefact and reasonable to place the burden of proof on the one in possession to prove that they own it or that their possession is otherwise lawful. In cases of looting and illicit trafficking the owner ultimately bears the loss and thus the deterrent effect will operate.

There have been auctions of material raised from wreck sites. Christie's auction in Amsterdam of a cargo of ceramics raised from the *Geldermahlsen* has already been mentioned.[119] The auction house was undoubtedly in possession of the material consigned for sale. Under Article 14 a State Party would now be obliged in similar circumstances to take measures to put an end to such possession; almost certainly by seizure under Article 18.

Underwater cultural heritage may be located within a State that is party to the Underwater Convention in order to be conserved. For example, the material raised from the Belitung wreck site in Indonesia[120] was sent to New Zealand for conservation. Such artefacts would be in the

---

115   The Cambridge Online Dictionary defines a free port as 'as area near a port or airport to which goods from foreign countries can be brought without tax being paid if they are sent to another country when they leave this area'.
116   See further O'Keefe, P.J. fn. 10 above, 136.
117   Above 12.
118   Van Heese, M. 'The Fight Against Illicit Traffic in Cultural Goods – The Dutch Approach' (2000) XI *Art Antiquity and Law* 85, 88.
119   Page 4.
120   Page 129.

possession of the laboratory where the work is being done and thus fall under Article 14.

WHICH STATE?

Article 14 is very broad in allocating powers to States attracting measures of prevention. For example, it is not specified that the illicit export has to take place from the territory of the State where the object was brought ashore. Nor is it said that that State must be a Party to the Convention. For example, underwater cultural heritage may be recovered and brought ashore in State A and then exported to State B which has legislation prohibiting the export of underwater cultural heritage recovered contrary to the Convention. If it is then likely to be exported from State B to State C contrary to the legislation of State B, State C, a State party to the Convention, would have to take measures to prevent its entry into its territory, or dealing in it once brought into the country or possessing it there. This situation would not be dependent on recovery contrary to the Convention but only on illicit export from State B.

A similar situation applies when underwater cultural heritage is recovered contrary to the Convention. If it is brought ashore in State A and then exported to State B it does not matter if State A is a party to the Convention nor does it matter whether State A has an export prohibition. The crucial factor is recovery contrary to the Convention. If this occurs, then State B would have to take measures to prevent entry into its territory, dealing in it or its possession there.

An object may have passed through many hands in many States. For example, it was at a restorer's in Munich in March 1973 that an ancient bronze sculpture, reputedly by Lysippus (though this has since been doubted), first became widely known, although it had apparently been found in waters off the Italian coast in 1964, bought by a dealer, sold on to a South American collector, sold by him to an English firm who then sent it to the restorers in Munich before it eventually ended up in the collection of the J. Paul Getty Museum in the United States of America.[121] States should consider what happens when there have been many transactions with the object concerned and the current possessor bought it without knowing the circumstances of its retrieval. Purchasers should note that appropriate enquires into provenance, in accordance with the principles of the 1970 UNESCO and 1995 UNIDROIT Conventions, may also reveal evidence of illicit recovery from an underwater site and consequent risk of seizure.

It must also be considered that dealing in an object or having possession of it may take place even though the object itself is not within the territory of the State. For example, a person may deal in or possess an object which is physically located in State A while he or she is located in State B. Article 14 would require State B, if it were party to the Underwater Convention, to take measures 'to prevent … the dealing in, or the possession' of that object if it constituted underwater cultural heritage recovered in a manner not in conformity with the Convention. Taking such measures could raise constitutional and human rights issues which are discussed further under Article 18.

The imposition of sanctions under Article 17 and seizure of underwater cultural heritage under Article 18 can be considered as measures going in part to satisfaction of the duty under Article 14. In administering the Underwater Convention, States will have to consider the interaction of these clauses.

LIMITATION PERIODS

Limitation periods in relation to sales are another factor. These allow a person to gain good title to an object even though one of the previous owners did not have this. For example, the law may provide that on unlawful export the object becomes the property of the State and is considered stolen. The person in possession may sell it to another and so on. Basically the limitation period means that, once it is bought by a person acting *bona fide*, after a certain lapse of time the then holder at the end of that period is recognized as having good title. There is no mention of this in Article 14. There is no limitation periods specified in the 1970 Convention although there is a complex formula dealing with them in the 1995 UNIDROIT Convention.

---

121 O'Keefe, P.J. and Prott, L.V. *Law and the Cultural Heritage: Volume III; Movement* (Butterworths, London, 1989) 543.

ARTICLE 15 – NON-USE OF AREAS UNDER THE JURISDICTION OF STATES PARTIES

> States Parties shall take measures to prohibit the use of their territory, including their maritime ports, as well as artificial islands, installations and structures under their exclusive jurisdiction or control, in support of any activity directed at underwater cultural heritage which is not in conformity with this Convention.

The purpose of this Article is to deny certain facilities to persons acting contrary to the provisions of the Underwater Convention. Such facilities could include access to food and fuel; communications and recreation. For example, a company seeking underwater cultural heritage may be based in the United States of America but be using a vessel registered in Panama to search on the continental shelf of Algeria. Even if neither the United States nor Panama were party to the Underwater Convention, the operations of the vessel would be severely constrained if all the States in the vicinity where it was working refused to make facilities available. Of course, as Article 15 states, the activities directed at the underwater cultural heritage would have to lack conformity with the Underwater Convention which means the Rules in the Annex and international law including UNCLOS.

Article 15 is very important. It applies to non-conforming activities directed at underwater cultural heritage wherever these may take place. But it is particularly important for a coastal State which can take action to prevent such activities on its continental shelf or in its exclusive economic zone without having to rely on the procedures in Paragraphs 9 and 10. Importantly, Article 15 is totally in conformity with international law including UNCLOS.[122] The measures a State Party takes must be restricted to prohibitions on the use of territory or other structures within that State's exclusive jurisdiction or control. UNCLOS sets out in detail the nature of these other structures. Moreover, a State has a right under international law to close even its international ports to protect its vital interests 'and it would be difficult to establish that any interests invoked by a State were inadequate to justify closure'.[123] States may also impose conditions for access to their ports – a right which is recognized in UNCLOS itself[124] - as well as other international agreements particularly those dealing with pollution.

> During discussion one expert raised the question whether Article 6 [now 15] contradicted other conventions on access to and use of ports. The most significant multilateral agreement in the field is the Geneva Convention and Statute on the International Regime of Maritime Ports (1923). Under Article 2 of that Statute, contracting parties are obliged, subject to certain exceptions, to grant on the basis of reciprocity the vessels of other contracting parties freedom of access and equality of treatment with their own vessels in maritime ports. However, only a relatively small number of States have ratified the 1923 Convention, which is generally considered as unsatisfactory. Most importantly, coastal authority to deny access is implied by Article 211(3) of the LOS Convention [i.e. UNCLOS] and it is assumed in a number of multilateral treaties relevant to marine pollution.[125]

Consequently, Article 15 contains no new powers on the part of the coastal State but rather an obligation to implement those already existing, albeit in a new context.

The full impact of Article 15 will only become apparent when most of the States in a particular geographic region become party to the Underwater Convention and implement the obligation. Until then vessels and their crews will be able to use the facilities available in non-Party States. The only region that would seem to be approaching a situation where it may be difficult for vessels to find port facilities is the Caribbean.

---

122   Articles 60 and 80, UNCLOS.
123   Churchill, R.R. & Lowe, A.V. fn. 43 above, 62; see also Kasoulides, G.C. *Port State Control and Jurisdiction: Evolution of the Port State Regime* (Martinus Nijhoff, Dordrecht, 1993) 20.
124   For example, Article 25(2).
125   Strati, A. *Draft Convention on the Protection of Underwater Cultural Heritage: A Commentary Prepared for UNESCO*, April 1999 UNESCO Doc. CLT-99/WS/8 p.40.

ARTICLE 16 – MEASURES RELATING TO NATIONALS AND VESSELS

> States Parties shall take all practicable measures to ensure that their nationals and vessels flying their flag do not engage in any activity directed at underwater cultural heritage in a manner not in conformity with this Convention.

Article 16 is directed at the fulfilment of a State's obligations under other provisions of the Underwater Convention. It will require action to be taken in advance of certain activities directed at underwater cultural heritage in a manner not in conformity with the Convention.

This provision applies in full force in internal waters. Those nationals and flag ships that engage in an activity directed at underwater cultural heritage have to conform to the Convention which includes the Rules in the Annex as well as the provision on dealing and possession in Article 14.

States Parties to the Underwater Convention have a range of obligations under Articles 9 and 11 in relation to their nationals and vessels flying their flag. These apply when those nationals and vessels discover or intend to engage in activities directed at underwater cultural heritage beyond the territorial sea of States Parties and the activities are not in conformity with the Underwater Convention. Article 16 does not use the same language. The measures to be taken must ensure that nationals and vessels do not engage in the activity. For example, there may be a discovery of underwater cultural heritage but no move to engage in any activities directed at it. In addition, Article 16 appears to apply to situations where such activities are actually occurring whereas Articles 9 and 11 apply also to those where so far there is only an intention to undertake the activities. Although there is this discrepancy, Article 16 is directed at the most pressing problem – the actual undertaking of the activities. There is nothing to prevent States going beyond Article 16 in implementing the Convention and applying the measures to both of the situations mentioned above. Indeed, their obligations under Articles 9 and 11 would seem to require them to do so.

However, it is likely in some cases that these activities will take place at a far remove from the State of the national or of the vessel. States Parties cannot wait until the activities have commenced. Under Article 16 there is an obligation on them to have in place an arrangement to prevent nationals and vessels flying their flag from engaging in the activities.

This will require a mixture of legislative and administrative provisions. The legislation would impose obligations on the national and the master of the vessel both to refrain from engaging in the activities mentioned and act so as to satisfy the obligations laid on the States under Articles 9 and 11. However, passing legislation by itself is not sufficient. The requirements of the legislation must be spelt out to those most concerned as well as made known to the general public. For example, even where this is not now done, instructions will have to be issued to masters of vessels as to their duties. Any known salvor of historic vessels as well as diver organizations must be circulated with details of what they are obliged to do.

ARTICLE 17 – SANCTIONS

> 1. Each State Party shall impose sanctions for violations of measures it has taken to implement this Convention.
>
> 2. Sanctions applicable in respect of violations shall be adequate in severity to be effective in securing compliance with this Convention and to discourage violations wherever they occur and shall deprive offenders of the benefit deriving from their illegal activities.
>
> 3. States Parties shall cooperate to ensure enforcement of sanctions imposed under this Article.

Sanctions are intended to forward the purpose of the Underwater Convention. They are part of the overall scheme of the Convention which must be seen as a whole with the object being, as stated in Article 2, to 'ensure and strengthen the protection of the underwater cultural heritage'. To this end, States Parties are required to take certain measures as set out in the Convention. These include action under Articles 14 and 15. Sanctions supplement such actions.

PARAGRAPH 1

This Paragraph is uncompromising. States Parties have to impose sanctions. On the other hand, the nature of the sanctions is not specified and will depend on the legal structure of the State in question. In most cases, they will be of a penal nature – fines and/or imprisonment. However, in some cases the sanctions may be administrative. For example, seizure of underwater cultural heritage under Article 18 may fall into this category depending on how it is classified. Another sanction that appears in national legislation is seizure of equipment used in bringing about the offence. For example, in Australia the *Historic Shipwrecks Act* 1976 authorizes the court, where a person is convicted of an offence against the Act, to order the forfeiture of 'any ship, equipment or article used or otherwise involved in the commission of the offence'.[126]

PARAGRAPH 2

States Parties have to give serious consideration as to how they implement this Paragraph. The difficult is that what is an adequate sanction in one part of the world may be regarded as insignificant in another. For example, a fine of 500 euros would be small in European countries but would be a large amount in some developing countries. Moreover, a State would have to consider whether it be necessary that the sanctions imposed be aligned with sanctions applicable to offences against land sites or to other anti-social activities in the country.

Paragraph 2 states that the sanction must be adequate in severity to be effective in securing compliance with the Convention and discouraging violations wherever they occur. But also the sanctions must deprive offenders of the benefit deriving from their illegal activities. A number of issues must be considered here. For example, if the underwater cultural heritage raised is an exquisite bronze statue, there will be more than monetary considerations involved. It must be realized that the offender and the statue may be situated in different States and the statue could have been raised from the continental shelf of a third State. The person raising it may well be prepared to pay a fine in one State if that means he or she retains possession and the benefit of aesthetic appreciation or can sell it in a non-State Party for a handsome profit.

It could be said that a gaol term of sufficient severity and length could accomplish both goals of Article 17. But does that relate to current theories on the purpose of gaol? Some consider the purpose of gaol is to rehabilitate the prisoner while others consider it needs to reflect punishment. Do both of these views relate to the purpose of adequacy and, if so, what period of gaol would achieve it? Similar arguments apply to fines. A fine may be sufficiently large as to deprive a person of the economic value of the object but not its aesthetic value if possession remains. However, whether classified as a sanction or not, the most effective means of preventing damage

---

[126] S. 25(3).

to underwater cultural heritage is seizure under Article 18. The real possibility of seizure removes any incentive to excavate in a way not in conformity with the Convention. By way of comparison, the philosophy underlying the 1995 UNIDROIT Convention is that the acquirer should be compelled to hand over unique objects because monetary compensation is not adequate recompense to the original owner for the loss.

Violations are to be discouraged 'wherever they occur'. This has to be read in context. The 'violations' are against measures a State Party has undertaken to implement the Underwater Convention. Consequently, they will not involve actions within the territorial jurisdiction of States not party to the Convention.

Paragraph 3

Co-operation between States Parties is essential to ensure enforcement of sanctions imposed under Article 17. That said, the Article gives no indication of what type of co-operation is envisaged and States Parties are left to their own conceptions of what would be appropriate. At the very least there should be exchange of information on the nature of sanctions applicable and the policy of States in applying them. At the other extreme there is extradition of the offender. But extradition is a highly complex procedure on which many States have already established policies and applicable legal procedures. Extradition for violations of measures taken under the Underwater Convention would need to fit within those policies and procedures. Early versions of this Article were much more detailed but a decision was taken to retain only the simple Paragraph 3 on the basis that there were many existing agreements which already dealt with recognition of judgments and extradition.

ARTICLE 18 – SEIZURE AND DISPOSITION OF UNDERWATER CULTURAL HERITAGE

> 1. Each State Party shall take measures providing for the seizure of underwater cultural heritage in its territory that has been recovered in a manner not in conformity with this Convention.
>
> 2. Each State Party shall record, protect and take all reasonable measures to stabilize underwater cultural heritage seized under this Convention.
>
> 3. Each State Party shall notify the Director-General and any other State with a verifiable link, especially a cultural, historical or archaeological link, to the underwater cultural heritage concerned of any seizure of underwater cultural heritage that it has made under this Convention.
>
> 4. A State Party which has seized underwater cultural heritage shall ensure that its disposition be for the public benefit, taking into account the need for conservation and research; the need for reassembly of a dispersed collection; the need for public access, exhibition and education; and the interests of any State with a verifiable link, especially a cultural, historical or archaeological link, in respect of the underwater cultural heritage concerned.

Seizure of underwater cultural heritage works on two levels: it acts as a deterrent and it deprives the person concerned of the underwater cultural heritage recovered in a manner not in conformity with the Convention. It is vital for the protection of the heritage. Consequently, States Parties should take care in how it is implemented. It must be effective and this means that its relationship to other significant legal principles has to be taken into account. Chief among these would be property interests particularly where they are guaranteed as a human right. The true nature of seizure as being both an aspect of punishment for wrongdoing and as furthering the public interest by reclaiming material for the public domain must be emphasized.

PARAGRAPH 1

As in Articles 14 and 15, the measures to be taken are unqualified. There is no mention of 'necessary', 'all necessary' or 'all practicable' measures. The form and function of the measures to be taken depends on the State Party concerned operating within its general legal structure. However, the measures will involve both the physical taking of the object and the legal consequences of this. It is obvious that Article 18 requires a State to do more than physical seizure alone. Paragraphs 2, 3 and 4 require it to take various actions which can only be done by someone with substantial rights in relation to the object.

The legal measures must ensure that seizure can be carried out effectively and without challenge. Seizure may, and usually does, involve a deprivation of property if the holder has acquired a property interest in the underwater cultural heritage. Whether this is the case will depend on the facts in question and the operation of applicable laws as affected by Article 4 of the Underwater Convention which excludes the operation of the law of finds except in specified limited circumstances.

Underwater cultural heritage may be abandoned or it may not be. This fact can be tested in a court with appropriate jurisdiction and the issue will be decided by that court according to the principles applicable in that jurisdiction. If it is not abandoned, the original owner, if one can be found, still has title. If it is found to be abandoned, Article 4 prevents the finder gaining any property interest. Consequently, if an item of underwater cultural heritage is found in the Area and brought ashore, it may belong to the person who lost it or, if abandoned, it will be ownerless. Seizure will result in the owner being deprived of his or her property or, where there is no owner, the State should become the owner. The Underwater Convention does not deal with these matters as it was decided early in the negotiations that property issues lay outside its scope.

Deprivation of property may lead to a claim for compensation. For example, many European States are party to the First Protocol of the *European Convention on Human Rights*, Article 1 of which states:

> Every natural or legal person is entitled to the peaceful enjoyment of his possessions. No one shall be deprived of his possessions except in the public interest and subject to the conditions provided for by law and by the general principles of international law.
>
> The preceding provisions shall not, however, in any way impair the right of a State to enforce such laws as it deems necessary to control the use of property in accordance with the general interest or to secure the payment of taxes or other contributions or penalties.

There is no space here to give a detailed account of how this provision may be applicable. In general, property may be taken provided there is payment of compensation. However, it must be remembered that Article 18 only applies when the underwater cultural heritage has been recovered 'in a manner not in conformity with this Convention'. This could bring into play the second paragraph of Article 1 of the Protocol and remove the need for payment of compensation. Thus, if the owner of underwater cultural heritage raised it without conforming to the Underwater Convention, it may be able to be seized without paying compensation. On the other hand, if someone else has raised it and the owner is not involved, then compensation may have to be paid.

Article 18 requires a State to seize underwater cultural heritage in its territory if it 'has been recovered in a manner not in conformity with this Convention'. The heritage only has to be within the State's territory. It does not matter how it got there. To take an example from the commentary to the ILA Draft:

> Suppose that European excavators of material excavated off the Malaysian coast proceed directly from the Far East to the Netherlands and suppose that the Netherlands is not party to the Convention. There the excavated material is sold by auction. One of the purchasers is French and brings his ceramics home. Under the Convention, if France was a Party, it would have an obligation to seize the ceramics. This obligation exists whatever the number of intervening transactions in an object.[127]

Nevertheless, the number of intervening transactions will be significant in certain respects. For example, the greater the number of such transactions, the more difficult will it be to prove that the object in question was 'recovered in a manner not in conformity with the Convention' as the evidence will just not be available. Moreover, courts may be less inclined to uphold seizures. In relation to Article 1 of the First Protocol to the *European Convention on Human Rights* referred to above, one rule that the courts have adopted is that there must be proportionality between the degree of control imposed and the effect on the owner. Applying this to measures imposed under Article 18, the greater the number of transactions in the heritage concerned after its recovery not in conformity with the Convention the less willing will the courts be to find the necessary degree of proportionality exists.

Paragraph 2

Paragraph 2 sets out the steps that should logically follow seizure but States must be ready to provide the necessary facilities, experts and finance to enable this to be done. It may not be easy.

Recording may seem a simple task but will depend on what has been seized. For example, in 2000 the Australian Government, at the request of the Indonesian Government, seized seven shipping containers packed with Chinese ceramics from the wreck of the *Tek Sing*. This was done under the *Protection of Movable Cultural Heritage Act* 1986. A practical difficulty with this case flowed from the requirement in s.36 of the Act that the 'Notice of Seizure' containing a description of the objects being seized be issued 'as soon as practicable' following physical seizure. The seven containers held 71,939 pieces of porcelain which had to be unpacked, catalogued and repacked

---

127 'Cultural Heritage Law Committee: Buenos Aires Draft Convention on the Protection of the Underwater Cultural Heritage: Final Report' in Crawford, J. and Williams, M. (eds) *International Law Association: Report of the Sixty-Sixth Conference* (International Law Association, Buenos Aires, 1994) 432, 442. This example assumes that the export from the Netherlands was not unlawful.

– a task taking experts several months to complete.[128]

What is involved in giving protection and taking stabilization measures will depend very much on the material of which the underwater cultural heritage is composed and the circumstances in which it has been preserved. However, virtually all objects will require specialized treatment for stabilization although, as Forrest notes, stabilization probably implies a less onerous duty than conservation.[129] The difficulties may be lessened by the circumstances. The major difficulty will be with heritage coming directly from the site. This will normally require immediate treatment. However, the fact that seizure applies only to material recovered not in conformity with the Convention means that this will probably be of high commercial value made of relatively stable substances. It is unlikely, for example, to comprise ship's timbers requiring decades of treatment.

Paragraph 3

Notification of the Director-General and States with a verifiable link[130] would normally take place after recording what has been seized. To do this before would serve no purpose as other States would not know the objects in which they may have an interest. It would seem that the Director-General is free to make his own decision on what to do with the information following notification. Perhaps placement on a web site would be sufficient. It must be recognized that the State making the seizure may have no connection with the underwater cultural heritage concerned. The State with the verifiable link may have much closer connections.

Paragraph 4

This Paragraph is aimed basically at ensuring seizures be for the public benefit. Without this, seizure loses its broader moral justification through bringing material back into the public domain and becomes simply a punishment. However, placing seized material in a storage area and leaving it there, even if it be stabilized, defeats one of the main purposes behind seizure and leaves the process open to criticism.

There does not appear to be any priority among the actions listed provided all are done within the context of the public benefit. The Paragraph specifically mentions re-assembly of a dispersed collection. This was one matter dealt with in a section of the *Arrangement Setting out the Guiding Principles for the Committee to Determine the Disposition of Material from the Shipwrecks of Dutch East India Company Vessels off the Coast of Western Australia*.[131] It is worth quoting the section in full for its explanation of the underlying principles.

> In modern archaeological practice sites are no longer regarded merely as a source of important individual items, but rather as a body of material whose collective value far outweighs the importance of the individual pieces and in which the relationship of the individual objects within the sample are a major part of its historical value. Accordingly, the sharing of material from an archaeological site is best regarded as the accommodation in several localities of a corporate entity rather than its division into parts.
>
> If the decision is made that the contents of an archaeological site are to be apportioned between two or more institutions, the first principle to be observed is that the total assemblage should be capable of reassembly to allow further statistical and scholarly analysis. It follows, therefore, that unnecessary splitting of a sample of closely similar objects capable of statistical treatment should be avoided and, where samples are accommodated in more than one institution,

---

128 Porcelain that had left Australia before the Indonesian request was received was taken to Munich and auctioned on the Internet. Apparently the auction was not a success with about half of the lots not selling and the company responsible failing to recover its costs: Bawden, T. 'Salvage Dividend Hopes Sunk' *Adelaide Advertiser* 1 March 2001.
129 Forrest, C. fn. 42 above, 353.
130 See discussion at p.54.
131 This is an attachment to the *Agreement Between the Netherlands and Australia Concerning Old Dutch Shipwrecks* (1972 Aust. T.S. N. 18).

those institutions should contract not to disperse them further and, moreover, to agree to allow samples to be brought together for analysis and study as required. The second principle is that where unique or rare objects, themselves, form a meaningful assemblage within the whole, this assemblage should not be split or, if split, perfect replicas be made to complete the assemblage. As in the case of the division of statistical samples an agreement should be made between the recipients to reconstitute the original assemblage if it is required for scholarly research.

Relations between the State making the seizure and that with a verifiable link will be influenced by their relative connections to the underwater cultural heritage concerned. The interests of the latter could be met in the first instance by its experts having access to the seized material for purposes of research. The use of film, photographs etc. for display to the public of that State is another option. But there may be situations where the link of the second State to the seized material is so strong that the division of the material is necessary or even transfer of the entire collection to that State.

If the material is to be divided, the Arrangement attached to the Agreement between the Netherlands and Australia referred to above provides guidance. The situation there was different in that the excavation was being run by the responsible authorities, but the principles are still relevant.

Operating Principles

Code of Operation
The Committee will operate by reviewing proposals for distribution made, from time to time, by the Director of the Western Australian Museum; it could decide that the proposed samples be increased or decreased in content in the light of the total material collected and other factors.

General aims
In its deliberations the Committee will have, as its general aim, the purpose of ensuring that representative series of statistical samples and sufficient examples of the rarer objects will be deposited in the museums of the Netherlands and Australia to convey the variety and contents of each wreck to both the public and to scholars while, at the same time, ensuring that major projects of scholarly research will not be impeded by overfragmentation of the collection. Dispersal in this way, among separate repositories will also help to ensure the permanent safety of representative material in the event of the destruction of any one repository.

Statistical samples
Most material so far recovered from the vessels are samples capable of statistical treatment.

A representative collection of the contents of each statistical sample should be made available to a museum of the Netherlands Government and a museum of the Commonwealth Government. Thus, in the case of coin, for example, both the Netherlands and Commonwealth Governments would receive as complete a series as possible representing the mintings and values contained within each of the wrecks. These will provide their museums with ample material of this class of objects for display purposes and sufficient to enable a scholar to make the initial qualitative studies which would possibly lead him to a more detailed statistical treatment of the bulk sample retained in the Western Australian Museum.

Less common or rare objects
In order to ensure that both the Netherlands and Commonwealth Governments acquire, in due course, representative collections of the less common and even unique objects, the following procedure will be adopted. Since the relationships of such objects to the whole sample cannot be known until excavation is complete, the distribution of specimens of this nature cannot be considered during the continuing process of recovery. However, at reasonable intervals (of say two or three years) it should be

possible to assemble a representative sample with fair certainty that all duplicates of any rare object present in a particular excavation should have been recovered and their nature taken into consideration during the deliberations of the Committee.

ARTICLE 19 – CO-OPERATION AND INFORMATION-SHARING

1. States Parties shall cooperate and assist each other in the protection and management of underwater cultural heritage under this Convention, including, where practicable, collaborating in the investigation, excavation, documentation, conservation, study and presentation of such heritage.

2. To the extent compatible with the purposes of this Convention, each State Party undertakes to share information with other States Parties concerning underwater cultural heritage, including discovery of heritage, location of heritage, heritage excavated or recovered contrary to this Convention or otherwise in violation of international law, pertinent scientific methodology and technology, and legal developments relating to such heritage.

3. Information shared between States Parties, or between UNESCO and States Parties, regarding the discovery or location of underwater cultural heritage shall, to the extent compatible with their national legislation, be kept confidential and reserved to competent authorities of States Parties as long as the disclosure of such information might endanger or otherwise put at risk the preservation of such underwater cultural heritage.

4. Each State Party shall take all practicable measures to disseminate information, including where feasible through appropriate international databases, about underwater cultural heritage excavated or recovered contrary to this Convention or otherwise in violation of international law.

Co-operation among States is crucial for achieving the objectives of the Underwater Convention. It underlies Articles 9, 10, 11 and 12. Article 19 expresses this underlying imperative in a broad and functional way.

PARAGRAPH 1

There is here created a duty on the part of States Parties to 'co-operate and assist each other in the protection and management of underwater cultural heritage under this Convention'. The impact of this statement is somewhat lessened by the qualification 'where practicable' which applies to the most significant elements where co-operation may occur. Nevertheless, casting the duty in absolute terms means that States are required to consider carefully the circumstances and limit as much as possible those where co-operation is not considered practical.

The duty to co-operate is general and not restricted to any particular group of States. Earlier drafts of this paragraph had referred to a State Party which 'had expressed a national heritage interest in particular cultural heritage' as collaborating with the State Party having that heritage. Ultimately, this was thought to raise too many difficulties[132] in establishing the nature of the interest required and the more general duty of Paragraph 1 was substituted.

Co-operation is also highly desirable for developing expertise among persons from different disciplines. The overall standard of work on underwater cultural heritage will improve as those with greater knowledge of particular aspects of the work pass it on to their colleagues. This is one of the goals of the regional capacity building programme run by UNESCO in Bangkok. It does this through 'professional training in field techniques on underwater archaeological site inventory and mapping, non-invasive techniques of site identification, inventory and investigation, museology techniques, and site monitoring and protection according to international professional standards. The application of the provisions of the Annex to the Convention is particularly stressed'. Participants

---

132   Strati, A. fn. 125 above, 56.

are expected to pass on what they have learnt to their colleagues on their return home.[133]

Co-operation can also contribute to international harmony as people of different races, with different languages, realize that, if they can work together on technical problems, then they should be able to appreciate each other's differences. Broadly speaking there is already an informal network of underwater archaeologists from many countries keeping each other informed of current developments.

Paragraph 2

The distribution of information is central to the purpose of this Paragraph which is unchanged from the original ILA Draft. The commentary on that Draft read:

> Rarely does the underwater cultural heritage beyond the territorial sea concern only a single, still existing State. If a shipwreck, the vessel will often have been making for a port in what is now another State. The site will reveal information about trading routes as well as details of the lives of the crew and passengers, construction of the vessel, and so on. It is essential that this information be distributed as widely as possible among interested parties, not only so that others know of what has been found but also so that their expertise may be brought to bear on interpretation and understanding of the information.[134]

A good example of the multiple contacts a ship had even in antiquity is provided by the Belitung wreck in Indonesian waters.[135] The archaeologist who supervised work on the site during the second excavation season concluded that it had been an Arab vessel.

> This is the first ancient Arab shipwreck to be found and investigated. Its cargo of Chinese ceramics and its location in Indonesian waters provide irrefutable archaeological evidence that there was direct trade between the western Indian Ocean and China during the latter part of the first millennium.[136]

This indicates a wider concern with distribution of information than perhaps is comprehended by the specific examples given in Paragraph 2. But the specific examples are only illustrative of the broader requirement to share information. Information on the discovery of heritage and its location is quite easily given if the State knows about it. Information flowing from study of discoveries is another matter. This will often be the intellectual property of specific researchers and it is only when their research is published that it becomes available to the public. To comply with Paragraph 2, States will have to consider how best to encourage researchers to publish their results as quickly as possible in accordance with Rule 36 of the Annex.

Certain of the Articles already discussed – 14, 15, 16 and 18 – require States Parties to take action when activities not in conformity with the Convention have resulted in underwater cultural heritage coming into their territory. But States can only act on the basis of information received. Paragraph 2 requires States Parties to share information concerning heritage excavated or recovered contrary to the Underwater Convention. For this to be effective there has to be someone in authority to whom such information can be directed. The authority then has to be able to send the information to whoever in their own administration is capable of recognizing what it means and acting on it.

The sharing of 'pertinent scientific methodology and technology' will be affected by agreements on technology transfer. It effectiveness will also depend on the relative development of the States concerned.

---

133   <http://unesdoc.unesco.org/images/0021/002172/217234e.pdf>
134   'Cultural Heritage Law Committee: Buenos Aires Draft Convention on the Protection of the Underwater Cultural Heritage: Final Report' fn. 127 above, 444.
135   See page 129.
136   Flecker, M. 'A Ninth-Century Arab Shipwreck in Indonesia: The First Archaeological Evidence of Direct Trade With China' in Krahl, R. *el al.* (eds) *Shipwrecked: Tang Treasures and Monsoon Winds* (Smithsonian Institution, Washington, 2010) 101.

At the present moment there is no body which collects information on legal developments relating to underwater cultural heritage. There is very little sharing of information on this among States. One reason is that most legal developments are related to municipal law and there has been little contact between lawyers from different States and legal systems. The need for shared information has not been considered a priority.

Paragraph 3

Widespread knowledge of the existence of a cultural heritage site can lead to its being damaged. This is not inevitable but is a recognized risk as far as land archaeology in concerned. Paragraph 3 draws the attention of States Parties to this risk in relation to the underwater cultural heritage. Information regarding the discovery or location of this heritage shall 'be kept confidential and reserved to competent authorities' if its disclosure might put at risk its preservation. Assessment of the risk will depend on many factors peculiar to particular situations. In a case involving the wreck of a vessel called the *Central America*[137], a salvage company, Columbus-America Discovery Group, was terrified that rival salvors would invade the site, so much so that it excavated the gold for a time before informing the court that they were not operating in the area covered by the injunction lest information on the true location be inadvertently be revealed. The site lay 2.4 kilometres beneath the Atlantic Ocean. Thus, if the site in question lies in very deep waters, the question will involve consideration of who has the capabilities of reaching such a depth and what their reaction would be on learning the information.

The requirement to keep information confidential can be qualified by contrary rules in national legislation. These would usually be freedom of information provisions whereby citizens have a right of access to government papers. It would be unfortunate, however, if the effect of such legislation would be to put information transmitted by a coordinating State or UNESCO immediately into the hands of looters.

It must be remembered that there is already a requirement to share information under Articles 9 and 11. That information has to be sufficient for a State to decide if it has a verifiable link to the underwater cultural heritage concerned.

Paragraph 4

The reason for including this Paragraph is obscure. It virtually repeats what is in Paragraph 2 with the addition that information is to be disseminated 'where feasible through appropriate international databases'. These databases do not exist. There are a variety of databases dealing with stolen cultural heritage, sale of art etc. but none on material excavated or recovered contrary to the Underwater Convention. None of the existing databases seem to be appropriate to carry this information. If a new database is ever established, it would be sufficient to have one, not a number.

The duty to disseminate information in this way is cast on States Parties but it will require at least one such State to take the lead. It might be appropriate for States Parties to delegate the task of establishing and operating the database to a private entity such as a museum or a university.

The quality of the information placed on the database has to be considered. A procedure for vetting its accuracy would be necessary. False or misleading information could give rise to legal proceedings for defamation. Requirements of privacy law would also have to be observed.

---

137   Page 6.

ARTICLE 20 – PUBLIC AWARENESS

> Each State Party shall take all practicable measures to raise public awareness regarding the value and significance of underwater cultural heritage and the importance of protecting it under this Convention.

Awareness and understanding are prerequisites for participation in society. If the population as a whole is to appreciate the value and significance of underwater cultural heritage, an understanding of history and the relationship of heritage to it has to be developed from an early age.

It is common now in some countries for school children to learn about archaeology and what it can do to reveal the past life of people. Underwater archaeology should have a place in such curricula. But education of school children is only a start. If the objectives of the Underwater Convention are to be achieved, public perceptions must be changed. Too often are the pure treasure hunters portrayed as adventurous, colourful characters and archaeologists as dull academics. There is also a perception encouraged by treasure hunters that archaeologists try to keep everything for themselves while they, the treasure hunters, are endeavouring to bring beautiful things back into the world. These approaches must be countered and the wider values and significance of underwater cultural heritage be emphasized.

Awareness raising also needs to be tailored to the particular situation which may be unique in time and place. For example, Chuuk Lagoon in the Federated States of Micronesia contains the remains of many Japanese ships and aircraft sunk during World War II. These are subject to a variety of dangers including the following.

> Some of the many munitions found on the shipwrecks are also being recovered and used to make into smaller bombs for fishing – on the many reefs as well as on the shipwrecks. This action not only kills the fish life and other marine fauna, but it damages the fabric of the ships accelerating the rates of corrosion and contributing to their collapse … Perhaps the most important factor in the management of the shipwrecks is not whether the law is adequate and enforced, or whether the programme is comprehensive, but whether the Chuukese have a desire to manage the shipwrecks and in what manner.[138]

The wrecks are obviously not covered by the Underwater Convention as they are not 100 years old but the situation illustrates the need for public awareness of this very specific problem otherwise they will not survive for 100 years.

There are many ways of raising public awareness but it will work best if these are designed for the specific audience. The attention of the general public can be attracted through television and film documentaries as well as museum exhibitions. If these are well done, they can produce an audience receptive to arguments for protection of underwater cultural heritage. But specialist groups need to be influenced and this may require specific and detailed material. For example, it is essential that divers have the Underwater Convention explained to them through their magazines and leaflets distributed by dive shops. There has been much incorrect information circulated among divers regarding the Convention which must be countered by a simple and concise description of how it operates. Journalists should be provided with background material stressing the cultural and historical value and significance of this heritage rather than its commercial value. Groups involved in administration and law enforcement should also be specifically targeted for education in their duties regarding enforcement of law implementing the Underwater Convention. In many cases they will need to have the law explained and the problems involved in enforcing it illustrated. They should be introduced to the values underlying the legal and administrative arrangements put in place by a State Party so that they do not regard

---

[138] Jeffery, B. 'Federated States of Micronescia' in Droomgoole, S. (ed.) *The Protection of the Underwater Cultural Heritage: National Perspectives in Light of the UNESCO Convention 2001* (Martinus Nijhoff, Leiden, 2006) 145, 155.

destruction of, or damage to, underwater sites as 'victimless crime' to be addressed with only minimal penalties. The irreplaceability of underwater cultural heritage in context must be stressed.

It will be obvious that much of the awareness raising outlined above will only be possible if there is adequate information on which to base it. This gives emphasis to the necessity for information sharing required by Article 19.

ARTICLE 21 – TRAINING IN UNDERWATER ARCHAEOLOGY

> States Parties shall cooperate in the provision of training in underwater archaeology, in techniques for the conservation of underwater cultural heritage and, on agreed terms, in the transfer of technology relating to underwater cultural heritage.

Training in underwater archaeology is a significant task. The discipline is a very recent one being barely 60 or so years old. The Underwater Convention is based on the availability of specialists to make assessments of sites, preserve and protect them, as well as excavate when there is need. States have sought assistance form one another to supply those needs. For example, China decided to begin by having field archaeologists trained in diving techniques and the methodology of underwater archaeology in Japan, the Netherlands and the United States of America. National training began in 1989-1990 with a course run in conjunction with a centre from the Western Australian University. Similar courses have followed.[139] The UNESCO website states that, since 2008, it has trained more than 400 specialists from more than 80 countries in underwater archaeological research with courses lasting from two weeks to three months.[140] A university twinning programme for universities teaching underwater archaeology and promoting co-operation has recently been established. There are currently five universities from Australia, Denmark, Egypt, Turkey and the United Kingdom taking part. The UNESCO Regional Office in Bangkok has established a capacity building programme called 'Safeguarding the Underwater Cultural Heritage in Asia and the Pacific'. This has been supported by the Norwegian and Thai governments. Three six-week Foundation Courses and two ten-day Advanced Courses were run from 2009 to 2011. Seventy experts from sixteen Asia-Pacific Member States and one from Kenya have taken part.[141] These very brief, and highly selective, examples of what is being done, show the extent to which UNESCO and individual States are working to provide trained underwater archaeologists.

Training does not consist only of formal study. There may be short professional courses in particular aspects of underwater archaeology or conservation offered by recognized international bodies such as the International Centre for the Study of the Preservation and Restoration of Cultural Property (ICCROM) in Rome. There can also be training provided by professional underwater archaeologists employed in museums and universities to amateurs so as to enable them to achieve a degree of competence to assist in site surveys or excavation. States Parties should be aware of these different levels of training and be prepared to consider them in their implementation of Article 21.

In the United Kingdom, the Nautical Archaeology Society, founded in 1981, aims to advance education in underwater archaeology.

> The NAS Training Programme was instigated in the UK in the 1980s and has subsequently been adopted by many countries throughout the world. It is structured in progressive levels beginning with a one-day 'Introduction to Foreshore and Underwater Archaeology' and ending with a 'Part IV Advanced Certificate in Foreshore and Underwater Archaeology'.[142]

A diver training course developed by the Society to develop better understanding of archaeological work and qualifications to assist specialists under water is now used in many countries under licence.

---

139 Zhang Wei 'Exploring History Underwater: The Development and Current Status of Underwater Archaeology in China' in Prott, L.V. (ed.) *Finishing the Interrupted Voyage* (UNESCO/Institute of Art and Law; Paris/Builth Wells; 2006) 81.
140 <http://www.unesco.org/new/en/culture/themes/underwater-cultural-heritage/unescos-work/>. Consulted 26 July 2013.
141 <http://unesdoc.unesco.org/images/0021/002172/217234e.pdf>.
142 Bowens, A. (ed.) *Archaeology Underwater: The NAS Guide to Principles and Practice* (Nautical Archaeology Society, Portsmouth, 2nd edn 2009) Ch. 3.

The possibilities for engaging divers who take such courses in archaeological research are eloquently described by Robert Grenier, former President of the ICOMOS International Scientific Committee for the Underwater Cultural Heritage:

> The discovery of the oldest American-built vessel ever found was made on Christmas Eve 1994 on the north shore of the St. Lawrence River by a local diver. Marc Tremblay used to be, up until a few months prior to his discovery, one of the best wreck looters on the shipwreck littered coast of Québec.
>
> A few weeks after taking the N.A.S. course, Marc found the 1690 wreck uncovered by the 'storm of the century' in front of his summer cottage, in a few feet of water. Appearing in front of him was a shopping-centre-like display of swords, muskets, axes, pistols and many other types of artifacts. Instead of gathering them up for his private collection or for selling a few as he would have done before taking the N.A.S. course, he took photographs, video, and measurements without touching anything. He then provided all of this information to the Provincial and Federal authorities which very quickly collaborated to launch a multi-year project involving Tremblay and his dive partners who had also taken the course. For the better part of two dive seasons, these individuals had the times of their diving lives, working long hours in the cold North Atlantic waters, excavating alongside Parks Canada archaeologists to uncover this significant part of their history (for a total of over 2000 hours of diving). The wreck, which turned out to be the *Elizabeth & Mary*, is now a National Historic Site of Canada and a Provincial historic site as well. It is the most significant shipwreck find of the last twenty years in our country. These sports divers, former looters, have now become cultural protectors, literally historic shipwreck wardens: they now feel they have a mission to protect this heritage for their successors, their future generations.
>
> … Only one artifact among the thousands found on site proved to be the smoking gun leading to the identification of the ship and of its relationship to the thirty-two ship fleet Phips had led to Québec. A simple, well recorded pewter porringer found on the upper layer of the wreck site was inscribed with the initials of its owner and of his wife: 'M.I.S.', standing for one sergeant Increase Moseley and his wife Sarah. Further research in the Boston archives revealed that this militiaman was part of the Dorchester regiment, which had been on the lost vessel *Elizabeth & Mary*.
>
> This story is a gem since it underscores that artifacts should be left in context for proper recovery by a specialist: had Marc Tremblay followed … advice 'that the best protection is the retrieval of artifacts as they are discovered', this vital archaeological link to historical records could have been lost. Had he mishandled this vital clue or had he sold it very shortly afterwards, the identification of the wreck could have been lost or at the very least rendered doubtful. The wreck then would not have been named of National Historic Importance to Canada and would have been deprived of most of its significance. Such a hasty; not controlled retrieval by man would have done more damage than nature had done over 304 years![143]

An example of co-operation in training for conservation comes from the Argentine where local archaeologists were excavating the wreck of the *Swift*, a British sloop, which lies off Puerto Deseado in Santa Cruz province.

> As for conservation, the INAPL underwater archaeology team decided not to lift objects from the wreck until an accurate preservation treatment could be ensured. This decision is in conflict with the criteria of the Brozowski museum, which is mainly interested in recovering as many objects as possible to put on display, but without disregarding conservation treatments. Hence, international co-operation … became a crucial issue regarding conservation training. During

---

143   Copy of letter dated 19 Oct. 2001 on file with the author.

the February 2001 fieldwork season the British Embassy in Buenos Aires supported an exchange programme with the Collections Department of the Mary Rose Trust (United Kingdom). Through this institutional exchange, staff are receiving qualified training in conservation techniques and treatments applicable to submerged artefacts. This is an initial step in the continued development of long-term international co-operative programmes that aim to preserve finds and retard deterioration, safeguarding the shipwreck material for further interpretation and display.[144]

It will be obvious that this example goes beyond co-operation in conservation training into museum policies, funding and the treatment of warships.

The final aspect of Article 21, the transfer of technology, raises complex issues of trade, patents and finance which are far beyond the scope of the Underwater Convention. Its inclusion in Article 21 is qualified by 'on agreed terms' which recognizes these realities.

---

[144] Dellino, V. and Luz Endere, M. 'The HMS *Swift* Shipwreck: The Development of Underwater Heritage Protection in Argentina' (2001) 4 *Conservation and Management of Archaeological Sites* 219, 224.

Article 22 – Competent Authorities

> 1. In order to ensure the proper implementation of this Convention, States Parties shall establish competent authorities or reinforce the existing ones where appropriate, with the aim of providing for the establishment, maintenance and updating of an inventory of underwater cultural heritage, the effective protection, conservation, presentation and management of underwater cultural heritage, as well as research and education.
>
> 2. States Parties shall communicate to the Director-General the names and addresses of their competent authorities relating to underwater cultural heritage.

Most States already have authorities responsible for protection of the archaeological heritage. In some instances there is a division in management between land and underwater archaeology. From an organizational point of view, it is preferable that there be one body responsible for all aspects of the archaeological heritage with the underwater cultural heritage forming a distinct unit within that body. Precisely where this body is placed in the overall structure of government is a matter for the State concerned. However, there are some connections which by their nature seem inappropriate. For example, Ministries of development and that of mining could by their very nature create a clash of interests.

Paragraph 1

This paragraph casts a duty on States to establish a competent authority or reinforce an existing one to carry out the functions listed which generally are all those associated with management. An inventory is a significant tool for management of the heritage and should be developed using electronic databases, digitized imagery etc. The *European Convention on the Protection of the Archaeological Heritage (Revised)* 1992 requires each State Party to make provision for the 'maintenance of an inventory of its archaeological heritage'.[145] It is also worth quoting from the ICOMOS *Charter for the Protection and Management of the Archaeological Heritage*:

> … inventories constitute primary resource databases for scientific study and research. The compilation of inventories should therefore be regarded as a continuous, dynamic process. It follows that inventories should comprise information at various levels of significance and reliability, since even superficial knowledge can form the starting point for protective measures.[146]

Once objects have been found, their inclusion in an inventory should mean that their whereabouts thereafter is known. It allows the physical condition of the object to be monitored if desired.

The activities listed as appropriate for the attention of the competent authorities are basically aimed at management of, and caring for, underwater cultural heritage. At the same time, those authorities will inevitably become involved in the sanctions and seizure provisions under Articles 17 and 18. This will require careful management so that all activities are properly performed and one is not favoured to the detriment of the other.

> If a heritage management body becomes involved in compliance, there is an unfortunate tendency to become more involved in restrictive aspects of the work rather than concentrating solely on the constructive aspects.[147]

Paragraph 2

The flow of information is essential for the smooth functioning of the Underwater Convention. This means not only information about the heritage itself but also information about its protection

---

145 Article 2.
146 Article 4.
147 Green, J. book review of Fenwick, F. and Gale, A. *Historic Shipwrecks – Discovered, Protected and Investigated* in (1998)27 *International Journal of Nautical Archaeology* 265, 266.

and management. It is vital that authorities in one State are able to contact those in other States, either to pass on information or to request it. Often it is very difficult to find the address of the correct official or, in current times, their e-mail address. A central databank of such information held by UNESCO would be of great importance for improved access. UNESCO does have a list of competent authorities but only seven States are listed.[148] Because officials often change their duties, it would be preferable for each State to supply the title and address of an official who is able to ascertain where in the particular administrative structure information should be passed, or where it may be found, depending on the nature of the contact.

---

148 <http://www.unesco.org/new/en/culture/themes/underwater-cultural-heritage/2001-convention/competent-authorities/>

ARTICLE 23 – MEETINGS OF STATE PARTIES

1. The Director-General shall convene a Meeting of States Parties within one year of the entry into force of this Convention and thereafter at least once every two years. At the request of a majority of States Parties, the Director-General shall convene an Extraordinary Meeting of States Parties.

2. The Meeting of States Parties shall decide on its functions and responsibilities.

3. The Meeting of States Parties shall adopt its own Rules of Procedure.

4. The Meeting of States Parties may establish a Scientific and Technical Advisory Body composed of experts nominated by the States Parties with due regard to the principle of equitable geographical distribution and the desirability of a gender balance.

5. The Scientific and Technical Advisory Body shall appropriately assist the Meeting of States Parties in questions of a scientific or technical nature regarding the implementation of the Rules.

One significant problem with the efficiency of international conventions is that often there is no mechanism for overseeing their implementation or resolving difficulties between States Parties as to how they view the convention. Certainly there often are procedures for dispute settlement but invocation of these is a serious step and usually marks an escalation of the problem. It is much better to foresee the emergence of the problem and discuss it before it becomes significant. Article 23, with its procedure for convening of a Meeting of States Parties, can play an important role in the smooth and efficient operation of the Underwater Convention.

PARAGRAPH 1

The first session of the meeting of States Parties took place in Paris, 26-27 March 2009. This was followed by a session that same year in December and further sessions in April 2011 and May 2013. This complies with Article 23(1).

PARAGRAPHS 2 AND 3

The Meeting of States Parties is to decide on its own functions and responsibilities and adopt its own rules of procedure. This gives it great scope to investigate and make recommendations for improving the way the Convention is implemented. Under Article 31 it can be presented with proposals for amending the Convention and has the power to adopt them. Apart from this Article, the Meeting has no express power to make any order or issue any instruction. On the other hand, Article 24 speaks of the UNESCO Secretariat implementing the 'decisions' of the Meetings of States Parties. This would seem to indicate an intention on the part of States to have a body with considerable powers. The original version of this Article spelt out a number of functions in detail. However, it was decided at the Fourth Meeting of Governmental Experts that it was not necessary to do so and that the Meeting of States Parties could take decisions on these matters itself. Article 24 obviously sees decisions of the Meeting as having substantive effect. Coupled with the power of the Meeting to decide its own functions and responsibilities, Article 24 gives great scope for the Meeting to influence future developments in the protection of underwater cultural heritage.

In reality, the Sessions so far held have not done anything truly significant. The Fourth Session in 2013 made recommendations to States Parties to raise awareness among promoters of development and resource extraction projects, fishers, divers and other stakeholders. It also recommended various steps States could take in respect of such projects and also with respect to fishing and trawling activities. While these are useful as an educational tool they are far short of what is needed. Most of these and other resolutions are aspirational in nature and are a reiteration of matters that have been raised and discussed in numerous *fora*. For example, there has been much discussion of the impact of fishing and trawling operations on underwater cultural heritage.

But for many States these represent very powerful vested interests that it would be hard for any cultural administration to influence without solid scientific evidence. The Meeting of State Parties could try to gather such evidence – even commissioning special studies into the issues.

The Meeting of States Parties has also adopted the 'Operational Guidelines' to the Underwater Convention. More could have been done with these than what has been done. Many meetings have been held promoting the Underwater Convention. These are essential for a new convention but much more needs to be done regarding substantive issues. For example, The Third Session adopted a Resolution[149] encouraging States Parties, particularly small island States, to review their national legislation protecting underwater cultural heritage. It went on to say that such legislation 'should consider', among others, the application of Article 16 of the Convention. It is more a matter of all States Parties being 'required' to implement that Article in their legislation or administrative practice as a condition of their membership. Failure to do so is a breach of the Convention.

One of the problems is that the resources to fund the Sessions of the Meeting of States Parties and the Advisory Body are woefully small. Much of the work has been done using funds donated by States Parties. How much longer can this continue? Staffing provided by UNESCO is minimal but once again that Organization is under intense financial pressures.

Paragraphs 4 and 5

Paragraph 4 gave the Meeting of States Parties the power to establish a Scientific and Technical Advisory Body (STAB). The Meeting did not have to do this. It was expressed as an option on the part of the Meeting but, as the author put it before the Convention came into force:

> Although the wording is permissive - 'may' – States will certainly seize the initiative for it gives them potentially significant influence.'[150]

States Parties moved to establish the Advisory Body at the first session of their Meeting. Membership of STAB was controversial. A clause in the proposed statutes of the body – 'The Members shall be independent and shall sit in their personal capacity' – was struck out even though that had been the intention of the drafters of the Convention. The current Statutes state that 'the members of the Advisory Body shall work impartially and in compliance with the principles of the Convention'.[151] There are twelve members of the Body although there is provision in the Statutes for up to 24. The biographies given on the UNESCO website indicate that ten of the current members have a background in archaeology with the remaining two having been trained in law. All are employed either in government administration or are connected with academic institutions. There is some indication that members do value independence. At the fourth session of the Meeting of States Parties, a proposal was made to deal with problems in STAB caused by members who could not attend meetings through illness, work functions etc.[152] Replacements had been sent but not accepted as 'the Advisory Body function had been understood to be a personal function'. Some States were uncomfortable with the possibility of States nominating a replacement. In the end the proposal was not adopted.[153] In that same session, Mexico 'reminded States Parties that they should focus on the expertise and experience of the experts, rather than relying on political reasoning'.[154]

The only mention of the functions of STAB in the Convention is in Article 23(5), which says that it 'shall appropriately assist the Meeting of States Parties in questions of a scientific or technical nature regarding the implementation of the Rules'. This author noted before the Convention came into force:

---

149 6/MSP3.
150 O'Keefe, P.J. 'The Implementation of the 2001 Underwater Convention' in González, A.W., O'Keefe, P.J. and Williams, M. 'The UNESCO Convention on the Protection of the Underwater Cultural Heritage: a Future for our Past?' (2009) 11 *Conservation and Management of Archaeological Sites* 54, 58.
151 Article 2(b), Statutes of the Scientific and Technical Advisory Body: <http://unesdoc.unesco.org/images/0018/001821/182130E.pdf>
152 <http://unesdoc.unesco.org/images/0021/002195/219528e.pdf>
153 UNESCO Doc. UCH/15/5.MSP/220/3, 18 June 2013, p.12.
154 Above 7.

This appears to be merely a specific example of the possible activities of a STAB. There is no suggestion that a STAB should be restricted to these questions. It could advise on a variety of matters requiring expertise affecting the implementation of the Convention.[155]

The mandate of STAB was questioned by the United States of America present as an observer delegation at the third meeting in 2012.[156] An item on the agenda raised the question whether activities directed at underwater archaeological sites financed through the deaccessioning of artifacts from the concerned site would be in harmony with the Rules. The United States wanted to know if the response to this question fell within the mandate of STAB and whether, as here, an accredited non-governmental organization could bring the matter to STAB's attention. The Secretariat relied on the Statutes, referring to Article 1(e):

> The Advisory Body shall consult and collaborate with non-governmental organization (NGOs) having activities related to the scope of the Convention ….

The Secretariat commented:

> Consultation and collaboration could be understood to include not only questions posed by the Advisory Body to the accredited NGO, but also an active contribution of the NGO to the Advisory Body's work in drawing its attention to emerging issue in the field of underwater archaeology.

The Secretariat also referred to Article 1(b)(ii)

> The Advisory Body shall propose to the Meeting of States Parties standards of and means to promote best practice in underwater cultural heritage sites protection and materials conservation protection by:
>
>> identifying and monitoring practical common and emerging issues in underwater cultural heritage sites protection and materials conservation.

and observed

> This could be interpreted that the Advisory Body could and should address emerging issues, for example the financing of activities directed at such sites, and recommend a relevant best practice in light of the Rules annexed to the Convention. It was therefore accepted that the Advisory Body had the right and the duty to address the question that was put up for discussion.

This gives an indication of the expansive role STAB is envisaged to have.

---

155   O'Keefe, P.J. fn. 150 above, 58.
156   <http://www.unesco.org/new/en/culture/themes/underwater-cultural-heritage/advisory-body/meetings/third-meeting/>

Article 24 – Secretariat for this Convention

> 1. The Director-General shall be responsible for the functions of the Secretariat for this Convention.
>
> 2. The duties of the Secretariat shall include:
>
> (a) organizing Meetings of States Parties as provided for in Article 23, paragraph 1; and
>
> (b) assisting States Parties in implementing the decisions of the Meetings of States Parties.

As more and more States become party to the Underwater Convention, UNESCO will have to devote increasing funds to its tasks as laid out in the various Articles. The particular duty to assist States Parties in implementing decisions of the meetings of States Parties could require substantial resources depending on how the role of those meetings develops.

The Secretariat has, however, a much more extensive role than organizing meetings of States Parties and assisting in the implementation of decisions. First, it has formal functions arising from its role as the depository for instruments of ratification, acceptance, approval or accession under Article 26(3). For example, it is to handle communications regarding amendments (Article 31(1)) and denunciations (Article 32(1)). Secondly, under Article 25(2), it may be called upon to act as mediator in a dispute among States Parties. Thirdly, and this is where most of the work will arise, it is to act as conduit for passage of information between States Parties. Such duties arise under Articles 9(3), 10(5)(c), 11(2)(3) and (4), 12(2)and (5), 18(3) and 22(2). Some of these provisions just say that States Parties shall communicate the information to the Director-General, but implicit in that requirement is an understanding that the Director-General will pass the information on to other States Parties or make it available on request. Any other interpretation would be nonsensical. But, as the number of States Parties grows, this will become a significant task. UNESCO will have to make plans for carrying out these functions well in advance of the time they are needed. The Underwater Convention will only function effectively if there is co-operation between States Parties and that will need to be supported by an effective system of information distribution. It is not something that can just be allowed to grow haphazardly as occasion demands.

Funds for the various functions have come from the UNESCO regular budget which States Members of UNESCO vote at the Organization's General Conference. However, in times of shrinking financial resources virtually world-wide, there is an issue of how long this will continue. States which did not vote to adopt these Conventions and are not party to them are being asked to finance the activities of UNESCO in servicing those who are party. This applies not only to the Underwater Convention but also to all the other UNESCO Conventions with supervising committees (six in the Culture Sector). As stated above these committees can play a very useful role but the financing of them has not been thought out. Perhaps there should be a special line in the UNESCO budget for expenditure on each such convention with each State Party being required to pay a minimum amount and other States having a discretion.

ARTICLE 25 – PEACEFUL SETTLEMENT OF DISPUTES

> 1. Any dispute between two or more States Parties concerning the interpretation or application of this Convention shall be subject to negotiations in good faith or other peaceful means of settlement of their own choice.
>
> 2. If those negotiations do not settle the dispute within a reasonable period of time, it may be submitted to UNESCO for mediation, by agreement between the States Parties concerned.
>
> 3. If mediation is not undertaken or if there is no settlement by mediation, the provisions relating to the settlement of disputes set out in Part XV of the United Nations Convention on the Law of the Sea apply mutatis mutandis to any dispute between States Parties to this Convention concerning the interpretation or application of this Convention, whether or not they are also Parties to the United Nations Convention on the Law of the Sea.
>
> 4. Any procedure chosen by a State Party to this Convention and to the United Nations Convention on the Law of the Sea pursuant to Article 287 of the latter shall apply to the settlement of disputes under this Article, unless that State Party, when ratifying, accepting, approving or acceding to this Convention, or at any time thereafter, chooses another procedure pursuant to Article 287 for the purpose of the settlement of disputes arising out of this Convention.
>
> 5. A State Party to this Convention which is not a Party to the United Nations Convention on the Law of the Sea, when ratifying, accepting, approving or acceding to this Convention or at any time thereafter shall be free to choose, by means of a written declaration, one or more of the means set out in Article 287, paragraph 1, of the United Nations Convention on the Law of the Sea for the purpose of settlement of disputes under this Article. Article 287 shall apply to such a declaration, as well as to any dispute to which such State is party, which is not covered by a declaration in force. For the purpose of conciliation and arbitration, in accordance with Annexes V and VII of the United Nations Convention on the Law of the Sea, such State shall be entitled to nominate conciliators and arbitrators to be included in the lists referred to in Annex V, Article 2, and Annex VII, Article 2, for the settlement of disputes arising out of this Convention.

To date there have been no significant disputes between States concerning underwater cultural heritage. Archaeologists routinely share information about their projects. For them, this is a vital necessity because information necessary to solve a problem may be found in a number of different countries. States have entered into agreements to regulate matters affecting their interests.[157]

This is not to say that disputes will not occur in relation to the Underwater Convention. For example, the procedures for reporting and protection of underwater cultural heritage, whether it be on the continental shelf, in the EEZ or the Area, are complicated and require the co-operation of a number of States. There are possibilities for misunderstandings and mistakes to be made. Disputes could also arise from application of the Rules in the Annex. One State may allege that the Rules, or some of them, have not been complied with and forbid entry of a vessel working on underwater cultural heritage to its ports. The flag State of that vessel may complain that the port State was unaware of the true circumstances. Consequently, it is necessary that the Underwater Convention contain an Article setting out means of settlement of such disputes as may arise within its terms of reference.

PARAGRAPH 1

This Paragraph refers to disputes concerning the interpretation or application of the Convention. As Aust notes: 'when the meaning is clear, the text is applied: when it is not clear, it has to be interpreted'.[158]

---

157 Page 52.
158 Aust, A. fn. 4 above, 285.

Paragraph 1 gives the States Parties complete freedom to choose what procedure they want for settlement of disputes provided it is peaceful. The normal methods are negotiation, conciliation, mediation, arbitration, litigation. Others, such as 'good offices', could also help.

Negotiation in good faith is the only procedure specifically mentioned in Paragraph 1. This would normally be the first step in any move to settle a dispute. The process is completely under the control of the parties. The only qualification in the Underwater Convention is the time period in Paragraph 2 but this itself is very flexible. It is difficult to say what is essential for a successful negotiation because everything depends on the circumstances. In some negotiations it may be desirable to keep the negotiations going whereas in others periods of inactivity could allow for reflection and consideration of compromises. Aust makes the point that, if the negotiations are successful, it is essential for the parties to record what they have agreed.[159]

Paragraph 2

Here UNESCO is given the role of mediator. Once again the procedure is entirely at the discretion of the States Parties. They have to decide whether a reasonable period of time has passed and no success has been achieved with negotiations. They then have to mutually agree to ask UNESCO to act as mediator. UNESCO is given a similar role under the *Convention on the Means of Prohibiting and Preventing the Illicit Import, Export and Transfer of Ownership of Cultural Property* 1970 but, in the 40 years that Convention has existed, has never been called upon to act.

Mediation is a process whereby a third party hears both sides and then makes his or her own proposals as to how the dispute may be resolved. Precisely how mediation works in a particular dispute depends very much on the character of the mediator. Some will make a suggestion and then stand back to allow the parties to discuss it among themselves. Others will actively join in the discussion of the parties and try to bring them to an acceptance of the proposal.

Paragraph 3

The procedures laid down in Paragraphs 1 and 2 are unexceptional. Paragraphs 3, 4 and 5 raise more complex issues. They are the result of a political decision rather than an assessment of the likely needs of the States Parties.

Paragraph 3 has only limited scope. By its own terms, it is only relevant 'if mediation is not undertaken or if there is no settlement by mediation'. Mediation is only undertaken if negotiations do not settle the dispute. Consequently, Paragraph 3 applies when negotiations do not settle the dispute and there is no mediation or when there is an attempt at mediation after negotiations but it fails. If the States Parties to the Underwater Convention have chosen a method of dispute settlement other than negotiations under Paragraph 1, Paragraph 3 is not applicable.

Paragraph 3 should provide a good incentive for any States Parties who are in dispute to make sure that those procedures are successful because, when Paragraph 3 applies, the complex dispute settlement procedures set out in Part XV of UNCLOS might apply. Some have read this as being the case whether or not one of the States Parties to the Underwater Convention is also party to UNCLOS. They say it has the effect of imposing on States not party to UNCLOS foreign procedures which may be anathema to them. Turkey indicated at the time that it could not become party to the Underwater Convention because of the cross reference. However, Article 291(2) of UNCLOS itself would seem to prevent such an interpretation. It reads:

> The dispute settlement procedures specified in this Part shall be open to entities other than States Parties only as specifically provided for in this Convention.

Clearly, Article 291(2) of UNCLOS explicitly prevents the use of the dispute settlement procedures in Part XV in circumstances where a State Party to the Underwater Convention is not also Party to UNCLOS. That cannot be overridden by the phrase 'whether or not they are also Parties to the United Nations Convention on the Law of the Sea' in Article 25(3) of the former.

Apart from that, the provisions of Part XV are to apply *mutatis mutandis* to disputes arising out

---

159   Above.

of the Underwater Convention. The Latin phrase means 'the necessary changes being made as far as possible'. As such it is a formula for producing further disputes, though frequently used in older treaties. Not all negotiators were happy with the use of this phrase, but the desire to achieve the Convention in the waning hours of the last meeting led to its acceptance.

As already stated, procedures under Part XV are complex. It is optimistic in the extreme to think that two parties already in a dispute which has failed to be settled under Paragraphs 1 and 2 will be able to agree on what changes would be 'necessary' to Part XV of UNCLOS to be practical for the workings of the Underwater Convention.

The whole of Part XV of UNCLOS is to apply to disputes arising out of the Underwater Convention. This includes the conciliation procedures under Article 284 as well as those outlined in Article 287.

Paragraph 4

This covers the situation of a State party to both the Underwater Convention and UNCLOS. It would have to be read as clearly applying only to disputes covered by Paragraph 3 and not to any other disputes. Any other interpretation would undercut paragraph 3 of this Article. Article 287 of UNCLOS gives a State Party the right to choose, by means of a written declaration, one or more of four listed means for the settlement of disputes:

. The International Tribunal for the Law of the Sea

. The International Court of Justice

. An arbitral tribunal constituted in accordance with Annex VII of UNCLOS

. A special arbitral tribunal constituted in accordance with Annex VIII of UNCLOS
for one or more of the categories of disputes specified therein.

The result of Paragraph 4 is that, if a State in its role as party to UNCLOS has chosen, for example, the International Tribunal for the Law of the Sea as its preferred procedure that choice applies also to disputes concerning the Underwater Convention. However, the State involved does have the option, when it becomes party to the Underwater Convention, of choosing one of the other three procedures for the settlement of disputes arising out of the Convention. However, it is unclear how this will work. Article 287(8) of UNCLOS requires declarations to be deposited with the Secretary-General of the United Nations 'who shall transmit copies thereof to the States Parties'. This does not seem an appropriate procedure for a declaration made under Article 25(4) of the Underwater Convention. The *mutatis mutandis* provision would not solve this problem.

Of the four procedures listed in Article 287, an arbitral tribunal constituted in accordance with Annex VII would seem the preferable procedure for settlement of disputes arising out of the Underwater Convention. A second choice would be the International Court of Justice. The International Tribunal for the Law of the Sea is a highly specialized and expert body but has no expertise in archaeological matters or those concerning underwater cultural heritage. It is true that, under Article 289 of UNCLOS, the Tribunal may select experts in consultation with the parties to sit with the Tribunal but they have no vote. It is unclear how much weight a body that considers itself expert would be prepared to give the views of these persons. There is a further problem if the dispute involves the relationship between the Underwater Convention and UNCLOS. It would be unfair to call on the Tribunal for the Law of the Sea to act in these circumstances where its partiality might be challenged. The International Court of Justice would have more general expertise and is likely to be seen as neutral in respect of the two Conventions.

On 28th May 2013 the Tribunal for the Law of the Sea gave judgment in a case entitled *The M/V "Louisa" Case (Saint Vincent and the Grenadines v. Kingdom of Spain)*[160]. This was not a case where issues of underwater cultural heritage were argued but they formed an underlying element. Spain had detained the *Louisa* in a Spanish port in 2006. The Spanish authorities alleged that

---

160 <http://www.itlos.org/fileadmin/itlos/documents/cases/case_no_18_merits/judgment/C18_Judgment_28_05_13-orig.pdf> accessed 17 June 2013

during the search of the vessel 'diverse pieces of undersea archaeological origin were found, as well five assault rifles, considered weapons of war, and a handgun'. Criminal proceedings were instituted in the Spanish courts for 'the crime of possession and depositing weapons of war […] together with the continued crime of damaging Spanish historical patrimony'. The *Louisa* was registered in Saint Vincent and the Grenadines. The vessel officially was conducting surveys of the sea floor off Spain with a view to locating oil and gas deposits but an agreement between the main parties contained clauses dealing with the discovery and allocation of underwater cultural heritage. Saint Vincent and the Grenadines raised various arguments that Spain was in breach of certain provisions in UNCLOS. The Tribunal rejected these arguments and thus concluded it had no jurisdiction to entertain the case.

The special arbitral tribunal constituted in accordance with Annex VIII might be appropriate where there is a dispute concerning the application of Article 10(2) of the Underwater Convention. It will be remembered that this Article gives a State Party the right to prohibit or authorize any activity directed at underwater cultural heritage on its continental shelf or in its EEZ in order to prevent interference with its sovereign rights or jurisdiction. The Tribunal set up under Annex VIII of UNCLOS is for disputes involving, *inter alia*, 'protection and preservation of the marine environment' and 'marine scientific research'. The arbitrators preferably are to be chosen from established lists of experts. Unfortunately, these would probably not include persons expert in the underwater cultural heritage.

Under Article 287 of UNCLOS, the fall back procedure in all cases is arbitration. For example, if a party has not made a declaration as to which of the procedures set out in Article 287(1) it chooses, it is deemed to have accepted arbitration. If the parties to a dispute have chosen different procedures in their declarations regarding Article 287(1), the dispute goes to arbitration unless the parties otherwise agree.

Paragraph 5

While Paragraph 4 deals with a State party to both the Underwater Convention and UNCLOS, Paragraph 5 purports to treat the situation of a State which is party to the former but not the latter. Here it would first have to overcome the problem of Article 291(2). Accepting that, Paragraph 5 states that, when becoming party to the Underwater Convention, a State may make a declaration choosing one or more of the procedures set out in Article 287(1). It does not say how this declaration is to be made nor to whom it is to be made. No such declaration is listed by UNESCO.[161]

The next sentence of Paragraph 5 is ambiguous. It reads: 'Article 287 shall apply to such a declaration, as well as to any dispute to which such State is party, which is not covered by a declaration in force'. This appears to mean that if there is no declaration, then arbitration in accordance with Annex VII applies under Article 287(3). But what of the situation where parties have chosen different procedures under Article 287(1)? This is not a case of Article 287 applying to such a declaration under the first part of the sentence above. It is a situation where the declaration fails because there is no mutuality. The *mutatis mutandis* provision cannot apply to fill the *lacunae*. In such case, it seems the procedure fails unless the parties otherwise agree.

The final sentence of Paragraph 5 purports to allow States party to the Underwater Convention but not UNCLOS to nominate conciliators and arbitrators 'to be included in the lists referred to in Annex V Article 2 and Annex VII Article 2 for the settlement of disputes arising out of this Convention' that is, the Underwater Convention. There are a number of difficulties with this. Taking Article 2 of Annex VII as an example, it states specifically that States Parties to UNCLOS shall be entitled to nominate four arbitrators to a list of arbitrators drawn up and maintained by the Secretary-General of the United Nations. It must be noted that the Secretary-General would not have the authority to add to that list nominations from States which are not party to UNCLOS. Even if the Secretary-General did have that authority, the persons concerned must be 'experienced in maritime affairs'. A State acting under Article 25(5) of the Underwater Convention may well wish to nominate an archaeologist or a conservator – someone outside

---

[161]   4 Aug. 2013.

the range of those covered by the qualification 'experienced in maritime affairs' (and what does this phrase mean?). Assuming that the Secretary-General has the necessary authority and the qualification can be stretched to cover the categories of person a State might want to have represented in a dispute arising from the Underwater Convention, it is only the State not party to UNCLOS which can make such nominations. States Parties to UNCLOS would have to include these persons in their normal allotment of four nominations under Article 2 of Annex VII.

The debate on Article 25 was only taken up at the fourth of the four negotiating sessions and was dealt with under considerable pressure. The ambiguities in these arrangements relate to the lack of a functional drafting committee[162]; the determination of Germany, in particular, to give as much power as possible to the Hamburg tribunal (the International Tribunal for the Law of the Sea which is based in Hamburg); the strong support for that position by those States which had throughout tried to minimise the impact of the Underwater Convention on the basis that it was inconsistent with UNCLOS and the imminent expiration of the negotiation period (the meeting closed at 0h35 on the day following the negotiation period). The result was tolerated by all States for the advantage of having concluded the text.

---

162   Page 19.

Article 26 – Ratification, Acceptance, Approval or Accession

1. This Convention shall be subject to ratification, acceptance or approval by Member States of UNESCO.

2. This Convention shall be subject to accession:
(a) by States that are not members of UNESCO but are members of the United Nations or of a specialized agency within the United Nations system or of the International Atomic Energy Agency, as well as by States Parties to the Statute of the International Court of Justice and any other State invited to accede to this Convention by the General Conference of UNESCO;
(b) by territories which enjoy full internal self-government, recognized as such by the United Nations, but have not attained full independence in accordance with General Assembly resolution 1514 (XV) and which have competence over the matters governed by this Convention, including the competence to enter into treaties in respect of those matters.
3. The instruments of ratification, acceptance, approval or accession shall be deposited with the Director-General.

It should be noted that there is no clause providing for signature by States. According to the Rules of Procedure concerning recommendations to UNESCO Member States and international conventions covered by the terms of Article IV, paragraph 4, of the UNESCO Constitution, once a convention has been adopted by the requisite two-thirds majority of Member States present and voting at a General Conference of UNESCO, the Convention is signed by the President of the General Conference and the Director-General of UNESCO. It is then immediately open to the deposit of instruments by Member States. Other States not Members of UNESCO but participating as Members of the United Nations or other United Nations agencies are also authorized to participate by Article 2(a).

Article 2(b) was inserted at the Fourth Meeting of Governmental Experts as an effort to show political support for Palestine and was an initiative of the Arab group of States. It was based on a precedent in UNCLOS itself – Article 305(1)(e). That clause was not intended to cover Palestine, but rather entities in the process of decolonization. After negotiations it was agreed that the clause could be inserted in the Underwater Convention in application of this principle but it had to use verbatim the UNCLOS formula which it has. Palestine ratified the Underwater Convention on 8th December 2011.

Article 27 – Entry into Force

> This Convention shall enter into force three months after the date of the deposit of the twentieth instrument referred to in Article 26, but solely with respect to the twenty States or territories that have so deposited their instruments. It shall enter into force for each other State or territory three months after the date on which that State or territory has deposited its instrument.

Choosing the number of States necessary to bring an international convention into force is usually a political decision. It reflects many things, such as the degree of opposition or support and the relative balance between the two; the significance of the treaty; the extent it will change the existing situation. During the negotiations, Germany proposed 60 States and another State 30. It was pointed out that these numbers were unusually high for a convention dealing with cultural heritage. The Convention for the Protection of Cultural Property in the Event of Armed Conflict required 5; its First Protocol 5; its Second Protocol 20; the 1970 Convention 3. Finally the number 20 was agreed on. This figure was attained on 2 January 2009.

ARTICLE 28- DECLARATION AS TO INLAND WATERS

> When ratifying, accepting, approving or acceding to this Convention or at any time thereafter, any State or territory may declare that the Rules shall apply to inland waters not of a maritime character.

'Inland waters not of a maritime character' refer to rivers, lakes, wells, moats and possibly marshes where the site becomes inundated as it is excavated. Most of these areas will already be covered by a State's legislation applying to sites on land. States would of course be perfectly free to apply the Rules to any such site if they so choose and this was in accordance with their law.

A number of States with important inland underwater sites were keenly interested in the Underwater Convention. They included Belgium (important riverine sites used more or less continuously from Neolithic times right up to the recent past for shelter and safety from enemies); Hungary (lake and Danube River sites) and Switzerland (Neolithic lake sites). The emphasis in the later negotiations on maritime matters tended to overshadow these important issues. Nonetheless, some of these sites are of world significance and archaeologists believe that any interference with them should follow the Rules in the Annex in the same way as required for maritime sites. On other hand, some countries argued that they already had legislation applying to these sites which might need to be amended if the Rules of the Annex were to be applied and that this might therefore slow down the rate of ratification and entry into force of the Convention.

The compromise solution was to allow States to make a declaration at the time of ratification which would enable them to show their support for the universality of these Rules but not impede ratification by those States which would first need to make legislative adjustments. No such declarations have been made.

Ratification even by landlocked States is important. Firstly, some of them have a very important direct link with underwater cultural heritage outside their current jurisdiction (such as Austria in ships of the former Austro-Hungarian Empire which once operated out of Trieste). Others may have a more indirect link, for example, through passengers and cargo on sunken vessels. They may want to assert their interests through those Articles of the Underwater Convention which provide for consultation with States which have a 'verifiable link' with underwater cultural heritage.

ARTICLE 29 – LIMITATIONS TO GEOGRAPHICAL SCOPE

> At the time of ratifying, accepting, approving or acceding to this Convention, a State or territory may make a declaration to the depositary that this Convention shall not be applicable to specific parts of its territory, internal waters, archipelagic waters or territorial sea, and shall identify therein the reasons for such declaration. Such State shall, to the extent practicable and as quickly as possible, promote conditions under which this Convention will apply to the areas specified in its declaration, and to that end shall also withdraw its declaration in whole or in part as soon as that has been achieved.

International conventions are entered into by States which are then responsible for carrying out whatever duties are imposed on them by the agreement. A State may be a grouping – a federation – of smaller political units. For internal reasons the subject matter of the international convention may be the responsibility of those unites. For example, Australia is a federation of six states each of which has responsibility for cultural matters within its own borders. The Federal or Commonwealth Government has no direct power to legislate on cultural matters but may do so incidentally in the exercise of one of the powers which it does have. It has power to enter into treaties and it is through this that the Commonwealth Government plays a significant role in certain aspects of cultural management. Australia's membership of the *Convention concerning the Protection of the World Cultural and Natural Heritage* 1972 has enabled the Commonwealth Government to override state development plans adversely affecting Australian sites on the World Heritage List.[163] But the extent of the Commonwealth's power under a treaty is not without limit. On many treaties there must be negotiations with the states before Australia can become a party. This can take many years and thus delays Australia's membership. Speaking generally, Aust makes the point:

> Such sharing of power, and particularly legislative power, between a federation and its constituent units can cause huge problems for the federal state when it wishes to become party to a treaty which will require to be implemented also in the law of the constituent units. This can be dealt with to some extent by the use of territorial and federal clauses, and federal reservations and declarations.[164]

However, unitary States (that is States without such distributed power) are often unhappy with federal clauses because they allow a federal State to become party to the treaty in a 'piecemeal' way. Normally, when a State is party to a treaty it is responsible to the other States Parties for any failure to carry out its obligations. However, where there is a federal clause in a treaty, the obligations of the federal State are limited in respect of matters outside its constitutional powers. On the other hand, some federal States also dislike such clauses, fearing that it will encourage internal litigation and claims at the constitutional level. When Canada proposed a federal clause for the Underwater Convention, it met considerable opposition on the ground that this gave federal States an unjustified advantage in allowing differential application of the Convention. Canada explained that under its complex federal system, certain small areas of its territorial sea and internal waters remained within provincial jurisdiction. The problem in fact prevented Canada from becoming party to UNCLOS for many years, although it was a strong supporter of that Convention. Canada had played a particularly active role in refining the concepts and negotiating compromises to achieve the Underwater Convention: its arguments were therefore heard with some sympathy.

After negotiation, Article 29 was eventually accepted. This acknowledges the problem for federal States and those with self-governing territories. These States may make a declaration to the depository regarding those areas to which the Convention shall not be applicable. However, Article 29 departs from the standard federal clause as exemplified by Article 34 of the *Convention*

---

163   O'Keefe, P.J. 'Foreign Investment and the World Heritage Convention' (1994) 3 *International Journal of Cultural Property* 259.
164   Aust, A. fn. 4 above, 50.

concerning the Protection of the World Cultural and Natural Heritage where federal States were obliged merely to inform their individual units of the provisions of the Convention with a recommendation that they be adopted. Article 29 of the Underwater Convention goes much further: States are under a duty to bring the areas specified within the scope of the Convention as quickly as possible and then withdraw the declaration. No such declaration has yet been made.[165]

---

[165] 4 Aug. 2013.

ARTICLE 30 – RESERVATIONS

> With the exception of Article 29, no reservations may be made to this Convention.

The Vienna Convention on the Law of Treaties defines a reservation as

> … a unilateral statement, however phrased or named, made by a State, when signing, ratifying, accepting, approving or acceding to a treaty, whereby it purports to exclude or to modify the legal effect of certain provisions of the treaty in their application to that State.[166]

The legal effect of reservations is highly complex. By use of this device, States try to avoid those parts of a treaty they dislike and accept only those parts they favour. Consequently, whether or not reservations are allowed is a significant point. For example, the original draft of the UNESCO *Convention on the Means of Prohibiting and Preventing the Illicit Import, Export and Transfer of Ownership of Cultural Property* 1970 prohibited reservations. However, when it met in 1970, the Special Committee of Governmental Experts decided to allow reservations, recognizing that there would be varying degrees of implementation. The use of a reservation is especially problematic where the draft is a 'package', that is, a State's acceptance of certain provisions is dependent on concessions it has made elsewhere. Whether there should be reservations in relation to the Underwater Convention did result in some sharp exchanges particularly in relation to salvage but there was no extensive debate. It was felt that the delicate balance of interests achieved in the Convention should not be subject to upset by allowing reservations. This 'package' included concessions concerning salvage, the wording of provisions on public access, the provisions on State vessels and aircraft as well as control of operations on the continental shelf and in the EEZ. These concessions were made by all States in different areas to achieve what each regarded as essential.

The exclusions of reservations may lead States to attempt to make their acceptance of the Underwater Convention subject to 'observations' or an 'understanding' in relation to, or 'explanations' of, a particular Article. The substance of the statement is crucial. If it excludes or modifies the legal effect of a provision of the Convention in its application to that State, it is a reservation and prohibited.

These disguised reservations must not be confused with a genuine interpretative declaration which is an accepted part of international treaty making. Such a declaration may be used by a State to clarify the meaning or scope it attributes to a provision in the treaty. The rules on interpretation already discussed apply.[167]

---

166 Article 2(1)(d).
167 Page 27.

ARTICLE 31 – AMENDMENTS

1. A State Party may, by written communication addressed to the Director-General, propose amendments to this Convention. The Director-General shall circulate such communication to all States Parties. If, within six months from the date of the circulation of the communication, not less than one half of the States Parties reply favourably to the request, the Director-General shall present such proposal to the next Meeting of States Parties for discussion and possible adoption.

2. Amendments shall be adopted by a two-thirds majority of States Parties present and voting.

3. Once adopted, amendments to this Convention shall be subject to ratification, acceptance, approval or accession by the States Parties.

4. Amendments shall enter into force, but solely with respect to the States Parties that have ratified, accepted, approved or acceded to them, three months after the deposit of the instruments referred to in paragraph 3 of this Article by two thirds of the States Parties. Thereafter, for each State or territory that ratifies, accepts, approves or accedes to it, the amendment shall enter into force three months after the date of deposit by that Party of its instrument of ratification, acceptance, approval or accession.

5. A State or territory which becomes a Party to this Convention after the entry into force of amendments in conformity with paragraph 4 of this Article shall, failing an expression of different intention by that State or territory, be considered:
   (a) as a Party to this Convention as so amended; and
   (b) as a Party to the unamended Convention in relation to any State Party not bound by the amendment.

This Article is quite complex compared to the provision on amendments in most international conventions. One factor in bringing this about was the possible need to amend the Rules in the Annex from time to time. These are technical rules arising from archaeological practice in relation to underwater cultural heritage as modified to a certain extent by political considerations. They can be expected to change as methodology and technology changes.

The ILA Draft had proposed that the International Council for Monuments and Sites should be responsible for revision of the Annex (then called the Charter). Any revision proposed by ICOMOS would be binding on States Parties subject to specific objection by a State signifying its non-acceptance. Activities affecting underwater cultural heritage would be judged against the version of the Charter existing at the time a particular activity occurred. However, the meetings of governmental experts were not prepared to have ICOMOS – a non-Governmental organization – make rules binding on States Parties, even with this provision which would allow them to 'contract out' of such new obligations.

The Annex containing the Rules is now an integral part of the Underwater Convention. Consequently, the amendment procedure in Article 31 now applies equally to both the body of the Convention and the Annex. The procedure for amendment must be started by a State Party making a proposal. It only moves forward if not less than one half of the State Parties signify within six months that they are in favour. This is a substantial hurdle. Unless there is lobbying among States or by interested non-governmental organizations, this would seem a short period of time in which to get States to act. The procedure would have been easier if it had required not less than one half of States Party to positively object. Nevertheless, if the requisite consent of States Parties is obtained, the proposal is put to the meeting of States Parties. This would allow the Scientific and Technical Advisory Body to examine the proposal if it raises questions of a scientific or technical nature regarding implementation of the Rules. The amendment may be adopted by the meeting of States Parties by a two thirds majority of those present and voting. It is then subject to ratification, acceptance, approval or acceptance by the States Parties.

It would seem that this is the only way amendment of the Rules can be brought about. Although the Meeting of States Parties is entitled to decide on its own functions and responsibilities, under Article 31 it has no power to adopt an amendment which has not come from a State Party. In practice, the Meeting could discuss an amendment which it, or the Advisory Body, thinks is necessary and then encourage one of the States Party to propose it.

ARTICLE 32 – DENUNCIATION

1. A State Party may, by written notification addressed to the Director-General, denounce this Convention.

2. The denunciation shall take effect twelve months after the date of receipt of the notification, unless the notification specifies a later date.

3. The denunciation shall not in any way affect the duty of any State Party to fulfil any obligation embodied in this Convention to which it would be subject under international law independently of this Convention.

This is a standard clause included in most international treaties but very rarely used. No denunciation has ever been made of a UNESCO convention dealing with cultural heritage matters. Denunciation must not be confused with the situation when a State Party withdraws from UNESCO as did Singapore, the United Kingdom and the United States of America in the 1980s. Withdrawal from the Organization did not affect their status as parties to UNESCO cultural conventions or lessen their obligations under them.

ARTICLE 33 – THE RULES

The Rules annexed to this Convention form an integral part of it and, unless expressly provided otherwise, a reference to this Convention includes a reference to the Rules.

The Cultural Heritage Law Committee of the ILA realized early in its work on its Draft Convention that States would need objective standards by which to judge the appropriateness of actions in respect of the underwater cultural heritage. As already explained, in 1991 the newly established ICOMOS International Committee on the Underwater Cultural Heritage was approached and asked to assist in the preparation of a set of principles which could be attached to the Draft Convention in a document called the 'Charter for the Protection and Management of the Underwater Cultural Heritage'. The relevant principles were developed at meetings in Paris, 1994, and London, 1995, and forwarded to UNESCO.[168] At the Second Meeting of Governmental Experts which was held in 1999, Canada stated that the standards set out in the Charter formed a good basis for the principles that should guide any authorized activity directed at underwater cultural heritage but they needed adjustment to fit the context of a Convention. Following on this, Canada circulated a working paper incorporating such adjustments. This became the basis for work in a special group during that and the Third Meeting of Governmental Experts. At the Fourth Meeting, the Rules were discussed in Plenary Session and adopted unanimously. During the debate in Commission IV of the UNESCO General Conference, some States that found problems with the Underwater Convention said they supported the Rules and would apply them unilaterally.[169]

Article 33 states that the Rules are an integral part of the Underwater Convention. Consequently, although drafted mainly by archaeologists and administrators of cultural heritage programmes, they are now a legal document to be interpreted according to the methods already explained.[170]

---

168 Page 15.
169 Page 119.
170 Page 27.

Article 34 – Registration with the United Nations

> In conformity with Article 102 of the Charter of the United Nations, this Convention shall be registered with the Secretariat of the United Nations at the request of the Director-General.

The original draft did not include this clause which was only put in when the text was being finalized after the end of the fourth meeting of governmental experts. This was done at the request of certain delegations who felt that the omission must have been an oversight. In fact it is not strictly necessary because registration of treaties with the United Nations is standard practice of all specialized agencies of the United Nations. However, specific mention does no harm.

This requirement to register treaties with the United Nations arose out of the practice of so-called 'secret treaties' endemic in international diplomacy prior to and around the time of the First World War. Article 18 of the Covenant of the League of Nations required every new treaty entered into by any Member of the League to be registered and published. It would not be binding until registered. This practice was followed in Article 102(1) of the United Nations Charter.

Article 35 – Authoritative Texts

> This Convention has been drawn up in Arabic, Chinese, English, French, Russian and Spanish, the six texts being equally authoritative.

It may seem strange to say that the texts are equally authoritative. However, the languages indicated are those used officially in the United Nations. To favour one above the other would be politically impossible. On the other hand, the use of multiple languages does have advantages. There may be occasions when a meaning that is obscure in one language can be clarified by referring to one or more of the other languages. Where this is not the case, the meaning which best reconciles the texts, having regard to the object and purpose of the treaty, is to be adopted.[171]

---

[171] Article 33(4) Vienna Convention on the Law of Treaties.

ANNEX: RULES CONCERNING ACTIVITIES DIRECTED AT UNDERWATER CULTURAL HERITAGE

The Annex, as stipulated in Article 33, is an integral part of the Underwater Convention. However, there is a tendency to consider it apart from the 35 Articles. This way of looking at the Convention derives in part from the different subject matter of the two sections – the first comprising legal and public relations aspects of the subject and the second the more specific provisions controlling activities directed at underwater cultural heritage. But, as stated, it is part of the Underwater Convention and, as such, has the status of an international treaty. It has to be interpreted as a treaty and can only be changed by the procedure laid down in Article 31.

Certain governments have indicated that they will apply the Annex where appropriate even though they are not party to the Convention. For example, at a 2009 meeting of the States Parties to the Convention, the observer delegation of the United States of America stated:

> A number of United States federal and state agencies currently use the Annexed Rules as a guide in the protection and management of underwater cultural heritage located in national marine sanctuaries, national parks, and national monuments, including in the national marine monument in the Northwestern Hawaiian Islands, the Papahanaumokuakea National Monument.[172]

The Government of the United Kingdom has formally adopted the Rules of the Annex as a matter of policy since 2005.[173] In 2001 Norway indicated that it would apply the Rules on a unilateral basis.

There have been allegations that the Rules were devised by academic and bureaucratic archaeologists to prevent shipwreck hunters from accessing the underwater cultural heritage and to keep it for themselves. For example, Stemm, Chief Executive Officer of Odyssey Marine Exploration Inc., has written:

> … it was somewhat disconcerting to see what started out as a relatively straight-forward Code of Ethics for underwater archaeology evolve into a politicalized [sic] set of regulations, promoted and drafted for the most part by desk-bound cultural heritage managers and lawyers.[174]

This is wholly inaccurate. As the history of the Underwater Convention shows[175] the rules were never intended by the drafters of the Convention as a code of ethics but as part of a regime to establish benchmarks for acceptable conduct in work on the underwater cultural heritage. It was intended to be part of an international agreement to which States could turn in assessing what people had done in relation to that heritage. Antony Firth, who, from the very beginning was closely involved in preparation of the Charter/Rules, has expressed what he sees as the philosophy underlying them in these terms:

---

172   UNESCO Doc. UCH/09/2.MSP/220/4, 15 Sept. 2009: <http://unesdoc.unesco.org/images/0018/001853/185392e.pdf>

173   Hansard, House of Commons, Written Answers for 24 Jan. 2005, Col. 46W. See also Yorke, R. 'Introduction: Protection of Underwater Cultural Heritage in International Waters Adjacent to the UK – a JNAPC Perspective 21 Years On' in Yorke, R. (ed.) *Protection of Underwater Cultural Heritage in International Waters Adjacent to the UK: Proceedings of the JNAPC 21st Anniversary Seminar, Burlington House, November, 2010* (Nautical Archaeology Society, Fort Cumberland, 2011) 1, 3.

174   Stemm, G. 'Preface' in Stemm, G. and Kingsley, S. (eds) *Oceans Odyssey 2: Underwater Heritage Management & Deep-Sea Shipwrecks in the English Channel & Atlantic Ocean* (Oxbow Books, Oxford, 2011) vii, viii.

175   Page 15.

The Charter-to-be was all about making proposals transparent, comprehensive, and explicit in terms of the detailed standards that were going to apply. The document was not especially normative - it requires process not specific results. This is because archaeology is fundamentally an ethic, not a collection of methods. A prescriptive Charter would not have been able to anticipate all possible circumstances; indeed, this was not its purpose. Rather, the Charter requires people to show how they are going to approach the key issues that attend the investigation of underwater cultural heritage. That is to say, Project Designs - as required by the Charter - provide evidence of the exercise of thought and judgment, which can be gauged to establish if the activity is 'archaeology'. A highly intrusive and destructive investigation could be regarded as 'archaeology' through this mechanism, so long as the Project Design made proper provision in terms of rationale and all the necessary arrangements. Hence the approach in the Charter is highly practical and flexible, drawing upon existing practice-based standards such as those of the Institute for Archaeologists.

From the start, drafting of the Charter was shaped by the need to arrive at something that archaeologists could achieve practically; which would distinguish what they did from others; and which would be enforceable for the purposes of the Convention. For an archaeologist, preparing a Project Design should be demanding but not onerous. For others, simply using the right headings in a Project Design is unlikely to disguise the underpinning motivations.[176]

Thus the Rules were always to be part of the Convention – much more than a simple code of ethics which could be accepted or rejected at will.

There are no UNESCO records of who actually attended the negotiations of the group working on the Rules. However, there were many people present who had extensive practical experience in activities directed at underwater cultural heritage and very few lawyers.

The following commentaries on the various Rules are not intended to be definitive. They are designed to emphasize the basic purpose and role of each Rule within the context of the Convention. Thus, there is extensive discussion of Rule 2 dealing with commercial exploitation as it fleshes out Article 2(7). It also provides standards for the illicit trade provisions of the Convention. Other Rules, dealing with the practical aspects of work on the underwater cultural heritage, should be supplemented by reference to the UNESCO Manual for Activities Directed at Underwater Cultural Heritage.[177]

---

176 Personal communication on file with the author: 18 August 2013
177 <http://www.unesco.org/culture/en/underwater/pdf/UCH-Manual.pdf>

I. GENERAL PRINCIPLES

RULE 1

> The protection of underwater cultural heritage through in situ preservation shall be considered as the first option. Accordingly, activities directed at underwater cultural heritage shall be authorized in a manner consistent with the protection of that heritage, and subject to that requirement may be authorized for the purpose of making a significant contribution to protection or knowledge or enhancement of underwater cultural heritage.

Commentary: It is quite clear that this provision does not prohibit work on the site of underwater cultural heritage or even its excavation. *In situ* preservation is the first option only. However, that does not stop criticism of the principle: it is said to be 'clearly not working'[178] and is 'a myth'[179]. Sinclair states that:

> One of the most outrageous statements that the UNESCO Convention advocates is that *in situ* preservation should be considered as a first option.[180]

Kingsley, following on underwater searches done by Odyssey in the English Channel and Western Approaches, concludes that '*in situ* preservation emerges as an inappropriate all-encompassing managerial policy for the protection of maritime heritage, either in the short- or long-term'.[181]

On the other hand, Robert Grenier, who was President of the ICOMOS International Scientific Committee for the Underwater Cultural Heritage at the time of the negotiation on the Underwater Convention in Paris and is a Canadian underwater archaeologist of world renown, takes a much more nuanced view:

> Although it is very easy to generalize, metal wrecks, like the *Titanic*, tend to remain more intact for a while after sinking. On the other hand wooden vessels exposed in salt water tend to weaken more rapidly and to collapse onto the bottom or into mud or sand, opening up like a book. This relatively quick collapsing and burying of a good portion of wooden hulls and their contents can however help them to withstand the long-term, damaging effect of the elements. I do not want to give … the impression that I think most of a given ship will be necessarily preserved in this way. I simply want to point out that significant and important parts of the wreck and its contents can be preserved. Hence the very well preserved hull of a 2,400 year old Greek merchantman on which I worked in Kyrenia, Cyprus, in 1968; hence the extremely well preserved hulls of four hundred year old Spanish galleons in Red Bay at the edge of the North Atlantic; hence the very stable partial remains of two of the largest French warships of the mid seventeenth-century, preserved *in situ* in the harbour of Louisbourg, Nova Scotia, also on the North Atlantic seaboard. And so on.
>
> It is sad that they [relatively modern vessels] do deteriorate and do finally collapse, given that they are not always well-protected by a deep blanket of sand or silt to help them retain structural integrity. But, all that being said, the collapsing of these hulls does not necessarily destroy their contents and their archaeological potential to provide us with … their 'history'. They can still be valid sites to record and even

---

178 Stemm, G. 'Preface' in Stemm, G. and Kingsley, S. (eds) *Oceans Odyssey: Deep-sea Shipwrecks in the English Channel, Straits of Gibraltar & Atlantic Ocean* (Oxbow Books, Oxford, 2010) vii, viii.

179 Tolson, H. 'The Jacksonville 'Blue China' Shipwreck & the Myth of Deep-Sea Preservation' in Stemm and Kingsley, fn. 7 above, 145, 156.

180 Sinclair, J. 'Threats to Underwater Cultural Heritage – Real and Imagined' in Stemm, G. and Kingsley, S. (eds) *Oceans Odyssey 2: Underwater Heritage Management & Deep-Sea Shipwrecks in the English Channel & Atlantic Ocean* (Oxbow Books, Oxford, 2011) 17.

181 Kingsley, S.A. 'Deep-sea Fishing Impacts on the Shipwrecks of the English Channel & Western Approaches' in Stemm and Kingsley, fn 7 above 191, 231.

excavate, if done properly, to extract an enormous amount of information. This is true even supposing they go undiscovered for hundreds of years from now. Given this degradation, the challenge before us is, I believe, to preserve the history of these wrecks, record and identify them non-intrusively before they collapse, and make these findings accessible to the public: all of this, though, without excavation or removal of objects.

Notwithstanding the harsh environmental conditions …, this long-term potential for archaeological survival has proven true for other North Atlantic shipwrecks we have studied: like HMS *Sapphire*, 1696; like the *Prudent* and the *Célèbre*, 1758; like the *Machault*, 1760; like the *Breadalbane*, 1853; and like the partial remains of the *Elizabeth and Mary*, 1690, the oldest American-built vessel ever found. And many others. It has been well demonstrated that shipwrecks can last thousands of years underwater as valid and fruitful archaeological sites. If shipwrecks are seriously damaged by natural destruction in given areas, and I have witnessed this myself, the damage generally occurs well within the first century of immersion. … After that initial period, the degradation can be more or less stopped or slowed down until the site reaches an equilibrium and stabilizes itself for centuries. In this context, the '*in situ preservation*' concept is an effective one and has been tried in sites in the United States, Australia, Denmark and Canada, to name just a few countries having employed it.[182]

The desirability of *in situ* protection was raised in argument before the US District Court for the Eastern District of Virginia in 2000 in one of the cases involving the *Titanic*. Counsel for the United States stated:

In situ preservation has meant … that the preference is to keep it [*Titanic*] in place because it is preserved best in place. However, if there is a reason for bringing it up, then that would be done according to proper methodology and provided that there were resources to properly conserve and curate those artifacts once they came up.[183]

The *in situ* principle has also been recognized in the *Agreement Concerning the Shipwrecked Vessel RMS Titanic*.[184] Article 4(2) reflects the principle as set out in Article 1 of the Annex:

Each Party agrees that the preferred management technique is *in situ* preservation and that project authorizations referred to in this Article involving recovery or excavation aimed at RMS *Titanic* and/or its artifacts should be granted only when justified by educational, scientific, or cultural interests, including the need to protect the integrity of RMS *Titanic* and/or its artifacts from a significant threat.

It would be impossible to apply the *in situ* principle as an absolute worldwide. There are numerous statements that modern fishing methods destroy shipwreck sites[185] and the possibility of this would need to be taken into account. In certain parts of the world shipwrecks are discovered by poor fishermen who take anything that seems of value. These are relatively shallow wrecks and they are often in places where it is difficult to know what is happening. Consequently, *in situ* protection can be nothing more than a first option for those administering the Underwater Convention. Any administrator who goes further than this is not complying with the Convention and should be held to account. Tolson alleges that some resource managers and archaeologists embrace *in situ* preservation 'as a preference and excuse to justify an absence of protective or preservative measures on many shipwreck sites'.[186] Unfortunately, he does not indicate who

---

182   Copy of letter dated 19 Oct. 2001 on file with the author.
183   *RMS Titanic v. Wrecked and Abandoned Vessel*, Transcript of Proceedings, 3 April 2000.
184   Page 52 .
185   For example, Foley, B. 'Impact of Fishing on Shipwrecks' <http://www.whoi.edu/sbl/liteSite.do?litesiteid=2740&articleId=4965>
186   Tolson fn. 8 above, 145.

these managers and archaeologists are or what country they come from. If statements of this nature are made they should be supported by evidence.

Over enthusiastic implementation of the *in situ* preservation principle is just as reprehensible as inadequate implementation. There must be an actual process of assessing *in situ* preservation as a viable method of dealing with the situation. It must take into account all the influences, both natural and man-made, affecting the site and its long term prospects.[187] A report must be prepared and presented to the appropriate authority, in general, the relevant Minister.

If, having done this, and the decision is for *in situ* preservation, then the site cannot be excavated.

If interference with the site can be justified then it may be authorized. Justification may consist of the need for scientific investigation of the site to establish what lies there: to save material from a site threatened by some sort of construction work, natural deterioration etc. Interference with the site, particularly excavation, should involve full investigation of the alleged reasons and, in accordance with Rule 1 must be 'consistent with the protection of that heritage'. This means that adequate conservation facilities are available; full reports are made and anything raised is properly curated and exhibited.

Any decision to excavate for the purpose of making a scientific contribution to knowledge must be made only with a full understanding of other techniques that may be available. These may not have the glamour of an excavation but may be more cost effective and provide the answers sought. This is one reason why, under Rule 22, activities directed at underwater cultural heritage should be undertaken only under the direction of a qualified underwater archaeologist. Such a person should be conversant with the most current techniques and devices. For example, at Red Bay in Canada, a technique was developed enabling reproduction in the laboratory of pieces from the wreck.

> An underwater moulding technique was developed in order to make exact replicas of certain important details of the construction of the ship. Diving conservators first used polysulfide rubber to make an imprint of the surface to be reproduced and then covered the object with a plaster that congeals rigidly, even in cold water, in order to capture and retain the original shape. In the comfort of the dry laboratory in Ottawa, an exact copy of the object could be reproduced. In this way, perfect reproductions were obtained of the traces left by tools showing how the pieces of the structure had been made or reproductions of the imprints of nails or treenails showing how or in what order various pieces had been assembled. The researchers even succeeded in capturing the imprint of rats' teeth on the ribs of the ship deep in the hold. The moulding technique was also used in the presentation of the ship: a section of the hull was reproduced in this way to show how it appeared when the archaeologists saw it underwater. This is useful for museological or educational purposes.[188]

The commitment to *in situ* preservation has been criticized on the grounds that wrecks are continually deteriorating, being buried in landfill projects or destroyed in dredging operations. In the first place, these criticisms ignore the fact that *in situ* preservation is only the first option. If a wreck is going to be destroyed, for example, during pipeline laying, and there is no way of

---

187 An excellent example is that done in respect of the *Vrouw Maria* (page 8). Biological, archaeological, hydrological, geological and physical methods were used to study the wreck with the conclusion being 'the present location of the *Vrouw Maria* is a good place to preserve her. …There are no actions which could be recommended for the improvement of the prevailing preservation circumstances'. Leino, M *et al*. 'The Natural Environment of the Shipwreck *Vrouw Maria* (1771) in the Northern Baltic Sea: an Assessment of her State of Preservation' (2010) 40 *International Journal of Nautical Archaeology* 133, 148.

188 Grenier, R and Berbier, M-A. *Challenges Facing Underwater Archaeology: the Red Bay Perspective* (Stichting voor de Nederlandse Archeologie, Amsterdam, 2001) 10.

avoiding this, then it can be excavated. Secondly, in many cases current criticisms also ignore the stipulation that to be eligible as underwater cultural heritage objects must be more than 100 years old. A great deal of concern is in relation to iron vessels many of which would not yet qualify for control under the Convention.

RULE 2

> The commercial exploitation of underwater cultural heritage for trade or speculation or its irretrievable dispersal is fundamentally incompatible with the protection and proper management of underwater cultural heritage. Underwater cultural heritage shall not be traded, sold, bought or bartered as commercial goods.
>
> This Rule cannot be interpreted as preventing:
>
> (a) the provision of professional archaeological services or necessary services incidental thereto whose nature and purpose are in full conformity with this Convention and are subject to the authorization of the competent authorities; (b) the deposition of underwater cultural heritage, recovered in the course of a research project in conformity with this Convention, provided such deposition does not prejudice the scientific or cultural interest or integrity of the recovered material or result in its irretrievable dispersal; is in accordance with the provisions of Rules 33 and 34; and is subject to the authorization of the competent authorities.

Commentary:[189] The first sentence of Rule 2 is somewhat peculiar in that it is worded not as a rule but rather as a policy. The second sentence is definitely a rule. The crucial phrase is 'commercial exploitation' which is not defined.

The words used in the Preamble and in the second sentence of Rule 2 are indicative of what is meant by commercial exploitation but are not to be taken as conclusive of that meaning. Indeed there is a large degree of overlap in the meaning of these words. 'Sale' is defined in the *Oxford English Dictionary* as the exchange of a commodity for money. To buy something is the obverse of sale; it means to obtain a commodity for payment of money. The result is that the person who buys underwater cultural heritage from its current holder is just as much affected by the prohibition as the person who sells it. Trading is the action of buying and selling goods and services and would thus cover both the activities already mentioned. It can also mean the exchange of one thing for another. This merges into the meaning of 'barter' which, according to the *Oxford English Dictionary*, involves the exchange of goods for other goods or immaterial things. That would cover an exchange of goods for services. It would go further and apply to the provision of favours such as political assistance or, indeed, any act which gives the other person an advantage in some way. To sum up, there must be an underlying transaction involving an exchange of underwater cultural heritage for something else, whether tangible or intangible.

The prohibited activities of trading, selling, buying or bartering cannot be used in a way which would convert underwater cultural heritage into 'commercial goods'. The prohibition takes this heritage out of the marketplace. It replicates the Latin phrase *res ex commercium*: 'objects excluded from trade'. This concept originated in Roman law and basically means that certain objects cannot be the subject of private rights. The application of the doctrine in private law varies according to the State concerned.[190] However, in Article 2(7) and Rule 2 we are dealing with an international obligation which States are obliged to implement when they become party to the Convention.

The phrase used is 'commercial exploitation'. Exploitation was first used in the sense of the 'productive working' of something and was regarded in a positive sense. However, in the 1850s

---

189 Much of the discussion on 'commercial exploitation' is based on an article already published in *Art Antiquity and Law*: O'Keefe, P.J. ' 'Commercial Exploitation': Its Prohibition in the UNESCO Convention on Protection of the Underwater Cultural Heritage 2001 and Other Instruments' (2013) XVIII *Art Antiquity and Law* 129.

190 For a brief summary of the doctrine and its development: Siehr, K. 'International Art Trade and the Law' (1993–VI) 243 *Recueil des cours de l'Académie de la Haye* 64

it developed an alternative, negative meaning of actions which took away the rights of others.[191] It is obvious that the second meaning is inherent in the use of the word in the Convention. The rights taken away by commercial exploitation are those of the public as set out in the Convention which sees underwater cultural heritage as the inheritance of humanity to be treated according to the Rules and preserved for the future.

This particular interpretation is reinforced by the first sentence of Rule 2 which is not cast in the form of a rule. Rather it is a policy statement to be used as a guide to interpretation of the second sentence. The statement that 'commercial exploitation of underwater cultural heritage for trade or speculation or its irretrievable dispersal is fundamentally incompatible with the protection and proper management of underwater cultural heritage' indicates that this form of heritage at least is to be treated as outside commerce.

Greg Stemm, from Odyssey Marine Exploration Inc., a salvage company, argues that 'the term 'exploit' has a wide range of meanings and so it needs to be placed in the context of other provisions'.[192] The provision he refers to is Article 18(4) which deals with the disposition of artefacts for the public benefit. He omits the opening words of that Article which confine its scope to situations where States have seized underwater cultural heritage. It is difficult to see what other provisions would govern the meaning of 'exploitation' so as to alter what has been indicated in the above discussion.

Stemm also tries to draw a distinction between 'trade goods' and 'cultural artefacts'. The former would be those objects eligible for sale.

> Trade Goods are also often characterized by large quantities of similar or duplicate items that have been mass-produced with the original goal of trade and dispersion of these artifacts. Their inclusion in the assemblage is a result of a simple twist of fate, not a clue to the shipboard culture. In other words, sale of artifacts from this portion of a collection would be a continuation of the original intent of the owners, as opposed to the shipboard artifacts, which are the remaining evidence of shipboard life prior to the disaster – or perhaps clues to the disaster itself. While cargo, freight, or trade status in and of itself does not necessarily justify separation from the cultural collection of a shipwreck site, three other issues may be useful in making this distinction. They are: 1) the number of duplicates on site, 2) the ease of recording or replicating the artifacts, and 3) archaeological value versus value of return to stream of commerce.[193]

Stemm's view, as the CEO of Odyssey, carries weight with those opposed to the approach taken in the Convention. It is a view which greatly favours the interests of persons exploiting the underwater cultural heritage. Trade goods are not so easily separated from the site as Stemm suggests. The fact that they might once have been part of commerce in no way requires that they should have that characteristic now. Indeed, so-called trade goods may be the most significant part of the wreck site. There are no academic or policy reasons why a line should be drawn between cargo and the remainder of the wreck site allowing the former to be regarded as outside the prohibitions of the Convention. 'Shipboard culture' is not the only aspect of history that can be gleaned from a wreck site. The cargo can provide evidence of life at the time in the much broader community. Its commercial dispersal, even subject to the strictures Stemm proposes, effectively means that it cannot be re-examined in the future.

COMMERCIAL EXPLOITATION IN PRACTICE

Recent events in the United Kingdom illustrate some of the problems that might arise if the

---

191   <http://dictionary.reference.com/browse/exploitation>
192   Stemm, G. 'Virtual Collectors and Private Curators: A Model for the Museum of the Future' in Stemm, G. and Kingsley, S. (eds) *Oceans Odyssey 2: Underwater Heritage Management and Deep-Sea Shipwrecks in the English Channel & Atlantic Ocean* (Oxbow Books, Oxford, 2011) 27, 32.
193   Stemm, G. 'Comment on Shipwreck Resources Management Issues' presented to the US Commission on Ocean Policy, 22 Feb. 2002: <http://www.oceancommission.gov/publiccomment/floridacomments/stemm_comment.pdf>

prohibition on commercial exploitation were to be applied in practice. The situation chosen is still developing but as it stands at the moment there are aspects that merit investigation.

At the centre of the controversy is HMS *Victory* – a British warship sunk in 1744 and regarded by the British Government as a state-owned vessel. According to work carried out by Odyssey, HMS *Victory* lies 'around 100km west of the Casquets off the Channel Isles, beyond the territorial seas or contiguous zone of any country'[194]. On 23rd January 2012, the Ministry of Defence issued a Press Release[195] announcing that HMS *Victory* had been gifted to a newly established Maritime Heritage Foundation. The Release states that the Foundation is a registered charity, 'established especially to recover, preserve and display in public museums artefacts from HMS Victory (1744)'.

The Release further indicates:

> The Maritime Heritage Foundation will be supported by an Advisory Group, with representatives of English Heritage and the National Museum of the Royal Navy. The Group will advise on the extent to which actions proposed by the Foundation are consistent with the archaeological principles set out in Annex A [*sic*] to the UNESCO Convention on the Protection of Underwater Cultural Heritage.

However, only fourteen days later, on 2nd February 2012, Odyssey Marine Exploration released a Press statement to the effect that it had entered into an agreement with the Foundation 'for the financing, archaeological survey and excavation, conservation and exhibit of HMS *Victory* (1744) and artefacts from the shipwreck site'.[196]

> The agreement calls for Odyssey's project costs to be reimbursed and for Odyssey to be paid a percentage of the recovered artefact's fair value. The preferred option is for Odyssey to be compensated in cash. However, if the Foundation determines, based on the principles adopted for its own collection management and curation policy, that it is in its best interest to de-accession certain artifacts, the Foundation may choose to compensate Odyssey with artifacts in lieu of cash.

Odyssey was to receive 80 per cent of the fair value of artefacts not associated with the operation of the ship and 50 per cent of all others.

If the Rules were to apply, Rule 2(a) would allow for:

> The provision of professional archaeological services or necessary services incidental thereto whose nature and purpose are in full conformity with this Convention and are subject to the authorization of the competent authorities.

It is difficult to say definitively that Odyssey has the authorization of the competent authorities. Considering the timing of the establishment of the Foundation and the entry into the contract with Odyssey, it is unlikely that there was any consultation with the Advisory Body.

Rule 2(a) is designed to accommodate contract archaeology whereby archaeological services are provided in exchange for payment. The UNESCO Manual for Activities Directed at Underwater Cultural Heritage states that all 'archaeological activity can be governed by commercial principles, as long as the activities are authorized in conformity with the Convention, and as long as the finds that belong to the site are not part of the commercial equation.'[197] Does the

---

194 Dobson, N.C. and Kingsley, S. 'HMS *Victory*, a First-Rate Royal Navy Warship Lost in the English Channel, 1744. Preliminary Survey and Investigation' in Stemm, G. and Kingsley, S. (eds), *Oceans Odyssey: Deep-Sea Shipwrecks in the English Channel, Straits of Gibraltar & Atlantic Ocean* (2010) 235, 239. This is not the *Victory* which was the flagship of Admiral Lord Nelson at the battle of Trafalgar.
195 <http://webarchive.nationalarchives.gov.uk/20121026065214/www.mod.uk/DefenceInternet/DefenceNews/PressCentre/PressReleases/0092012HmsVictory1744.htm>
196 Odyssey Marine Exploration, Press Release Archive, 2 Feb. 2012: <http://shipwreck.net/pr240.php>
197 <http://www.unesco.org/new/en/culture/themes/underwater-cultural-heritage/unesco-manual-for-activities-directed-at-underwater-cultural-heritage/unesco-manual/general-principles/commercial-exploitation/>

arrangement with Odyssey fit into this accommodation? Odyssey's preferred option is to be 'compensated in cash'. This would seem to suggest that Odyssey is simply a hired company performing a service for the Foundation. However, the latter has no funds and the chances of it obtaining sufficient funding to pay for the indicated work on the wreck and its contents is highly unlikely. That being the case, while it is set out as an alternative, both parties must be contemplating using the artefacts raised as compensation. This falls squarely within the terms of commercial exploitation. The artefacts are being bartered or exchanged for services rendered. What provision has been made for curation of the project archives – something that must be agreed before the project begins and be written into the project design?

Considering the contract in more detail, it states that 'Odyssey will receive the equivalent of 80% of the fair value of artefacts which were primarily used in trade or commerce' and further: 'For any private property including coins or other cargo administered through the Receiver of Wreck, the Foundation has agreed that Odyssey shall receive 80% of the value.' This incorporates the distinction Stemm made in his 2002 paper to the US Commission on Ocean Policy between trade goods and cultural artifacts. Odyssey has intimated that *Victory* was carrying a very substantial quantity of specie on behalf of merchants in Lisbon and elsewhere as well as prize money won by the captain and officers.[198] This seems to be based largely on conjecture and has been doubted by official sources.

As of 5th August 2013 the Government had not announced any decision on whether to authorize Odyssey to proceed with excavation. For the purposes of the above discussion, this is not relevant. It can fairly be claimed that, to date, all concerned have paid little attention to the Rules of the Annex.

COMMERCIAL EXPLOITATION IN OTHER CONTEXTS

The Convention is not the only document prohibiting commercial exploitation in dealings with underwater cultural heritage. For example, the Council of Europe has recommended that States be encouraged 'to ensure that the underwater cultural heritage is protected from commercial recovery operations from the high seas'.[199]

Non-governmental bodies whose role affects underwater cultural heritage have had the standard for many years. The Council of American Maritime Museums in 1987 adopted a by-law headed 'Archaeological Standards'. It reads:

> CAMM member institutions shall adhere to archaeological standards consistent with those of AAM ICOM and shall not knowingly acquire or exhibit artifacts which have been stolen, illegally exported from their countries of origin, illegally salvaged, or removed from commercially exploited archaeologically or historic sites in recent times.

That by-law has been adopted verbatim by the International Congress of Maritime Museums in a resolution on underwater archaeology at Barcelona in 1993. There it specifically states that member museums should follow the policy of the Council of American Maritime Museums; defining 'recent times' as since the 1990 full Congress of ICMM.[200] A commercially exploited site is said to be one 'in which the primary motive for investigation is private financial gain'.[201]

Another example comes from the Introduction to the ICOMOS Charter on the Protection and

---

198   Dobson, N.C. and Kingsley, S. 'HMS Victory, A First-Rate Royal Navy Warship Lost in the English Channel, 1744. Preliminary Survey and Identification' in Stemm, G. and Kingsley, S. (eds) *Oceans Odyssey: Deep-Sea Shipwrecks in the English Channel, Straits of Gibraltar & Atlantic Ocean* (Oxbow Books, Oxford, 2010) 235, 272.
199   Parliamentary Assembly, Council of Europe, Recommendation 1486 (2000): Maritime and Fluvial Cultural Heritage: <http://assembly.coe.int/Mainf.asp?link=/Documents/AdoptedText/ta00/EREC1486.htm>
200   <http://www.asia.si.edu/exhibitions/SW-CulturalHeritage/downloads/ICMMArchaeologyPolicy.pdf>
201   The ICMM resolution is reproduced at (1994) 2 *International Journal of Cultural Property* 308.

Management of Underwater Cultural Heritage (1996) which includes the following statement:

> Underwater cultural heritage is also threatened by activities that are wholly undesirable because they are intended to profit few at the expense of many. Commercial exploitation of underwater cultural heritage for trade or speculation is fundamentally incompatible with the protection and management of the heritage.[202]

Article 13 of the Charter emphasizes this: 'Underwater cultural heritage is not to be traded as items of commercial value'.

The International Council of Museums (ICOM) has a Code of Ethics for Museums.[203] Paragraph 7.2 lists the Convention as 'international legislation that is taken as a standard in interpreting' the Code. It further states that museum policy should acknowledge this. There are some 20,000 museums in ICOM which must follow this injunction.

Among non-specialist national organizations, the Museums Association in the United Kingdom has Ethical Guidelines on Acquisition which state that due diligence checks must be performed to ensure that there is no suspicion that an item may have been removed from a wreck[204] in contravention of international conventions on the protection of cultural property.

It cannot be argued that the prohibition against commercial exploitation in the Convention is an aberration. The above examples show that it is widespread, particularly in relation to the collecting and exhibition policy of museums.

IMPLICATIONS OF COMMERCIAL EXPLOITATION

If commercial exploitation has occurred, what are the implications? One is that the prohibition against engaging in this conduct establishes standards for implementation of the Convention by States Parties. For example, Article 14 of the Convention talks of 'recovery contrary to this Convention'.

> States Parties shall take measures to prevent the entry into their territory, the dealing in, or the possession of, underwater cultural heritage illicitly exported and/or recovered, where recovery is contrary to this Convention.

The implications of this paragraph have already been studied,[205] but it clearly covers recovery of underwater cultural heritage for the purpose of commercial exploitation. If this happens, States Parties are required to take the measures listed in Article 14 to deal with the situation. This has severe implications for transactions in the objects at issue.

Other Articles use the phrase 'in conformity with this Convention'. For example, Article 9 casts a general duty on all States Parties 'to protect underwater cultural heritage in the exclusive economic zone and on the continental shelf in conformity with this Convention'. Included within that would be the duty to prohibit commercial exploitation. Two other Articles of note are 16 and 18. The first obliges States Parties to take 'all practicable measures to ensure that their nationals and vessels flying their flag do not engage in any activity directed at underwater cultural heritage in a manner not in conformity with this Convention'. Article 18 is even more significant.

> Each State Party shall take measures providing for the seizure of underwater cultural heritage in its territory that has been recovered in a manner not in conformity with this Convention.

If the underwater cultural heritage has been recovered with the object of commercially exploiting it then it has not been recovered in conformity with the Convention.

Rule 2(b) dealing with commercial exploitation does not prevent 'the deposition of underwater cultural heritage, recovered in the course of a research project in conformity with this Convention

---

202 <http://www.icomos.org/charters/underwater_e.htm>
203 <http://icom.museum/who-we-are/the-vision/code-of-ethics.html>
204 Para. 4.2: <http://www.museumsassociation.org/download?id=11114>
205 Page 78 .

…'. This means that those objects not so recovered are outside the provisions of the Convention on deposition.[206] In other words they are subject to seizure under Article 18 and disposition by the State according to the provisions of that Article.

The prohibition against commercial exploitation is more than just a simple prohibition; it sets a standard against which activities directed at underwater cultural heritage are to be judged. That standard is clear and cannot be negotiated downward as into 'trade goods' and 'cultural artefacts'. States must implement it as it is.

But the prohibition is significant beyond what States do. It provides a measure by which organizations such as museums can assess their own activities. A museum may be offered a particularly fine or rare object from an underwater site for purchase, as a gift or for an exhibition. If the object comes from a commercially exploited site, it can pose a particularly difficult decision for all concerned – curators, senior management and the board of trustees. Thomas Hoving, then Director of the Metropolitan Museum of Art in New York, once wrote: 'The chase and the capture of a great work of art is one of the most exciting endeavours in life – as dramatic, emotional, and fulfilling as a love affair'.[207] Not all underwater cultural heritage will raise this degree of desire. But there is some that will, even if only available on loan.

In the ninth century an Arab dhow sank in what are now Indonesian waters. The dhow was discovered in 1998 by fishermen and reportedly was subject to looting. The Government of Indonesia issued a licence for salvage to a German company – Seabed Explorations GbR. In 1998 and 1999 a large quantity of glazed ceramics together with gold and silver vessels from the Tang Dynasty were raised. The contract between Seabed Explorations GbR and the Indonesian Government provided for an equal division of the proceeds of the excavation. In the end, the Indonesian Government asserted ownership of the Belitung wreck, as it is called, and cargo and transferred title to Seabed Explorations GbR for $2.5 million together with the return to Indonesia of objects raised from the Intan wreck excavated by Seabed Explorations in Indonesian waters. In 2005 most of the finds from the Belitung wreck were sold for $32 million to the Sentosa Leisure Group – a wholly-owned subsidiary of the Sentosa Development Corporation. This is a statutory board within the Singaporean Ministry of Trade and Industry.

The primary purpose of the Sentosa Leisure Group is the development for tourism of Sentosa Island – 'a theme-park like recreation island just south of the Singapore city centre'. There seems to have been little or no consideration of the way in which the collection was obtained or what would be done with it.[208] Singapore is not party to the Convention. Indeed, Singapore, almost alone in the world, is party to none of the international conventions dealing with cultural heritage matters. An exhibition – 'Shipwrecked – Tang Treasures and Monsoon Winds' – of part of the excavated material was opened at the Marina Bay Sands ArtScience Museum in Singapore in February 2011. This Museum is an attraction at a casino owned and operated by Las Vegas Sands Corporation of the United States.

The Singaporean authorities proposed a world tour for the exhibition. It would go first to the Freer and Sackler Galleries at the Smithsonian Institution in Washington. This proved highly controversial. It was criticized by the three major American archaeological associations and three of the internal research organizations at the Smithsonian Institution of which the Galleries are a part. The 'commercial exploitation' prohibition of the Annex was frequently quoted. The Smithsonian is not a member of ICOM but it is a member of the Council of American Maritime Museums. As we have seen, that Council's Code of Ethics states that member institutions shall not knowingly exhibit artefacts which have been removed from commercially exploited archaeological or historical sites and this policy has also been adopted by the International Congress of Maritime Museums. The Director of the Freer and Sackler Galleries is reported as

---

206   Page 150, 151.
207   Hoving, T. 'The Chase, the Capture' in Hoving, T. (ed.) *The Chase, the Capture: Collecting at the Metropolitan* (Metropolitan Museum of Art, New York, 1975) 1.
208   For example see the speech by Minister George Yeo at the launching of the exhibition 'Shipwrecked – Tang Treasures and Monsoon Winds' at the Marina Bay Sands ArtScience Museum, 18 Feb. 2011: <http://www.asia.si.edu/Shipwrecked/downloads/yeo021811.pdf>

saying: 'There are bound to be divergent opinions and I feel that the Smithsonian should not flinch from controversial exhibitions. It should use controversy to open debate'.[209] Many archaeologists and museum professionals believed that debate had already been held with the results reflected in Rule 2 of the Annex. Following the controversy, the Smithsonian is not proceeding with the exhibition. However, the door has been left open for a modified exhibition at some time in the future if certain concerns have been adequately addressed.

It seems clear that this should be regarded as a case of commercial exploitation. Both parties – Seabed Explorations GbR and the Indonesian Government – were intent on profiting from the cargo in accordance with the contract. It is further reinforced by the subsequent sale to the Singaporean entity. Other commentators have reached the same conclusion.

> According to the legal mechanisms then in place in Indonesia, no unlawful activity took place at Belitung. From an ethical perspective, however, the majority of the project cannot be described other than as commercial exploitation, which violates the ethos of archaeological best practice whether on land or underwater. Little of the Belitung project can be described as archaeological.[210]

The view has been expressed that this was a rare case where the excavator tried to keep the objects together as a collection and this should mitigate the effect of commercial exploitation.[211] However, the Convention allows for no exception. The various provisions adopted by non-governmental organizations also do not permit qualification. There will always be hard cases where arguments are made for the creation of an exception.

The exhibition of the Belitung wreck at the Smithsonian never eventuated and there was no public discussion of what would happen if it had gone ahead. In other cases this has been an issue. For example, if the museum is a member of one of the non-governmental organizations, is it feasible for the museum to be expelled? Would this be self-defeating?

The position taken by ICMM in 1993 was almost immediately confronted by the decision of the National Maritime Museum at Greenwich in England – a member museum – to stage an exhibition in 1994-95 of objects raised from the wreck of RMS *Titanic*. This had been found in 1985. Artefacts were raised in 1987, 1993 and 1994 by an American company – RMS Titanic Inc. In 1994, the US District Court for the Eastern District of Virginia ruled that R.M.S. Titanic Inc. (RMST) was salvor in possession of RMS *Titanic* on the understanding that all artifacts recovered would be kept as a collection, exhibited to the public and not sold or otherwise disposed of. The raising of the artefacts and their exhibition was highly controversial. The company insisted that the artefacts would not be sold. The Museum, a founding member of the Congress, threatened to withdraw from the ICMM if it were criticized. There was no public criticism and the Museum went ahead with the exhibition despite the opposition. It was hugely successful in terms of attendance figures. The official catalogue alleged that 'if RMS Titanic, Inc., and IFREMER were to stop work on the site, unscrupulous treasure hunters could take over'.[212] Afterwards the Museum held two seminars to study issues arising from the exploitation of shipwrecks. Whether the site of the *Titanic* was a 'commercially exploited heritage site' in terms of the Resolution of the International Congress of Maritime Museums was never determined.

Another incident involved the Merchant Marine Academy at Kings Point in the United States. It had accepted the gift of a boson's whistle said to be from the wreck of the *Atocha*. There was argument that the only sanction for violation of the by-law was expulsion from the organization.

---

209 Quoted in Pringle, H. 'Smithsonian Shipwreck Exhibit Draws Fire from Archaeologists' *Science Insider* 10 March 2011: <http://news.sciencemag.org/scienceinsider/2011/03/smithsonian-shipwreck-exhibit.html>

210 Leventhal, R.M. *et al*. '"Archaeology vs. Commercial Exploitation: How the Smithsonian Could Display Objects from the Belitung Shipwreck': <http://culturalheritagelaw.org/blog?mode=PostView&bmi=773188>

211 Gongaware, L. and Varmer, O. 'Public/Private Partnerships vs. 'Commercial Exploitation': The Belitung Shipwreck Controversy Continued': <http://www.culturalheritagelaw.org/blog?mode=PostView&bmi=739447>

212 G. Hutchinson, *The Wreck of the Titanic* (National Maritime Museum, London,1994) 47.

However, the Board of the Council of American Maritime Museums decided to send a letter to the museum pointing out the error and 'suggesting some remediation options'.[213]

Expulsion from the organization is not really a viable tool for ensuring compliance. If the museum is an important one, the organization may well suffer more from its departure than the museum itself. If it is not so important, the museum may feel that it is being bullied and conduct a public relations campaign on that basis. The low key approach suggested by the CAMM Board is most likely to achieve results. An official letter pointing out the failure to comply with policy could be sent. It might request that the history of the object, including its commercial exploitation, be spelt out in all documentation made by the museum including exhibition labels. A more severe reprimand would be to make the transgression public by judicious stories released to the media.

THE TITANIC AND COMMERCIAL EXPLOITATION

The *Titanic* has already been mentioned in reference to the National Maritime Museum exhibition in 1994-95 and the attempt by RMST to exclude all third parties from the site, especially any recording images of the wreck. The court had established RMST was salvor of the *Titanic* but not owner of the artefacts raised. The company earned an income from exhibiting them. However, by 2001 the company considered it was no longer earning enough money from exhibitions, sale of coal raised from the site, tourism and sale of visual images. It came up with a scheme to sell the artefacts it had raised to a specially created non-profit foundation and to various museums. The court refused permission to sell the artefacts as it was concerned that the same person was head of both RMST and the Foundation and that the latter's board of directors was filled with his relatives, friends and business associates. Then the company declared it needed more artefacts for new exhibitions. It proposed to obtain these by making a 'surgical incision' into the vessel. The Court would not allow this.

Over the years, RMST has had significant changes in management and ownership. In 2004 it became a wholly-owned subsidiary of Premier Exhibitions Inc. which organizes touring exhibitions. It currently runs exhibitions of artefacts from the Titanic and other exhibitions displaying cadavers preserved through plastination. Some 46 per cent of the shares in Premier are held by Sellers Capital LLC which, a report of November 2010 says, wanted out of the company. The only way it could do this was to 'monetize the *Titanic*'.[214]

The award of salvage rights to RMST was conditioned on the artefacts raised being kept together as a collection, exhibited to the public and not sold. This was based on an attempt by courts in the United States of America to expand the reach of salvage law, and therefore their own jurisdiction, to accommodate the special interests of historic wrecks.

> In this 'historical salvage' case, the Court finds that it is desirable to keep these artifacts together for the public display and, therefore, traditional salvage rights must be expanded for those who properly take on the responsibility of historic preservation.[215]

As we have seen, RMST attempted on a number of occasions to avoid this undertaking.

Against this background, in 2010 the court granted RMST a salvage award in the amount of 100 per cent of the value of the artefacts recovered during six dives on the wreck. No buyer having come forward, in 2011 RMST was granted ownership of the artefacts subject to covenants and conditions.[216] Basically, these required the artefacts, if disposed of, to be sold as a collection

---

213   Cohn, A.B. 'The Council of American Maritime Museums (CAMM) and a Re-examination of Its Role in the Protection of Underwater Cultural Heritage' paper delivered at CAMM Annual Meeting, Maine, 26 Sept. 2002: <http://www.acuaonline.org/assets/2010/09/21/1e6ffe7fa278adefe056b58525609f97.pdf>

214   <http://www.mlive.com/business/west-michigan/index.ssf/2010/11/grand_rapids_bar_owner_mark_se.html>

215   *RMS Titanic v. Wreck* [1996] American Maritime Cases 2497, 2499.

216   Aznar, M.J. and Varmer, O. 'The *Titanic* as Underwater Cultural Heritage: Challenges to its Legal International Protection' (2013) 44 *Ocean Development and International Law* 96. A critical review of the 'Covenants and Conditions', particularly from the point of view of English law, is

to a person who agreed to keep them together as a collection and available to the public. The collection was to be sold in April 2012 but not in a typical auction. Bidders had to submit their bids to Guernsey's, the auction house chosen by Premier Exhibitions. All bids would be reviewed. Guernsey's would then contact the leading bidders for further discussion, after which the winning bidder would be determined and announced. No announcement has been made, but there has been progress on the matter. The judge ordered a hearing on 29th November 2012 in Norfolk in regards to the status of the company and its potential sale or transfer of the collection.

Is this commercial exploitation? The artefacts were raised prior to the coming into force of the Convention. However, in view of the adoption of the principle by international organizations and museums it has been relevant since at least 1987. To make the sale of the *Titanic* artefacts subject to terms and conditions laid down by the US Government is laudable. However, it is still a sale and sales are in contravention of the prohibition on commercial exploitation.

RULE 3

> Activities directed at underwater cultural heritage shall not adversely affect the underwater cultural heritage more than is necessary for the objectives of the project.

Commentary: Rule 3 is a reminder that there should be minimal interference with underwater cultural heritage consistent with achieving the objectives sought. It is unlikely that a project would be approved to study only artifacts carried by a vessel without regard to information which might be provided by study of the hull. Incidental destruction of the hull or remaining ship's timbers to facilitate removal of artifacts would normally not be permitted.

RULE 4

> Activities directed at underwater cultural heritage must use nondestructive techniques and survey methods in preference to recovery of objects. If excavation or recovery is necessary for the purpose of scientific studies or for the ultimate protection of the underwater cultural heritage, the methods and techniques used must be as non-destructive as possible and contribute to the preservation of the remains.

Commentary: This Rule reflects Article 5 of the ICOMOS Charter for the Protection and Management of the Archaeological Heritage:

> It must be an overriding principle that the gathering of information about the archaeological heritage should not destroy any more archaeological evidence than is necessary for the protectional [sic] or scientific objectives of the investigation. Non-destructive techniques, aerial and ground survey, and sampling should therefore be encouraged wherever possible, in preference to total excavation.

There are of course great differences between what can be done on land compared to under water. But even in the latter context, new techniques and devices are being developed that can make it easier to investigate underwater cultural heritage without disturbing its equilibrium with its surrounds.[217]

Archaeological excavation is destruction in that the site is destroyed in order to extract the information and artefacts it contains. It can be done only once. The only things that are left are the artefacts and the documentary records. Consequently, if procedures less destructive than excavation can answer the questions being asked, then they should be used. Excavation may be necessary to answer particular questions or to save material from a threatened site. Even then it should cause the least amount of destruction possible which means that the material excavated must be thoroughly investigated, results established and then preserved. Documentation and records must be made to the highest standards.

RULE 5

---

to be found in Stevenson, P. 'A Titanic Struggle: An Update. Salvage Beyond the Scope of the UNESCO Underwater Cultural Heritage Convention' (2011) XVI *Art Antiquity and Law* 305.

[217] Quinn, R. *et al*. 'The Mary Rose Site – Geophysical Evidence for Palaeo-scour Marks' (1997) 26 *International Journal of Nautical Archaeology* 3.

> Activities directed at underwater cultural heritage shall avoid the unnecessary disturbance of human remains or venerated sites.

Commentary: The purpose of this Rule is different from Article 2(9) which was aimed at achieving proper respect for human remains.[218] Rule 5 is an injunction to those who carry out activities directed at underwater cultural heritage. They are to avoid disturbance of human remains unless it is necessary. In many cases this will only be when excavation is to take place. Then it could be necessary because the remains are an integral part of the site which cannot be excavated without disturbing them.

Venerated sites may be the graves of people who went down with a particular ship such as RMS *Titanic* or warships such as HMS *Hood*. There were suggestions during the negotiations that cases where there had been large-scale loss of life should receive special treatment in the opening Articles of the Underwater Convention, but for war graves this failed for the reasons given above.[219]

Venerated sites may also be those having a spiritual attachment for certain peoples such as Aborigines or First Peoples. Others may have close connections with such indigenous peoples. For example, certain worked objects lie on a plateau alongside the Channel of Many Ghosts near Moorea, a sister island of Tahiti. One report is that these are votive offerings made either before the Christianization of the Island or after, as a substitute for rites outlawed on the *marae*.[220]

There was considerable debate over the possible inclusion in Article 1(a) of the Underwater Convention of a Paragraph (iii) listing 'sites with spiritual associations for indigenous peoples'. Although strongly supported by Australia and Canada, it was questioned by some other States which were disturbed by the possibility that a site might have no distinguishing physical characteristic. The proposal was withdrawn just before the vote at the last moments of the Fourth Meeting of Governmental Experts in July 2001.

However, through Rule 5 it still survives as a factor to be taken into account in activities directed at underwater cultural heritage. For example, there are cases in Australia where wrecks have become havens for fish. Aborigines, hunting the fish, have incorporated the sites into their 'dreaming' thus giving them spiritual significance. Dreaming stories pass on important knowledge, cultural values and belief systems to later generations. Through song, dance, painting and storytelling which express the dreaming stories, Aborigines have maintained a link with the dreaming from ancient times to today, creating a rich cultural heritage.

> Thousands of years of rising sea levels have meant that many old burial grounds and sites have been submerged. Places of aesthetic value in land or sea country may include places that are underwater today, but were used as places to meet, eat, gather etc when sea levels were lower. They may have rock art and/or shell middens associated with them, and may also include places that people look to from the land. Places of aesthetic value are likely to be used in similar ways today (i.e. for meeting, eating, gathering etc.) and may occur on land or in sea. For some Traditional Owner groups, the Great Barrier Reef and lagoon contain a large number of heritage sites and cultural places that are presently underwater.[221]

Rule 6

> Activities directed at underwater cultural heritage shall be strictly regulated to ensure proper recording of cultural, historical and archaeological information.

Commentary: The precise effect of this Rule is difficult to establish. Certain Articles of the Underwater Convention require that in the matters they cover there be conformity with the

---

218   Page 42.
219   Page 43.
220   Veccella, R. 'The Gran Underwater Inventory of French Polynesia' in Prott, L.V. (ed.) *Finishing the Interrupted Voyage* (UNESCO/Institute of Art and Law; Paris/Builth Wells; 2006) 77, 79.
221   <http://onboard.gbrmpa.gov.au/home/marine_park/what_makes_the_reef_special/indigenous_heritage_in_the_great_barrier_reef_world_heritage_area> accessed 13 Aug.2013.

Convention or with the Rules. Rule 6 is not capable in itself of establishing that activities directed at underwater cultural heritage shall be strictly regulated. This is clearly the responsibility of States. The desirability of proper recording of cultural, historical and archaeological information cannot be doubted but the Rule itself cannot achieve this without the power of the State.

RULE 7

> Public access to *in situ* underwater cultural heritage shall be promoted, except where such access is incompatible with protection and management.

Commentary: This Rule recalls the Preamble and Paragraph 10 of Article 2. Encouragement of public access is seen as a goal of the Underwater Convention because underwater cultural heritage ultimately is protected for the benefit of the public. Thoughtful persons would acknowledge that sometimes access has to be regulated or, in extreme cases, prohibited. But such steps must not be taken lightly. An excess of protective zeal is as bad as no protection.

RULE 8

> International cooperation in the conduct of activities directed at underwater cultural heritage shall be encouraged in order to further the effective exchange or use of archaeologists and other relevant professionals.

Commentary: There are relatively few underwater archaeologists working full time at their chosen profession. The same is not true of other professionals such as conservators, although even their numbers are insufficient. But world-wide there is an imbalance in the location of such professionals, with the great majority coming from the developed world. The degree of expertise in managing sites and working on material from them can be much better utilized if there is co-operation between States in the conduct of activities directed at underwater cultural heritage. States can best assist by encouraging existing links and developing new ones between institutions. One of many examples of co-operative research at institutional level is that between the Western Australian Maritime Museum and the Museum of Overseas Communication History, China, under which Australian archaeologists made a number of visits to study a wreck at Houzhou as part of a co-operative China-Australia research and training programme.[222] This may be seen as another example of training and technology transfer under Article 21.

---

[222] Green, J., Burningham, N. and Museum of Overseas Communication History 'The Ship frpm Quanzhou, Fujian Province, People's Republic of China' (1998) 27 *International Journal of Nautical Archaeology* 277.

II. Project Design

Rule 9

> Prior to any activity directed at underwater cultural heritage, a project design for the activity shall be developed and submitted to the competent authorities for authorization and appropriate peer review.

Commentary: Given the objectives of the Underwater Convention, any activity directed at underwater cultural heritage must ensure its protection. This is best achieved if the goals of the activity and the methods by which these are to be achieved are thoroughly thought out before any action takes place. The project design is the outcome of these deliberations. According to the Rule, it has to be submitted to the competent authority, designated under Article 22, of the State empowered to issue authorizations under Article 10 in respect of the EEZ and continental shelf or Article 12 in respect of the Area. It is unclear from Rule 9 when the 'appropriate peer review' should occur but logically this should be before authorization is sought.

In archaeological practice as exemplified by the ICOMOS *Charter for the Protection and Management of the Archaeological Heritage*, excavation should take place in only two circumstances: firstly, where a site is threatened by 'development, land-use change, looting, or natural deterioration'; secondly, 'unthreatened sites may be excavated to elucidate research problems or to interpret them more effectively for the purpose of presenting them to the public'.[223] Preparation of the project design should take these guidelines into account.

Rule 10

> The project design shall include:
> (a) an evaluation of previous or preliminary studies;
> (b) the project statement and objectives;
> (c) the methodology to be used and the techniques to be employed;
> (d) the anticipated funding;
> (e) an expected timetable for completion of the project;
> (f) the composition of the team and the qualifications, responsibilities and experience of each team member;
> (g) plans for post-fieldwork analysis and other activities;
> (h) a conservation programme for artifacts and the site in close cooperation with the competent authorities;
> (i) a site management and maintenance policy for the whole duration of the project;
> (j) a documentation programme;
> (k) a safety policy;
> (l) an environmental policy;
> (m) arrangements for collaboration with museums and other institutions, in particular scientific institutions;
> (n) report preparation;
> (o) deposition of archives, including underwater cultural heritage removed; and
> (p) a programme for publication.

Commentary: Rule 10 sets out the basic structure for a project design. It is not exclusive and there would be nothing against adding additional requirements in a particular case. The structure is a logical progression for the conduct of activities directed at underwater cultural heritage. It enables the authorities to determine that the site will be properly treated and the information obtained recorded and distributed. The individual requirements for a project design are explained and expanded in the following Rules of the Annex.

Rule 11

> Activities directed at underwater cultural heritage shall be carried out in accordance with the project design approved by the competent authorities.

---

223   Article 5.

Commentary: Once the project design has been approved by the authorities responsible for this under the Underwater Convention, it must be performed according to its terms. This Rule is in the imperative in order to make sure that persons working on activities directed at underwater cultural heritage do not indulge their own interests at the expense of others. For example, it is not unknown for specialists in one era or civilization to ignore others outside their interests when excavating.

Rule 12

> Where unexpected discoveries are made or circumstances change, the project design shall be reviewed and amended with the approval of the competent authorities.

Commentary: Notwithstanding what was said above, it may sometimes be necessary to depart from the project design. For example, authorization may have been given for the survey of a particular site. During the course of this it begins to appear that there may be a second wreck on the same site. It might be necessary to remove part of the first to establish this, an action which would require amendment of the project design and approval by the authorities.

Rule 13

> In cases of urgency or chance discoveries, activities directed at the underwater cultural heritage, including conservation measures or activities for a period of short duration, in particular site stabilization, may be authorized in the absence of a project design in order to protect the underwater cultural heritage.

Commentary: The Underwater Convention establishes when authorization is needed for activities directed at underwater cultural heritage and which State has the power to give it. Under Rule 13, that State can issue an authorization for the conduct of such activities in the absence of a project design where there is an emergency or a chance discovery provided this is for the protection of the heritage. For example, where the chance discovery is of something the location of which may be lost if time is allowed to pass. Site stabilization is specifically mentioned. This may be necessary if a site has been exposed by a change in currents.

III. Preliminary Work

Rule 14

> The preliminary work referred to in Rule 10 (a) shall include an assessment that evaluates the significance and vulnerability of the underwater cultural heritage and the surrounding natural environment to damage by the proposed project, and the potential to obtain data that would meet the project objectives.

Commentary: Rule 13 essentially requires those preparing the project design to begin by making an assessment of the benefits sought against the damage that will be caused. This includes not only damage to the underwater cultural heritage but also to the natural environment in which the heritage exists. The assessment normally will be based on certain assumptions. For example, the true significance of a wreck may not be evident until work has been done on the site and its identity established. As regards the anticipated data, researchers will be looking to justify their activities directed at the underwater cultural heritage. It can be anticipated that the benefits will be well presented and the advantages stressed.

Rule 15

> The assessment shall also include background studies of available historical and archaeological evidence, the archaeological and environmental characteristics of the site, and the consequences of any potential intrusion for the long-term stability of the underwater cultural heritage affected by the activities.

Commentary: The Underwater Convention as a whole stresses the preservation of underwater cultural heritage *in situ* as a first option. Any potential intrusion on a site must be measured against that benchmark. Consequently, all available information must be collected and analysed as part of the assessment. Of course, this will depend on the site. Historical information will not be available for a wreck which is unidentified and whose nationality is not known. Archaeological evidence would have to come from previous activities on the site. However, in some cases, there is substantial archival material such as the Archivo de las Indias in Seville and the Netherlands Royal Archives in The Hague.

Study of the environment of the site is essential. Where a wreck, for example, has reached a stage of equilibrium, a change in the environment may well upset this and restart deterioration. Such a change may also cause damage of a more aggressive nature such as change in currents leading to scouring of the site.

IV. Project Objective, Methodology and Techniques

Rule 16

> The methodology shall comply with the project objectives, and the techniques employed shall be as non-intrusive as possible.

Commentary: Non-intrusive techniques are those which do not disturb the site. Basically this means survey, which can be an end in itself if it answers research questions posed in the project design. It can also provide much information as a basis for future work on the site if this is found to be necessary. For example, a survey may indicate what type of material or type of information is likely to be encountered thus allowing estimates to be made regarding funding: decisions on the experts that will be needed and the conservation facilities required.

Survey is the careful recording of accurate observations and measurements. There are various methods for doing this which are beyond the scope of this comment but can be found in textbooks on underwater archaeological investigation. The actual methods used will depend in the first place on the site. For example, setting up grids will be almost impossible on a site where the seabed is in constant motion.

V. Funding

Rule 17

> Except in cases of emergency to protect underwater cultural heritage, an adequate funding base shall be assured in advance of any activity, sufficient to complete all stages of the project design, including conservation, documentation and curation of recovered artifacts, and report preparation and dissemination.

Commentary: The cost of underwater archaeology will depend on what activity is planned and the location of the site. On the one hand, a survey in calm waters with good visibility using volunteer divers would generally cost very little. An excavation in deep waters with a full team of professionals would be very expensive – some mention US$75,000 per day. But, whatever the activity, Rule 17 requires that funding be established before any work takes place. Too often have projects proceeded without the necessary funding with the result that they have come to a halt part way to completion or the work has been defective. For example, in the eyes of the Irish courts the team that discovered the Armada wrecks – *La Lavia, Juliana* and *Santa Maria de la Vision* – off Sligo did excellent work in making the discovery and preliminary surveys. However, they had made no provision for future work or conservation – thinking that some of the cannon from the site might be sold for this purpose. In refusing a licence for continued work on the site, the Irish authorities said:

> The reason for this decision is that the conservation facilities and other resources available to the State at present would not be adequate to deal with the amount and range of archaeological material that is likely to be recovered from the wrecks in question and in the absence of such facilities and resources, it would not be in the public interest that the wrecks should be interfered with.[224]

Another example is provided by the history of what happened to the wreck of the first HMS *Invincible* which sank in 1758 and was discovered in 1976. The finders obtained a licence to investigate from the UK Government.

> Conservation would prove to be a considerable – and very expensive – part of the undertaking, as the next decade's surveys and excavations produced a vast and diverse array of equipment, stores, and personal effects. The Chatham Historic Dockyard Trust acquired representative examples of the finds in exchange for funding part of the conservation, but the project was never backed by a major museum or public institution. ICL was left with the challenge of preserving and maintaining everything else. In a move that stunned and dismayed archaeologists around the world, ICL's directors raised £64,000 for the project by auctioning 298 items at Christie's in 1988. Bingeman withdrew from the company around this time, and three years later ICL folded. More artifacts were then sold via the internet to pay off creditors.[225]

It may be alleged that requiring funding in advance will make it more difficult to conduct activities directed at underwater cultural heritage. For example, salvors have often relied on raising funds from shareholders; the sale of artifacts such as was envisaged in the case above or a combination of the two. The first carries notorious risks because, once the initial offering is made, shareholders will be unlikely to contribute further funds unless there is something to attract them. The sale of artefacts will fall under Rule 2 and the issues discussed there. The American company, RMS Titanic Inc., has experienced major financial problems over the course

---

[224] Letter quoted in the official transcript of the decision of Barr J. in the High Court of Admiralty of Ireland in *King and Chapman v. The Owners and All Persons Claiming an Interest in the 'La Lavia', 'Juliana' and 'Santa Maria de la Vision'*, 26 July 1994.

[225] Crisman, K. review of Bingeman, J.M. 'The First HMS *Invincible* (1747-58): her excavations (1980 – 1991)' in 2001 (40) *International Journal of Nautical Archaeology* 455, 456.

of its life. In 1996 it was said to have lost US$9.8 million since its inception.[226] Then its situation improved and the 1999 report indicated it had $3 million in cash but by 2001 that had dropped to $600,000.

Funding may come from both public and private sources. Robert Grenier, former President of the ICOMOS International Scientific Committee for the Underwater Cultural Heritage, illustrated this with reference to numerous examples. Although written in 2001 his comments are just as relevant today:

> Public funding has been, and continues to be central to some of the most extensive 'history learning' ... projects all around the world, including those in the United States. At the moment, two of the most exciting underwater archaeology projects in the world are conducted in the United States: the publicly-funded *H.L. Hunley* (1864) project, and the excavation of Louis Quatorze's ship *La Belle* (1683) a Texas state-funded project started during Governor W. Bush's governorship. These are truly and completely what you call 'history learning' projects, with no demonstrated equivalent in the private sector, now or anytime in the past. One has also to remember the late 1970s publicly funded project on the *San Esteban*, off the coast of Padre Island, Texas. ...
>
> But also non-profit, privately funded organizations have run, and continue to run outstanding projects around the world. One of the largest and most famous is perhaps the excavation in England of the *Mary Rose*, 1545, which began in the late 1970s. Several non-profit, privately funded projects are going on in Argentina. A large project is now taking place in Sri Lanka, with various sources of non-profit funding. But the most famous and longest running program of non-profit funded projects remain the United States based operations of Dr. George Bass' Institute of Nautical Archaeology, based in College Station, Texas. Some of the Institute's work is on wrecks off the coast of Turkey, some of which have been surviving *in situ* for thousands of years. These are true 'history learning projects', involving much more than the careful recovery of random objects ...; they are run with mostly American know-how, with mostly American private funding. And this outstanding American achievement and contribution to the world's maritime history has been going on for over forty years, since the early 1960s. As you can see, private funding *per se* does not run counter to this Convention, as long as it is not for profit through the selling of objects and/or through the dispersal of collections.[227]

A significant aspect of Rule 17 is that funding has to be secured in advance for report preparation and dissemination. Often this is seen as the orphan child of the archaeological process. No attention is paid to it until the work has been done, at which stage it is viewed as unglamorous and difficult to attract attention from donors. However, if the information is not preserved for the benefit of the public and is accessible to them, the site has been destroyed to no purpose and only a few individuals have had any advantage from an irreplaceable part of the heritage. Those who excavate without preserving and analyzing information from the site are in the same category as treasure seekers.

RULE 18

> The project design shall demonstrate an ability, such as by securing a bond, to fund the project through to completion.

Commentary: Rule 18 indicates that the availability of funding is not to be seen as a matter of hope or exaggerated expectation. Funding must be arranged during the course of establishing the project design. This does not mean that there has to be cash in hand. Undertakings backed by legal guarantees are sufficient.

---

226   Evidence of George Tullock, then President of the company, quoted by the Court in *RMS Titanic v. Wrecked and Abandoned Vessel* 924 F.Supp. 714 (1996) 717.
227   Copy of letter dated 19 Oct. 2001 on file with the author.

Rule 19
>The project design shall include a contingency plan that will ensure conservation of underwater cultural heritage and supporting documentation in the event of any interruption of anticipated funding.

Commentary: Preparing such a contingency plan may be difficult as it will not be known when there may be an interruption of the anticipated funding and how much conservation may be required. When the interruption occurs would be important because it will determine how much of the funding is left as well as the amount of conservation required. For example, if it occurs late in the projected timetable, available funds will probably be small and, if there has been excavation, conservation will be needed for a body of artefacts. It might be possible to indicate in the project design funding provisions that, if there is such an interruption, funds on hand will be immediately devoted to conservation and mitigation.

VI. Project Duration – Timetable

Rule 20

> An adequate timetable shall be developed to assure in advance of any activity directed at underwater cultural heritage the completion of all stages of the project design, including conservation, documentation and curation of recovered underwater cultural heritage, as well as report preparation and dissemination.

Commentary: A timetable is a most useful device for ensuring that everyone knows what is to occur and when. Of course, no timetable can be followed absolutely. There will inevitably be occurrences beyond the ability of anyone to control that will lead to delay. This must be accepted as the normal course of events. But the timetable should be drawn up as best as can be, foreseeing all eventualities. All should have the intention to follow it.

Rule 20 specifically mentions two matters for inclusion in the timetable that are often overlooked or left to the last minute, or longer. These are 'report preparation and dissemination'. They are discussed further under Rules 30 and 35 respectively. Suffice it here to say that sufficient time must be spent on this aspect of the timetable to ensure that publication is not forgotten once the fieldwork has been completed and personnel have returned to their universities, government departments or other occupations. A rule of thumb commonly mentioned is that the time allowed for report preparation and publication should be three times that for fieldwork, particularly excavation.

Rule 21

> The project design shall include a contingency plan that will ensure conservation of underwater cultural heritage and supporting documentation in the event of any interruption or termination of the project.

Commentary: Rule 21 obviously relates to Rule 19. While the latter tries to ensure funding, the former provides the practical steps to be taken to ensure conservation. This would require consultation with institutions and other bodies capable of providing what could be long-term facilities needed for care of the underwater cultural heritage and documentation. Episodes have occurred in the United States of America which illustrate what happens when such arrangements are not in place.

> A disturbing new trend has surfaced in the United States, wherein salvors who have obtained permits to recover artifacts from significant shipwrecks later lose interest or financing before completing their projects, and simply abandon the ships and associated artifacts of little monetary value. This has happened in the state of Delaware with the wreck of the 18th-century British warship *De Braak*, and in Massachusetts with the so-called *General Arnold*, attributed to the Revolutionary period. Ownership of both these wreck assemblages, which include large hull sections requiring extensive conservation, have reverted to the respective states, which are now forced to manage these resources without dedicated funding or staffing commitments.[228]

It could well be disastrous for both the heritage and any institution involved if it were suddenly presented with costly conservation and curation.

---

[228] Johnston, P.F. 'Treasure Salvage, Archaeological Ethics and Maritime Museums' (1993) 22 *International Journal of Nautical Archaeology* 53, 57.

VII. COMPETENCE AND QUALIFICATIONS

RULE 22

> Activities directed at underwater cultural heritage shall only be undertaken under the direction and control of, and in the regular presence of, a qualified underwater archaeologist with scientific competence appropriate to the project.

Commentary: Rules 22 and 23 recognize the role that may be played by persons who have competence in the field of underwater archaeology but no relevant academic qualifications and may well have spent most of their time in completely different occupations. Sometimes they are referred to as 'amateurs' but may in their own right have a great deal of knowledge and much practical experience. The two Rules in effect recognize the right of public access stressed in the Preamble and Article 2 of the Underwater Convention.

Rule 22 ensures that whatever activities are directed at underwater cultural heritage they must be under the direction and control of a qualified underwater archaeologist. Moreover, that archaeologist must himself or herself be appropriately qualified for the project. For example, an expert in medieval submerged harbour fortifications in Europe should not be working on the excavation of a colonial era wreck site in Asia. The concept of a 'qualified underwater archaeologist' is not established. At the least it should mean a person who has a degree in archaeology with a specialization in underwater archaeology and who is qualified to dive. But academic qualifications are not enough for a person who is to be in charge of the project. He or she must have practical experience of administering projects of similar size or larger and a proven track record of successful completion of the work including preparation and publication of reports.

The qualified underwater archaeologist is to direct and control the activities. The precise role of the archaeologist has long been controversial, particularly in relation to historic ship salvaging. The independence of the archaeologist in these circumstances has been questioned. Archaeologists themselves have spoken of the pressures they work under. Mathewson wrote a master's thesis in anthropology in which he states regarding work on the site of the *Nuestra Señora de Atocha*:

> There were, of course, countless disappointments and many difficulties to overcome in the data-gathering process. Many times it was impossible to get essential information because of the shortage of time, equipment breakdown or other operational difficulties. Often data were unreliable and had to be discarded. Other times it was impossible to get the divers to record data consistently enough to recognize incipient patterning.[229]

Jeremy Green writes of the position in these terms:

> Commercial salvage companies are going to be driven by profits, not archaeology. Any archaeologist becoming involved in salvage will be faced with the reality that objects are only going to be recovered if they have an economic value. Hence the stern of the Belitung wreck still lies on the sea-bed.[230]

Where the Rules apply, the matter of control is now beyond doubt. It is firmly in the hands of the qualified underwater archaeologist.

The archaeologist has to be present on a regular basis. In its unreported judgment of 18th November 1993 the Virginia District Court in the *Colombus America* case stated that a number

---

[229] Mathewson, R.D. *Archaeological Treasure: The Search for Nuestra Señora de Atocha* (Seafarers Heritage Library, Woodstock, Vt. 1983) 112.

[230] Green, J. review of Krahl, R. *el al.* (eds) *Shipwrecked: Tang Treasures and Monsoon Winds* (Smithsonian Institution, Washington, 2010) in (2011) 40 *International Journal of Nautical Archaeology* 449, 452.

of experts were aboard the search vessel 'from time to time'. The court seemed to regard this as satisfactory. 'On a regular basis' would seem to require more. The UNESCO Manual states that the project director should always be present on site unless he or she has a 'significant reason' not to be. This seems a sensible interpretation of the Rule and one that is long overdue.

> The bottom line is that the responsibility for the intervention and its results lies with the project director. The archaeologist thus controls the work being executed. He or she must be on site to ensure that the project is undertaken to the appropriate standard and according to the agreed project design.[231]

RULE 23

> All persons on the project team shall be qualified and have demonstrated competence appropriate to their roles in the project.

Commentary: Rule 23 would allow persons who have no formal qualifications but a basic knowledge of archaeological techniques to work on the project. The work would have to be appropriate to their ability and they would be working under supervision. This permits the use of divers who regard such activities as a pastime provided they have undertaken training in what will be required of them. Moreover, as Greene points out: 'An excavation is an ideal place for students or individuals to learn new techniques and skills'.[232]

---

[231] Maarleveld, T.J.; Guérin, U. and Egger, B. (eds) *Manual for Activities Directed at Underwater Cultural Heritage: Guidelines to the Annex of the UNESCO 2001 Convention* (UNESCO, Paris, 2013) 172.

[232] Green, J. Review of Palmer, R. 'Underwater Expeditions' (1988) 17 *International Journal of Nautical Archaeology and Underwater Exploration* 276, 277.

VIII. Conservation and Site Management

Rule 24

> The conservation programme shall provide for the treatment of the archaeological remains during the activities directed at underwater cultural heritage, during transit and in the long term. Conservation shall be carried out in accordance with current professional standards.

Commentary: Rule 24 stresses that conservation is a continuing process. It begins when the first interference is made at the site and never really ends. Certain materials begin to decay as soon as the equilibrium they have obtained is disturbed. Conservation must begin then as decay can be extremely fast. Even when the object has been stabilized and placed in a collection, its state of conservation must be monitored and remedial action taken if necessary. This may well be a costly process extended indefinitely.

An example of a lengthy conservation process is that of the legendary *Mary Rose*. Excavated between 1979 and 1982, off Portsmouth, England, from 1983 to 1996 the hull was constantly sprayed with chilled fresh water keeping the timbers below 5 degrees centigrade. Polyethylene glycol was then sprayed on from 1996 to 2006. The hull is currently undergoing air drying scheduled to finish in 2016 when the major phases of the conservation programme will be completed. The conservation will thus have taken 33 years.[233]

It may be difficult to establish 'current professional standards' on an international basis. Are these the standards applying in the best equipped laboratory in the most advanced and wealthy States? Who ascertains what these standards are and by what means? No guidance is given for these questions. The best approach would be to aim for the most effective process of conservation available considering the circumstances. For a shipwreck of significant historical or other value, it may be wise to consult conservation laboratories which have developed specialised treatments and can assess whether this would be effective for the newly found wreck. Such treatments are time consuming and resource intensive and it is important to get the best possible outcome for the site concerned.

Rule 25

> The site management programme shall provide for the protection and management in situ of underwater cultural heritage, in the course of and upon termination of fieldwork. The programme shall include public information, reasonable provision for site stabilization, monitoring, and protection against interference.

Commentary: The first sentence of this Rule is intended to deal with what happens to material that is not raised during the project or is raised but returned to the site after study. For example, at Red Bay in Labrador, Parks Canada excavated a Basque whaling vessel. It was disassembled, raised for recording and then systematically reburied as the cost of long-term conservation was prohibitive.

> The most obvious possibility is to leave the timbers on the bottom and to seal them as anaerobically as possible. ... During the reburial, steps were taken to ensure that timbers could periodically be recovered for testing and the reburial environment could also be analysed.[234]

Rule 25 stresses that the site must be fully protected during both fieldwork and afterwards.

Public information is essential. Not only does the public have a right to know what is being done

---

233 Dobbs, C. 'Interpreting and Displaying The *Mary Rose* to the Public in a New Museum' in *International Meeting on the Protection, Presentation and Valorisation of Underwater Cultural Heritage* – Chongqing, China (23 - 27 Nov. 2010) p. 341, 346: <http://www.unesco.org/culture/underwater/pdf/uch_publication_chine_en.pdf>

234 Waddell, P.J.A. 'Long Range Shipwreck Timber Storage' (1994) 18 *Bulletin of the Australian Institute for Maritime Archaeology* 1.

to its heritage, but it is also necessary to relieve possible misunderstandings and, at the same time, expound on the values of underwater cultural heritage.

The remaining requirements in Rule 25 relate to what happens following fieldwork.

> When a survey or excavation has come to an end the site does not suddenly develop an ability to take care of itself! Responsibility does not end with the project. You have changed the site, perhaps making it more vulnerable. Other workers may wish to investigate the site in the future and whether or not the material survives to that date should not be left totally to chance. No one can halt the march of time or prevent large scale changes in the environment, but keeping a check on the state of a site might allow some potentially damaging processes to be mitigated thus preserving more of the evidence contained in the remains.[235]

Sites that have stable conditions are easily disturbed by fieldwork which involves any interference with them. This may upset their stability which can be mitigated by observing what is happening and taking steps to reduce the impact. What steps are taken will depend on the circumstances and the imagination of those responsible. The process begins by a close examination and recording of the site followed by regular visits to see what changes have taken place and then the introduction of measures to prevent further change or to reverse what has occurred. For example, some sites may be stabilized by the placement of sandbags in appropriate spots whereas others may require more elaborate methods.

The fieldwork may actually have been carried out to ascertain the effect on a site of external changes. One of the many examples occurred in Spain when the construction of a marina changed the coastal dynamics, stripping the seabed in a bay and exposing the remains of a seventh-century Phoenician vessel and its cargo.

> In 1991, a short programme was carried out for the immediate protection of the remains as the coastal dynamics of the area continued to be unstable. In this programme, two 1 m² soundings were carried out, one at each end of the wooden structure, and Phoenician ceramics associated with the structure were observed. Later, the remains were given a protective coating of successive layers of sand, mesh and gravel.[236]

Although this was in Spanish internal or territorial waters, the same necessity to deal with the situation would hold true if it were outside those areas. In the Red Bay reburial mentioned above, a sandbag wall was created using 1,200 plastic bags that had originally contained salt used to salt fish at the local fish plant. The timbers were covered with sand, then a 36mm thick tarpaulin made of rubber with a reinforcing weave on which was placed 60 old tyres filled with concrete. The system has worked well and is an example of effective use of low cost local materials.

The effects of any particular method of covering a site must be carefully considered; especially any long term implications for future archaeological investigation. For example, on the site of HMS *Fowey* in Florida backfilling was done and a layer of sand spread to protect the site. Seagrass was transplanted from shallower areas and pinned to the seabed with steel nails. The sea grass died leaving 1,200 nails to contaminate the area.[237]

Protection against deliberate interference may require disguising the site by sand or some other method. Devices may be placed on the site to trigger an alarm if activity takes place.

---

235 Dean M. *et al*. *Archaeology Underwater: The NAS Guide to Principles and Practice* (Nautical Archaeology Society, Portsmouth, 1992) 218.
236 Negueruela, I. *et al*. 'Seventh-century BC Phoenician Vessel Discovered at Playa de la Isla, Spain' (1995) 24 *International Journal of Nautical Archaeology* 189.
237 Skowronek, R.K. and Fischer, G.R. *HMS Fowey Lost and Found* (University Press of Florida, Gainesville, 2009) 96.

IX. Documentation

Rule 26

> The documentation programme shall set out thorough documentation including a progress report of activities directed at underwater cultural heritage, in accordance with current professional standards of archaeological documentation.

Commentary: Archaeology through excavation is destruction. All activities directed at underwater cultural heritage, unless totally non-invasive, bring about some destruction. Documentation is the only way of preserving what was there and what was done. The project design should state, even before work commences, what documentation will be kept and how detailed this should be.

Rule 27

> Documentation shall include, at a minimum, a comprehensive record of the site, including the provenance of underwater cultural heritage moved or removed in the course of the activities directed at underwater cultural heritage, field notes, plans, drawings, sections, and photographs or recording in other media.

Commentary: The minimum level of documentation set out in Rule 27 shows why it is necessary that its degree and level must be established at the project design stage and followed throughout the project.

X. Safety

Rule 28

> A safety policy shall be prepared that is adequate to ensure the safety and health of the project team and third parties and that is in conformity with any applicable statutory and professional requirements.

Commentary: Safety is of paramount importance. This means not only in the diving operations but also in the handling of equipment, use of chemicals in conservation etc. For vessels operating beyond the territorial sea the statutory rules will be those of the flag State, if there are any. Various codes of practice are available which can be adopted for a project design.

XI. Environment

Rule 29

> An environmental policy shall be prepared that is adequate to ensure that the seabed and marine life are not unduly disturbed.

Commentary: Any intrusion in a site will disturb seabed and marine life of some kind. In some cases this will be minimal but where, for example, a wreck is embedded in coral there will be considerable disturbance if there is any excavation. The Rule is not in absolute terms. Seabed and marine life are not to be 'unduly' disturbed. This means that an assessment has to be made of the forms of life that exist on the site and the policy developed as part of the project design which will cause the least disturbance possible.

XII. Reporting

Rule 30

> Interim and final reports shall be made available according to the timetable set out in the project design, and deposited in relevant public records.

Commentary: Reports have already been mentioned in the above Rules; such as Rule 17 requiring funding to be allocated at the project design stage for preparation of reports and Rule 20 requiring specific inclusion in the project timetable of report preparation provisions. Rule 30 now requires those responsible for the project to abide by the timetable. This is a most significant provision.

There are different forms of publication and publications for different audiences. Rule 30 refers to interim as well as final reports. That both are required has been recognized for example by the *European Convention on the Protection of the Archaeological Heritage (Revised)* 1992 which requires States to take all practical measures to ensure that a summary scientific record is published before the 'necessary comprehensive publication of specialized studies'.[238]

Report preparation is regarded by some as an afterthought to their fieldwork. The editors of *Antiquity* write:

> A distinctly archaeological iconoclasm is non-publication of fieldwork. As all archaeologists know, excavation and survey are destruction and are only preserved by fieldwork, a record that only the original fieldworkers can present effectively. … What is required is an addition to the tradition of good fieldwork; the tradition of regular publication.[239]

One criticism made of the work of RMS Titanic Inc. on the *Titanic* site was its failure to assemble an archive of dive data and its failure to prepare an archaeological report.[240]

Those undertaking activities directed at underwater cultural heritage must realize that reporting is not a matter of personal choice. Not only is it now required by Rule 30 but also it can be seen as one component in the network of cultural rights as they relate to archaeology.

> It is not too much to say that there is emerging a recognition that, not only local communities, but also other specialists and the general public have a right to know the results of archaeological fieldwork.[241]

Rule 30 requires that the reports be deposited in relevant public records. What this means will vary greatly from State to State. Some, for example, require that a copy of all books published in the country be placed in the collection of the national library; others do not. Note that it must be a 'public' collection. Does deposit in a university library meet this criterion? The nature of the University and its policy on library access would need to be examined.

Rule 31

> Reports shall include:
> (a) an account of the objectives;
> (b) an account of the methods and techniques employed;
> (c) an account of the results achieved;
> (d) basic graphic and photographic documentation on all phases of the activity;
> (e) recommendations concerning conservation and curation of the site and of any underwater cultural heritage removed; and
> (f) recommendations for future activities.

---

238 Article 7(ii).
239 Stoddart, S. and Malone, C. 'Editorial' 75 *Antiquity* 233, 234-236.
240 Fewster, K.J. and Valliant, J.R. 'Titanic: Delving Beneath the Surface' (1997) (May-June) *Museum News* 29.
241 O'Keefe, P.J. 'Archaeology and Human Rights' (2000) 1 *Public Archaeology* 181, 192.

Commentary: Rule 31 sets out the minimum of what a report should contain. Advice on reports and how to write them can be found in a number of publications such as *Maritime Archaeology: A Technical Handbook* by Jeremy Green.[242]

---

242   Academic Press, London, 1990.

XIII. Curation of Project Archives

Rule 32

> Arrangements for curation of the project archives shall be agreed to before any activity commences, and shall be set out in the project design.

Commentary: Once again, the project design stage is the time for deciding what will be done with the documentation and any underwater cultural heritage discovered. There will necessarily be an element of estimation because it is impossible to predict with absolute accuracy what will eventuate once the project commences. However, projections can normally be made by experienced project leaders and the absence of absolute accuracy is no argument for avoiding a decision on what will be necessary for curation.

Quite apart from the ultimate destination of the archive, there must be agreement on how the documentation will be treated; when it will be made available to the public and when it will be assembled as the archive. One matter that needs consideration is that of copyright. Who is to have copyright in the documentation produced and will copyright held by individual researchers be transferred on formation of the archive.

Where underwater cultural heritage has been recovered in the course of a research project conforming to the Convention, the commercial exploitation provisions of Rule 2 do not prevent its deposition in accordance with paragraph (b). This sets out the conditions under which the archives of an excavation are to be deposited (i.e. placed in appropriate care) for long term curation. It does not go to the issue of ownership or the nature of the body that will hold it.[243] The conditions for deposition must be distinguished from the method of deposition. The method has to be agreed before work on a site commences. Article 22 is cast in the imperative. If it is not followed then there has been failure to comply with the Annex and all that entails in terms of the Convention.

Rule 33

> The project archives, including any underwater cultural heritage removed and a copy of all supporting documentation shall, as far as possible, be kept together and intact as a collection in a manner that is available for professional and public access as well as for the curation of the archives. This should be done as rapidly as possible and in any case not later than ten years from the completion of the project, in so far as may be compatible with conservation of the underwater cultural heritage.

Commentary: The project archive has two aspects – documentation and artifacts. Different considerations apply to these. For example, it is unlikely that documentation will have a commercial value although if it does (film and photographs are possibilities) then duplicates can be made without harm to the originals. Artifacts may be a different matter. They could well have commercial value and be attractive to collectors including museums. Replicas do not have the same qualities as originals in the eyes of many collectors.

Documentation arising from the project may be held by a number of people. Those doing the fieldwork will have their own notes including digital material; the conservators will have their records etc. These, or full copies, will need to be brought together and made available for professional and public access. Rule 33 states that this should be done as rapidly as possible but in any case not more than ten years after completion of the project. This should put a stop to any practice of fieldworkers claiming copyright in their notes and refusing access to other researchers. Stoddart and Malone comment on such practices and recommend:

> … a moratorium on exclusive rights after – say – 10 years? If the original excavator has not *commenced* publication within 10 years of completing fieldwork, then it is unlikely they ever will![244]

---

243   Cf. Forrest, C. *International Law and the Protection of Cultural Heritage* (Routledge, London, 2010) 344.
244   Stoddart and Malone, fn. 239 above, 235.

Ideally, for reasons of security and natural disaster such as fire, there should be two sets of documentation to be kept in separate locations.

Other considerations come into play regarding any artifacts raised. Here Rule 2 must be considered. This states that any deposition of underwater cultural heritage shall be made in accordance with Rules 33 and 34. Rule 33 says that material raised shall be kept together and intact as a collection 'as far as possible'. Indirectly, these two Rules recognize that, for political and other reasons, it may be necessary to split a collection and place artifacts in different locations. Thus, as has been noted, while most of the material from the *Batavia* is in the Western Australian Maritime Museum, some has been placed in its regional museum at Geraldton for public relations and educational reasons.

While Rule 33 sets a limit of ten years for assembly of the project archive, it recognizes that conservation may take longer than this and creates an exception. The *Batavia* is a good example. There the conservation of the timbers took some 30 years.

Rule 34

> The project archives shall be managed according to international professional standards, and subject to the authorization of the competent authorities.

Commentary: At some stage the project archives will become subject to standards set by the body responsible for them. This may be an academic institution, a museum or some other entity. Many such bodies have their own policies often prepared after careful study of the issues involved in caring for the material in their charge. There are also national and international codes of ethics such as that of the International Council of Museums to provide guidance.

The UNESCO Manual for Activities Directed at Underwater Cultural Heritage states that de-accessioning is not what the Rules try to avoid 'as long as it does not imply feeding the antiquities market with finds'.[245] Article 34 introduces 'management according to international professional standards'. De-accessioning is a recognized element in professional collection management. For example, the ICOM Code of Ethics recognizes the concept but imposes a strict set of conditions to be satisfied before disposal of an object from a collection:

> The removal of an object or specimen from a museum collection must only be undertaken with a full understanding of the significance of the item, its character (whether renewable or non-renewable), legal standing, and any loss of public trust that might result from such action.[246]

Particularly significant is the possible loss of public trust. There are strict rules governing the method of de-accessioning.

> Each museum should have a policy defining authorised methods for permanently removing an object from the collections through donation, transfer, exchange, sale, repatriation, or destruction, and that allows the transfer of unrestricted title to any receiving agency. Complete records must be kept of all deaccessioning decisions, the objects involved, and the disposal of the object. There will be a strong presumption that a deaccessioned item should first be offered to another museum.[247]

It will be obvious from these provisions in the ICOM Code and from Rules 2(b) and 34 that, while de-accessioning is a possibility, it is an exceptional step in management of the archive; one that is to be undertaken only in rare and pressing circumstances. Moreover, other reputable collections should be the first offerees. Finally, archives held in accordance with the Convention can only be de-accessioned 'subject to the authorization of the competent authorities'. This is implied in the structure of the Rules and mentioned specifically in Rule 34. As stated specifically in the UNESCO Manual, de-accessioning cannot be used as a means of feeding antiquities into

---

245   Fn. 177 above, p. 35.
246   Paragraph 2.13.
247   Paragraph 2.15.

the art market. Nor can it be used as a means of avoiding the commercial exploitation prohibition by laundering the objects recovered through a museum: i.e. objects are raised, placed in what purports to be a museum collection and then de-accessioned.

The members of the Scientific and Technical Advisory Body have attempted to spell out in more detail what is meant by using de-accessioning for the transfer of artefacts in lieu of payment for archaeological services.

> De-accessioning is the formal process of the removal of an object from a collection, register, catalogue or database based upon a number of sound considerations. Disposal is the physical removal of the object from the collection. De-accession and disposal are practices used in museums and other institutions which host natural or cultural materials. One of the reasons why materials can be de-accessioned and disposed of is that they are duplicates. De-accession and disposal normally take place after a thorough analysis, assessment and consultation.

> The members concluded that the practice of de-accessioning could be abused to justify a pre-planned over-recovery and trade of archaeological materials for the payment of professional recovery services employed on that same or other archaeological site. This could typically result in a commercial exploitation scheme on the ground that certain materials would be identified as duplicates, which is for instance often the case for coins and ceramics. In the end result sites would be excavated more for their monetary value rather than for their scientific interest. From the outset items could be recovered for no other reason than for sale and they would be commercialized for the payment of the salvor. This would be inconsistent with the intent and provisions of the 2001 Convention.

> While the Advisory Body recognized that the de-accessioning of material from a museum or other entity might in some cases not be inconsistent with the Rules annexed to the Convention, without issuing any view on that issue, it was of the opinion that a breach of the Rules would occur when the recovery of material from an archaeological site:

> - was made with the intention of transferring artefacts in lieu of payment for archaeological services;
> - was made without the goal of contributing considerably to the protection, knowledge about or enhancement of underwater cultural heritage; and /or
> - resulted in the unnecessary disturbance of the concerned archaeological remains and their context; and /or
> - would effectively result in the commercialization of underwater cultural heritage; and /or
> - when an activity on a site would be undertaken without first securing the necessary sound funding base for the activity.

> More specifically, the Advisory Body considered that:

> *On Rule 1 of the Annex:* A pre-planned de-accessioning of 'surplus' material from a submerged archaeological site would mean that Rule 1 of the Annex, which regulates that protection in situ should be considered as first option, is not respected. Recoveries would be made with the intention that artefacts would be transferred in lieu of payment for archaeological services while there was no intention to contribute through it considerably to knowledge, enhancement or protection. Even if there was a threat to the site by other causes, like trawling or looting, it was not justifiable to foresee from the outset to recover material for the financing of an activity (instead for instance to look for protective measures or other solutions).

On Rule 2 of the Annex: The Advisory Body members also opined that as soon as the artefacts from the excavated site were effectively and in whichever way used in lieu of payment to compensate a party to a pre-excavation agreement for archaeological or other services rendered, this was equivalent to trade in artefacts, so that the activity becomes a commercial one and violates Rule 2. This was not to be considered as a correct deposition of underwater cultural heritage, as mentioned in Rule 2, recovered in conformity with the Convention.

On Rule 3 and 4 of the Annex: A pre-excavation agreement for the transfer of artefacts in lieu of payment for archaeological services by means of de-accessioning would also mean the disturbance of an archaeological site with the pre-set goal of recovering items beyond any scientific need in order to finance the activity. This would typically result in a situation that would violate Rule 3, according to which activities directed at underwater cultural heritage shall not adversely affect the heritage more than is necessary for the objectives of the project. According to Rule 4 activities directed at underwater cultural heritage must also use non-destructive techniques and survey methods in preference to the recovery of objects. If excavation or recovery is necessary for the purpose of scientific studies or for the ultimate protection of the underwater cultural heritage, the methods and techniques used must be as non-destructive as possible and contribute to the preservation of the remains. This does not cover their de-accessioning pursuant to a pre-excavation agreement to serve as payment for archaeological or other services.

On Rule 17 of the Annex: Moreover, according to Rule 17 an adequate funding base shall be assured before undertaking any activity. This should however not include any sale of artefacts which is not in conformity with Rule 2. If no such funding is assured, the activity should not be undertaken.[248]

---

[248] Scientific and Technical Advisory Body, *Report, Recommendations and Resolutions*, Third Meeting, 19 April 2012: <http://www.unesco.org/new/en/culture/themes/underwater-cultural-heritage/advisory-body/meetings/third-meeting/>

XIV. Dissemination

Rule 35

> Projects shall provide for public education and popular presentation of the project results where appropriate.

Commentary: Archaeology does not take place in a vacuum. It requires funding for often increasingly complex and expensive scientific procedures and equipment. The bulk of the money for activities directed at underwater cultural heritage covered by the Underwater Convention will come from governments, sale of images, tourism, non-profit foundations and possibly public subscription. For all of these, an enthusiastic public is essential and enthusiasm can only be generated by education of the public in the values of the underwater cultural heritage. This does not mean simply photographs of gleaming hoards of gold or the stories of derring-do so beloved by the tabloid journalist. That has its place but much more important is the story of what the heritage can tell us of those who for thousands of year went down to the sea.

An excellent example of public education and popular presentation is provided by the *Mary Rose* excavation.

> Upon finding the ship, all possible publicity was recruited – publication in academic journals, local press and radio, the colour supplement, *Diver* magazine etc. plus *exhibition* and this was very important. There followed lectures round the country. 'We had an honours board of subscribers right round the warehouse'. It was essential to involve the public at every level – 'provided it's accurate don't mind how low you go'.[249]

Unfortunately, it seems that not all archaeologists are capable of communicating effectively to those outside their immediate colleagues.

> Too few archaeologists can write well, and too few can communicate really effectively. Instead, there is the desire to write overly detailed, technically dense and theoretically obscure text that communicates only with a small and initiated peer-group. … Teachers of archaeology need to promote the skills of writing, as well as knowledge and debate, if the future generations of archaeological report writers are to be more successful than those of the past or present.[250]

But education is not all done by the written word. On land, sites can be opened to the public and the work in hand be presented as part entertainment, part education. This is much more difficult underwater not only for reasons of access but also safety. Nevertheless, it should be possible for interested divers to be shown what is being done if this is integrated into the programme. For non-divers much can also be achieved through film, videos and photographs.

Rule 36

> A final synthesis of a project shall be:
> (a) made public as soon as possible, having regard to the complexity of the project and the confidential or sensitive nature of the information; and
> (b) deposited in relevant public records.

Commentary: Ideally the final report should always be made available to the public although sometimes information such as the location of a site may need to be kept secret. This could occur where the project has only involved a survey but the survey has revealed that the site contains a great deal of important material.

---

249 Croome, A. 'Underwater Archaeology in Britain: Discussion Meeting at the Royal Amouries, London, 30 January 1988' (1988) 17 *International Journal of Nautical Archaeology and Underwater Exploration* 113, 118 summarizing a paper by Margaret Rule.
250 Stoddart and Malone, fn. 239 above, 236 .

The final synthesis is to be made public 'as soon as possible'. This will vary greatly depending on the nature of the project. That at Red Bay mentioned above[251] involved the recording of 3,000 pieces of the ship's structure through more than 50,000 photographs and 2,500 minutes of film not to mention notes, measurements, drawings, plans etc. The 4,000 page manuscript took fifteen years to produce after completion of the excavation and commencement of work in the laboratory.[252]

How to make the final synthesis public is a difficult decision and one greatly influenced by cost. A full publication complete with plans and artifact catalogue may be so expensive to produce that only wealthy libraries and researchers will be able to acquire it.

> Hard-copy initial and interim reports alert scholars to the potential of a new discovery, the popular book secures public support and interest, but the sheer quantity of data that can be obtained from surviving ship structure, environmental analyses and atrefacts may make full paper publication unrealistic.[253]

Some see the way forward to be publication on the Internet but others find a need for caution in adopting this method.

> Microfiche had a phase of popularity but is now surpassed by the Internet. The difference is that microfiche has a conservation quality which, although not yet as well tested as paper, is not so dependent on refreshment and maintenance as are the many web sites now proliferating. Even now a search of the web, using a friendly engine, produces unlocatable sites, only realized a year or two ago. The Internet certainly has immediacy, but does it have continuity of record? The Archaeological Data Services (ADS) already has horror stories of the delivery of unindexed discs from a defunct archaeological agency, delivered to their door for storage and processing.[254]

---

251 Page 4.
252 Grenier and Bernier, fn. 17 above, 10-11.
253 Fenwick, V. 'Editorial' (1996) 25 *International Journal of Nautical Archaeology* 1,2.
254 Stoddart and Malone, fn. 239 above, 235.

CONCLUSION

The *Convention on the Protection of the Underwater Cultural Heritage* has now been in existence twelve years and in force some four years. Forty-five States are party to it which is a respectable number considering its complexities. UNESCO has done much work to promote both it and the actions it endorses such as training and raising public awareness.

The complexities arise more from political demands than the inherent nature of the subject. The International Law Association Draft Convention proposed a relatively simple scheme to protect underwater cultural heritage. However, some States, for which Norway acted as leader, insisted on a strict adherence to what they saw as the requirements of the *United Nations Convention on the Law of the Sea*. Others did not see any clash[1] but compromised on crucial points in the hope of reaching a consensus which did not eventuate. The result is a regime which requires States Parties and UNESCO to institute and follow detailed procedures to ensure that the Convention works as it should.

Much effort has been devoted to increasing the number of States Parties. More States have indicated they are preparing to join. Efforts should be directed to obtaining groups of States in sensitive areas so that the denial of port facilities will be an effective deterrent. Then there is the problem of the major maritime powers - France, Germany, Japan, Netherlands, Norway, Russia, United Kingdom and the United States of America. These States are home to the most significant treasure seekers and salvage interests. Here there has been some slight change. France has become party to the Underwater Convention thus indicating it no longer saw incompatibility between the two Conventions. On the other hand, as recently as 2009 the United States has stated that it could not 'join a Convention that is not consistent with the jurisdictional regime set forth in the United Nations Convention on the Law of the Sea'.[2] The United States is reiterating its position as it was in the late 1990s. There seems to have been no reconsideration of this, at least in official circles.

On the other hand, the Netherlands has been actively investigating the compatibility of the two Conventions. Its National Commission for UNESCO has recommended that the Dutch Government 'ratify the 2001 UNESCO *Convention on the Protection of the Underwater Cultural Heritage* as this treaty provides the only adequate tool at our disposal to ensure the effective worldwide protection of underwater cultural heritage'.[3] Furthermore

> The UNESCO convention does not undermine international maritime law (UNCLOS). The understandable fear that this might be the case, based on statements made by some Member States during the negotiations in 2001, has proved to be unfounded over the last ten years. To this day, the UNESCO treaty has not effected [sic] any precedent to disrupt the delicate balance between the rights and obligations of coastal and flag states within UNCLOS.[4]

The Dutch Advisory Committee on Issues of Public International Law has also responded to a request from the Minister of Foreign Affairs for answers to certain questions. One in particular was very pertinent; namely, that dealing with the issue of jurisdiction. The Committee advised

---

[1] The Chairman of the negotiating sessions in Paris in later years called it a division between the 'minimalist protectors of cultural heritage' and the 'progressive protectors of cultural heritage': Lund, C. 'The Making of the 2001 UNESCO Convention' in Prott, L.V. (ed.) *Finishing the Interrupted Voyage* (Institute of Art and Law, UNESCO; Builth Wells, Paris; 2006) 14, 17.

[2] <http://unesdoc.unesco.org/images/0018/001853/185392E.pdf>. p. 14.

[3] <http://isearch.avg.com/?cid={7BF8C62B-7D07-45F6-89FB-A766675636BA}&mid=8ef8b46f559b47d0ae9769e52939b814-ff8b48e04c753de542b04eae195a-3c607a8a2994&lang=en&ds=AVG&pr=pr&d=2013-01-21%2015:12:07&v=15.3.0.11&pid=avg&sg=0&sap=hp>. p. 1.

[4] Above p. 3.

that it was 'unlikely that the UNESCO Convention will set a precedent for the division of jurisdiction at sea in other areas. There is no evidence of any attempts to extend what, as noted above, is only a minor shift in the distribution of competences between coastal and flag States in the UNESCO Convention to areas other than the protection of underwater cultural heritage'.[5] This opinion from a most eminent group of government advisors should have great weight with others who still dispute the relationship between the two Conventions, particularly as far as jurisdiction is concerned.

Leading international lawyers have also criticized the failure by the remaining major maritime powers to re-examine their position. Ariel González who was leader of the Argentinian delegation to the negotiations in Paris has stated:

> Not a single line in an official document by any of those States has been written to clearly substantiate such allegations on any debatable legal basis. Not a single line to explain, in particular, the alleged incompatibility with UNCLOS of a text that establishes the very scheme of cooperation for the protection of underwater cultural heritage that Article 303 of UNCLOS requires: …[6].

Keun-Gwan Lee has observed:

> … the 'sanctification' of the relevant provisions of UNCLOS, the discussion of which took place in the late 1970s when the general awareness of the question and the relevant technology were in their infancy should be seriously reconsidered.[7]

The views of the major maritime powers can only be changed by persuasion over time. That is not impossible. It took 32 years for the United Kingdom to become party to the *Convention on the Means of Prohibiting and Preventing the Illicit Import, Export and Transfer of Ownership of Cultural Property* 1970. Constant persuasion brought the United Kingdom from a position of outright hostility to gradual acceptance that the 1970 Convention would not bring disaster to its art market. It took Russia 18 years; Japan 32 years; Germany and Norway 37 years; Netherlands 39 years to also accept that Convention. It is obvious that these States are not easily persuaded to become party to such international agreements but may do so over time if the arguments for and advantages available are continually presented to them.

Promotion is highly desirable and, indeed, necessary if the Convention is to play a significant role in protecting underwater cultural heritage. But the quality of State participation must also be considered. Have States that are party to the Convention considered and taken all the steps they must do to properly implement the Convention. For example, are all the reporting procedures required by Articles 9 and 11 in place? Do the masters of vessels flying their flag know what is required of them under those Articles and to whom reports of discoveries should be made? This applies particularly to flags of convenience States. Is there legislation in place to enforce the prohibitions under Article 14, particularly the dealing in or possession of underwater cultural heritage which may have been brought ashore in other States? Has the State Party mandated (or authorised) denial of the use of its ports in accordance with Article 15?

On these issues STAB could play a major role. While there is no express provision in the Convention for periodic reporting as there is in the other UNESCO cultural conventions, States Parties are still obliged to provide periodic reports under general UNESCO rules. But reporting of this nature has not been particularly successful. In recent years the sheer weight of national reporting, both for the States and for the UNESCO Secretariat, has led to the adoption of priorities

---

5   *Advisory Report on the UNESCO Convention on the Protection of the Underwater Cultural Heritage*, Advisory Report No. 21, The Hague, December 2001, p. 12.
6   González, A. 'The UNESCO Convention on the Protection of Underwater Cultural Heritage: A Future for Our Past' in González, A.W., O'Keefe, P.J. and Williams, M. 'The UNESCO Convention on the Protection of the Underwater Cultural Heritage: a Future for our Past?' (2009) 11 *Conservation and Management of Archaeological Sites* 54
7   Keun-Gwan Lee, 'An Inquiry Into the Compatibility of the UNESCO Convention 2001 with UNCLOS 1982' in in Prott, L.V. (ed.) *Finishing the Interrupted Voyage* (Institute of Art and Law, UNESCO; Builth Wells, Paris; 2006) 20, 26.

in their management, and the present priority is for the *Convention on the Means of Prohibiting and Preventing the Illicit Import, Export and Transfer of Ownership of Cultural Property* 1970.[8] A new Convention, such as the 2001 Convention, might suggest that a certain leeway be given before the reporting schedule is instituted in view of the lack of resources in the Secretariat (one member of staff to service this Convention in all its aspects, its promotion, its training programme the Meeting of States Parties). Consequently, there is here a role for STAB to play in ensuring the quality of State participation in the Underwater Convention. It could survey States on particular aspects and request them to provide detailed answers to the questions raised above as well as others arising from the procedures of the Convention. From these it would be possible to build up a picture of how well States Parties are complying with the Convention and give an idea of possibly differing ways they are coping with the same problems. States should realize that this is not an attempt to criticize their internal procedures but rather an effort to improve the overall operation of the Convention.

STAB could also examine various provisions of the Convention, providing guidance to States in particular situations. As I stated in my comment as the Convention was coming into force in 2009, STAB could certainly examine whether adequate attention has been paid to the principle of *in situ* preservation before activities were commenced on a site. It could interpret the meaning of 'commercial exploitation' in a specific situation and whether activities fall within its scope. Moreover, there would be nothing to prevent STAB from considering a situation where the Rules are being applied, or not applied, by a State which is not a party. If a non-State were to grant a licence for excavation in conditions where the Rules were not observed, STAB could consider the issues and make a report to the Meeting of States Parties. Of course, the Meeting would have no control over a non-party State, but as its power and status grows its reports could play a significant public relations role. States Parties obviously envisaged playing a major role in establishing how the Rules are interpreted.[9] Is it too much to envisage STAB giving an opinion on the current situation involving *HMS Victory*, Odyssey Marine International and the British Government?

STAB could investigate the situation in South East Asia where some argue that the principles of the Annex are not appropriate. It is said that any wreck site, once found, will be stripped by local people using all means at their disposal. In particular, the prohibition on commercial exploitation is unworkable as it is precisely the commercially valuable material that is likely to attract the attention of fishermen etc. Supporters of this view say that commercial salvors should be allowed to excavate under licence from the government otherwise sites would be stripped without any knowledge being obtained of what was there. These allegations and the use of salvage contracts should be investigated by STAB.

States should not rely on the UNESCO Secretariat to do this type of work for them. This would be beyond the functions of the Secretariat as set down in Article 24. It would be for the members of STAB themselves to organise these activities supported by the States Parties to the Convention. This would also give those States an opportunity to become directly involved in the mechanics of what, after all, is their own Convention.

The success of STAB in undertaking activities such as those mentioned should have an effect on States not yet party to the Underwater Convention. As these States see the impact STAB is having on developments in underwater archaeology and interpretation of the Convention, there will be pressure on them to also become party – even if only to ensure that their own viewpoints are represented and taken into account at the international level.

Many have contributed to the developments that have taken place since the Underwater Convention was adopted. The *Manual for Activities Directed at Underwater Cultural Heritage*

---

8 This is summarized in O'Keefe, P.J. & Prott, L.V. *Cultural Heritage Conventions and Other Instruments: A Compendium with Commentaries* (Institute of Art and Law, Builth Wells, 2011).

9 O'Keefe, P.J. 'The Implementation of the 2001 Underwater Convention' in González, A.W., O'Keefe, P.J. and Williams, M. 'The UNESCO Convention on the Protection of the Underwater Cultural Heritage: a Future for our Past?' (2009) 11 *Conservation and Management of Archaeological Sites* 54, 59.

is an example of what can be done to assist those working on this heritage. However, as has been shown in the previous pages, there are those who still find fault with the Convention: some because it curbs their own activities and some for political reasons. Hopefully, as the Convention continues to gain greater acceptance this will diminish.

Postscript

The discoveries at Red Bay in Canada have led to events beyond the excavation and analysis of the wrecks. The *San Juan* came from San Sebastian in the Basque country of Spain. That city has been selected as the cultural capital of Europe for 2016. As part of the celebrations, a full scale replica of the ship is being built. It will travel between European cities during 2016 and then sail across the Atlantic to Canada where it will take part in the 150th celebration of Canadian confederation. It will act as a reminder of the ties between Spain and Canada, particularly hundreds of years of commercial relationships, and act as a symbol of commerce between Europe and North America.

SELECTED BIBLIOGRAPHY

Advisory Committee on Issues of Public International Law (The Netherlands) *Advisory Report on the UNESCO Convention on the Protection of the Underwater Cultural Heritage*, Advisory Report No. 21, The Hague, December 2001.

'Cultural Heritage Law Committee: Buenos Aires Draft Convention on the Protection of the Underwater Cultural Heritage: Final Report' in Crawford, J. & Williams, M. (eds) *International Law Association: Report of the Sixty-Sixth Conference* (International Law Association, Buenos Aires, 1994) 432

Abbass, D.K. 'A Marine Archaeologist Looks at Treasure Salvage' (1999) 30 *Journal of Maritime Law and Commerce* 261

Adlercreutz, T. 'Sweden' in Dromgoole, S. (ed.) *Legal Protection of the Underwater Cultural Heritage: National and International Perspectives* (Kluwer Law International, The Hague, 1999) 155

Allotta, G. *Tutela del Patrimonio Archeologico Subacqueo* (Centro Studi Giulio Pastore, Palerno, 2001)

Alves, F.J.S. & Castro, F. 'New Portuguese Legislation on Management of the Underwater Cultural Heritage' (1999) 3 *Conservation and Management of Archaeological Sites* 159

Aust, A. *Modern Treaty Law and Practice* (Cambridge University Press, 2000)

Bascom, W. *Deep Water, Ancient Ships: the Treasure Vault of the Mediterranean* (Doubleday, New York, 1976)

Aznar, M.J. &Varmer, O. 'The *Titanic* as Underwater Cultural Heritage: Challenges to its Legal International Protection' (2013) 44 *Ocean Development and International Law* 96.

Aznar-Gómez, M.J. 'Spain' in Droomgoole, S. (ed.) *The Protection of the Underwater Cultural Heritage: National Perspectives in Light of the UNESCO Convention 2001* (Martinus Nijhoff, Leiden, 2006) 271.

Bederman, D. 'Historic Salvage and the Law of the Sea' (1998) 30 *Inter-American Law Review* 99

Bederman, D.J. 'The UNESCO Draft Convention on Underwater Cultural Heritage: A Critique and Counter-Proposal' (1999) 30 *Journal of Maritime Law and Commerce* 331

Bederman, D.J. &Prowda, J.B. 'In 'Titanic' Case, IP and Admiralty Laws Collide' *National Law Journal*, 19 October 1998, p. 2

Berns, P.A. 'A Sovereign's Perspective on Treasure Salvage' (1999) 30 *Journal of Maritime Law and Commerce* 269

Blackman, D. 'Archaeological Aspects' in *The Underwater Cultural Heritage: Report of the Committee on Culture and Education, Parliamentary Assembly* (Council of Europe Doc.4200. Strasbourg, 1978) 27

Blake, J. 'The Protection of the Underwater Cultural Heritage' (1996) 45 *International and Comparative Law Quarterly* 819

Blake, J. 'The Protection of Turkey's Underwater Archaeological Heritage - Legislative Measures and Other Approaches' (1994) 3 *International Journal of Cultural Property* 273

Blake, J. 'Turkey' in Dromgoole, S. (ed.) *Legal Protection of the Underwater Cultural Heritage: National and International Perspectives* (Kluwer Law International, The Hague, 1999) 169

Boesten, E. *Archaeological and/or Historic Valuable Shipwrecks in International Waters: Public International Law and What it Offers* (T.M.C. Asser Press, The Hague, 2002).

Braekhus, S. 'Salvage of Wrecks and Wreckage: Legal Issues Arising From the Runde Find' (1976) 20 *Scandinavian Studies in Law* 39

Brice, G. 'Salvage and the Underwater Cultural Heritage' (1996) 20 *Marine Policy* 337

Brodie, N. 'All at Sea' (2000) 74 *Antiquity* 662

Brown, E.D. 'Protection of the Underwater Cultural Heritage. Draft Principles and Guidelines for Implementation of Article 303 of the United Nations Convention on the Law of The Sea, 1982' (1996) 20 *Marine Policy* 325

Caflisch, L. 'Submarine Antiquities and the International Law of the Sea' (1982) 13 *Netherlands Yearbook of International Law* 3

Churchill, R.R. & Lowe, A.V. *The Law of the Sea* (Manchester University Press, Manchester, 3rd edn. 1999)

CCA *Proceedings of International Roundtable Meeting on the Protection of Underwater Cultural Heritage* (Taipei, Taiwan, 2010) 84.

Chuan-Kun Ho, 'Prehistoric Landbridge Mammalian and Human Fossils Discovered Under Taiwan Strait' in CCA *Proceedings of International Roundtable Meeting on the Protection of Underwater Cultural Heritage* (Taipei, Taiwan, 2010) 84.

Ciciriello, M.C. 'Italy' in Dromgoole, S. (ed.) *Legal Protection of the Underwater Cultural Heritage: National and International Perspectives* (Kluwer Law International, The Hague, 1999) 101

Cleere, H. 'The Underwater Heritage and the World Heritage Convention' (1993) 17 *Bulletin of the Australian Institute for Maritime Archaeology* 25

Clément, E. 'Current Developments at UNESCO Concerning the Protection of the Underwater Cultural Heritage: Presentation Made at the First and Second National Maritime Museum Conferences on the Protection of Underwater Cultural Heritage (Greenwich, 3 and 4 February 1995) (London, IMO, 25 and 26 January 1996)' (1996) 20 *Marine Policy* 309

Cohn. A.B. "The Council of American Maritime Museums (CAMM) and a Re-examination of Its Role in the Protection of Underwater Cultural Heritage" paper delivered at CAMM Annual Meeting, Maine, 26 September 2002: <http://www.acuaonline.org/assets/2010/09/21/1e6ffe7fa278adefe056b58525609f97.pdf>

Council of Europe *European Convention on the Protection of the Archaeological Heritage (Revised): Explanatory Report* Doc. MPC (91)

Council of Europe *The Underwater Cultural Heritage: Report of the Committee on Culture and Education, Parliamentary Assembly* (Council of Europe Doc.4200. Strasbourg, 1978)

Couper, A. 'The Principal Issues in Underwater Cultural Heritage' (1996) 20 *Marine Policy* 283

Crisman, K. review of Bingeman, J.M. 'The First HMS *Invincible* (1747-58): her excavations (1980 – 1991)' in 2001 (40) *International Journal of Nautical Archaeology* 455.

Dean, M. et al. *Archaeology Underwater: The NAS Guide to Principles and Practice* (Nautical Archaeology Society, Portsmouth, 1992)

Delgado, J.P. 'Diving on the Titanic' (2001) (January/February) *Archaeology* 52

Dellino, V. & Luz Endere, M. 'The HMS Swift Shipwreck: The Development ofUnderwater Heritage Protection in Argentina' (2001) 4 *Conservation and Management of Archaeological Sites* 219

Dobbs, C. 'Interpreting and Displaying The *Mary Rose* to the Public in a New Museum' in

International Meeting on the Protection, Presentation and Valorisation of Underwater Cultural Heritage – Chongqing, China (23 to 27 November 2010) p. 341, <http://www.unesco.org/culture/underwater/pdf/uch_publication_chine_en.pdf>

Dobson, N.C. and Kingsley, S. "HMS *Victory*, a First-Rate Royal Navy Warship Lost in the English Channel, 1744. Preliminary Survey and Investigation" in Stemm, G. and Kingsley, S. (eds), *Oceans Odyssey: Deep-Sea Shipwrecks in the English Channel, Straits of Gibraltar & Atlantic Ocean* (2010) 235.

Dromgoole, S. 'A Note on the Meaning of 'Wreck'' (1999) 28 *International Journal of Nautical Archaeology* 319

Dromgoole, S. 'Legal Protection of the Underwater Cultural Heritage: The United Kingdom Perspective' (1999) 4 *Art Antiquity and Law* 135

Dromgoole, S. 'Military Remains on and Around the Coast of the United Kingdom: Statutory Mechanisms of Protection' (1996) 11 *International Journal of Marine and Coastal Law* 23

Droomgoole, S. (ed.) *The Protection of the Underwater Cultural Heritage: National Perspectives in Light of the UNESCO Convention 2001* (Martinus Nijhoff, Leiden, 2006).

Dromgoole, S. 'United Kingdom' in Dromgoole, S. (ed.) *Legal Protection of the Underwater Cultural Heritage: National and International Perspectives* (Kluwer Law International, The Hague, 1999) 181

Dromgoole, S. 'United Kingdom' in Droomgoole, S. (ed.)*The Protection of the Underwater Cultural Heritage: National Perspectives in Light of the UNESCO Convention 2001* (Martinus Nijhoff, Leiden, 2006) 313.

Dromgoole, S. *Underwater Cultural Heritage and International Law* (Cambridge University Press, Cambridge, 2013)

Dromgoole, S. & Gaskell, N. 'Draft UNESCO Convention on the Protection of the Underwater Cultural Heritage 1998' (1999) 14 *International Journal of Marine and Coastal Law* 171

Dromgoole, S. & Gaskell, N. 'Interests in Wreck' (1997) 2 *Art Antiquity and Law* 103

Dromgoole, S. & Gaskell, N. 'Interests in Wreck: Part II' (1997) 2 *Art Antiquity and Law* 207

Dudley, W.S. 'CSS Alabama: The Evolution of a Policy' (1991) *Underwater Archaeology: Proceedings from the Society for Historical Archaeology Conference, 1991, Richmond, Virginia* 47

Elia, R.J. 'Titanic in the Courts' (2001) 54 *Archaeology* 54

Elia, R.J. 'US Protection of Underwater Cultural Heritage Beyond the Territorial Sea: Problems and Prospects' (2000) 29 *International Journal of Nautical Archaeology* 43

Fewster, K.J. & Valliant, J.R. 'Titanic: Delving Beneath the Surface' (1997) (May- June) *Museum News* 29

Firth, A. 'Making Archaeology: The History of the Protection of Wrecks Act 1973 and the Constitution of an Archaeological Resource' (1999) 28 *The International Journal of Nautical Archaeology* 1

Flecker, M. 'A Ninth-Century Arab Shipwreck in Indonesia: The First Archaeological Evidence of Direct Trade With China' in Krahl, R. *el al.* (eds) *Shipwrecked: Tang Treasures and Monsoon Winds* (Smithsonian Institution, Washington, 2010) 101.

Flecker, M. 'The Ethics, Politics, and Realities of Maritime Archaeology in Southeast Asia' (2002) 31 *International Journal of Nautical Archaeology* 12.

Fletcher-Tomenius, P. & Forrest, C. 'The Protection of the Underwater Cultural Heritage and the Challenge of UNCLOS' (2000) 5 *Art Antiquity and Law* 125

Fletcher-Tomenius, P. & Williams, M. 'Regulating Recovery of Historic Wreck in UK Waters: When is a Salvor Not a Salvor?' (2000) *Lloyd's Maritime and Commercial Law Quarterly* 208

Fletcher-Tomenius, P. & Williams, M. 'The Draft UNESCO/DOALOS Conventionon the Protection of Underwater Cultural Heritage and Conflict with the European Convention on Human Rights' (1999) 28 *International Journal of Nautical Archaeology* 145

Fletcher-Tomenius, P. & Williams, M. 'The Protection of Wrecks Act 1973: A Breach of Human Rights?' (1998) 13 *International Journal of Marine and Coastal Law* 623

Fletcher-Tomenius, P.; O'Keefe, P.J. & Williams, M. 'Salvor in Possession: Friend or Foe to Marine Archaeology?' (2000) 9 *International Journal of Cultural Property* 263

Forrest, C. *International Law and the Protection of Cultural Heritage* (Routledge, London, 2010).

Forrest, C.J.S. 'Salvage Law and the Wreck of the Titanic' (2000) *Lloyd's Maritime and Commercial Law Quarterly* 1

Giesecke, A.G. 'The Abandoned Shipwreck Act Through the Eyes of Its Drafter' (1999) 30 *Journal of Maritime Law and Commerce* 167

Green, J. Book review The Nanking Cargo by Michael Hatcher with Max de Rham and other books on the Geldermahlsen sale (1988) 17 *International Journal of Nautical Archaeology and Underwater Exploration* 357

Gongaware, L. and Varmer, O. "Public/Private Partnerships vs. 'Commercial Exploitation': The Belitung Shipwreck Controversy Continued": <http://www.culturalheritagelaw.org/blog?mode=PostView&bmi=739447>

González, A. 'The UNESCO Convention on the Protection of Underwater Cultural Heritage: A Future for Our Past' in González, A.W., O'Keefe, P.J. and Williams, M. 'The UNESCO Convention on the Protection of the Underwater Cultural Heritage: a Future for our Past?' (2009) 11 *Conservation and Management of Archaeological Sites* 54.

González, A.W., O'Keefe, P.J. and Williams, M. 'The UNESCO Convention on the Protection of the Underwater Cultural Heritage: a Future for our Past?' (2009) 11 *Conservation and Management of Archaeological Sites* 54.

Green, J. review of Krahl, R. *el al.* (eds) *Shipwrecked: Tang Treasures and Monsoon Winds* (Smithsonian Institution, Washington, 2010) in (2011) 40 *International Journal of Nautical Archaeology* 449.

Grenier, R &Berbier, M-A.*Challenges Facing Underwater Archaeology: the Red Bay Perspective* (Stichtingvoor de Nederlandse Archeologie, Amsterdam, 2001) 10.

Grenier, R.; Bernier, M-A.& Stevens, W. *The Underwater Archaeology of Red Bay: Basque Shipbuilding and Whaling in the 16th Century* (Parks Canada, Ottawa, 2007).

Grenier, R.: Nutley, D. & Cochran, I (eds) *Underwater Cultural Heritage at Risk; Managing Natural and Human Impacts* (ICOMOS, Paris, 2006).

Hatcher, M. (with Thorncroft, A.) *The Nanking Cargo* (Hamish Hamilton, London, 1987)

Hayashi, M. 'Archaeological and Historical Objects under the United Nations Convention on the Law of The Sea' (1996) 20 *Marine Policy* 291

He Shuzhong 'What Kind of Underwater Heritage Convention Do We Need?' (1999) 8 *International Journal of Cultural Property* 1999

Henderson, G. 'Significance Assessment or Blanket Protection' in Prott, L.V.; Planche, E. and Roca-Hachem, R. (eds) *Background Materials on the Protectio of the Underwater Cultural Heritage* (UNESCO & Ministère de la Culture et de la Communication (France), Paris, 2000) 350

Hess, P.E. 'The Trouble With Treasure: Ethical Dilemmas for the Salvage Attorney' (1999) 30 *Journal of Maritime Law and Commerce* 253

Hoagland, P. 'China' in Dromgoole, S. (ed.) *Legal Protection of the Underwater Cultural Heritage: National and International Perspectives* (Kluwer Law International, The Hague, 1999) 19

Hoagland, P. 'Managing the Underwater Cultural Resources of the China Seas: A Comparison of Public Policies in Mainland China and Taiwan' (1997) 12 *International Journal of Marine and Coastal Law* 265

Horan, E.W. 'Organizing, Manning, and Financing a Treasure Salvage Expedition' (1999) 30 *Journal of Maritime Law and Commerce* 235

Hutchinson, G. 'Threats to Underwater Cultural Heritage: The Problems of Unprotected Archaeological and Historic Sites, Wrecks and Objects Found at Sea' (1996) 20 *Marine Policy* 287

Jeffery, B. ''Activities Incidentally Affecting Underwater Cultural Heritage' in the 2001 UNESCO Convention' in Prott, L.V. (ed.) *Finishing the Interrupted Voyage* (UNESCO, Institute of Art and Law; Paris, Builth Wells; 2006) 96.

Jeffery, B. 'Australia' in Dromgoole, S. (ed.) *Legal Protection of the Underwater Cultural Heritage: National and International Perspectives* (Kluwer Law International, The Hague, 1999) 1

Jeffery, B. 'Federated States of Micronescia' in Droomgoole, S. (ed.) *The Protection of the Underwater Cultural Heritage: National Perspectives in Light of the UNESCO Convention 2001* (Martinus Nijhoff, Leiden, 2006) 145.

Jeffery, B. 'World War II Underwater Cultural Heritage Sites in Truk Lagoon: Considering a Case for World Heritage Listing' (2004) 33 *International Journal of Nautical Archaeology* 106.

Johnston, P.F. 'Treasure Salvage, Archaeological Ethics and Maritime Museums'(1993) 22 *International Journal of Nautical Archaeology* 53

Jones, J.P. 'The United States Supreme Court and Treasure Salvage: Issues Remaining After Brother Jonathan' (1999) 30 *Journal of Maritime Law and Commerce* 205

Keller, P.N. 'Salvor-Sovereign Relations: How the State of Illinois Destroyed the Lady Elgin' (1999) 30 *Journal of Maritime Law and Commerce* 245

Kinder, G. *Ship of Gold in the Deep Blue Sea* (Little Brown and Company, London, 1998)

Kingsley, S.A. 'Deep-sea Fishing Impacts on the Shipwrecks of the English Channel &Western Approaches' in Stemm, G. & Kingsley, S. (eds) *Oceans Odyssey: Deep-sea Shipwrecks in the English Channel, Straits of Gibraltar & Atlantic Ocean* (Oxbow Books, Oxford, 2010) 191.

Kowalski, W. 'Poland' in Dromgoole, S. (ed.) *Legal Protection of the Underwater Cultural Heritage: National and International Perspectives* (Kluwer Law International, The Hague, 1999) 119

Le Gurun, G. 'France' in Dromgoole, S. (ed.) *Legal Protection of the Underwater Cultural Heritage: National and International Perspectives* (Kluwer Law International, The Hague, 1999) 43

Leanza, U. 'Zona archeologica marina' in Francioni, F.; Del Vecchio, A.; De Caterini, P. (eds) *Protezione internazionale del patrimonio culturale: interessi nazionali e difesa del patrimonio comune della cultura* (Giuffrè Editore, Milan, 2000) 41

Lee, K-G. 'An Inquiry into the Compatibility of the UNESCO Convention 2001 with UNCLOS 1982' in Prott, L.V. (ed.) *Finishing the Interrupted Voyage* (UNESCO, Institute of Art and Law; Paris, Builth Wells; 2006) 20.

Leino, M *et al.* 'The Natural Environment of the Shipwreck *Vrouw Maria* (1771) in the Northern Baltic Sea: an assessment of her state of preservation' (2010) 40 *International Journal of Nautical Archaeology* 133.

Leventhal, R.M. *et al.* "Archaeology vs. Commercial Exploitation: How the Smithsonian Could Display Objects from the Belitung Shipwreck": <http://culturalheritagelaw.org/blog?mode=PostView&bmi=773188>

L'Hour, M. 'DRASSM 1996-2008: An Overview of the Accomplishments and Future of French Underwater Archaeology' in *International Meeting on the Protection, Presentation and Valorisation of Underwater Cultural Heritage – Chongqing, China* (23 to 27 November 2010): <http://www.unesco.org/culture/underwater/pdf/uch_publication_chine_en.pdf>

Lund, C. 'The Making of the 2001 UNESCO Convention' in Prott, L.V. (ed.) *Finishing the Interrupted Voyage* (UNESCO, Institute of Art and Law; Paris, Builth Wells; 2006) 16.

Maarleveld, T.J.; Guérin, U. & Egger, B. (eds) *Manual for Activities Directed at Underwater Cultural Heritage: Guidelines to the Annex of the UNESCO 2001 Convention* (UNESCO, Paris, 2013).

Martin-Bueno, M. 'Patrimonio cultural y arqueologia' (1985) (July-September) *Analisis e investigaciones culturales* 37

Mather, R. 'Technology and the Search for Shipwrecks' (1999) 30 *Journal of Maritime Law and Commerce* 175

Mathewson, R.D. *Archaeological Treasure: The Search for Neustra Señora de Atocha* (Seafarers Heritage Library, Woodstock, Vt. 1983)

Matikka, M. 'Finland' in Droomgoole, S. (ed.) *The Protection of the Underwater Cultural Heritage: National Perspectives in Light of the UNESCO Convention 2001* (Martinus Nijhoff, Leiden, 2006) 43.

McCarthy, M. 'HM Ship *Roebuck* (1690-1701) :Global Maritime Heritage' (2004) *33 International Journal of Nautical Archaeology* 54.

Migliorino, L. 'In Situ Protection of the Underwater Cultural Heritage Under International Treaties and National Legislation' (1995) 10 *International Journal of Marine and Coastal Law* 483

Miller, G.L. 'The Second Destruction of the Geldermalsen' (1987) 47 *The American Neptune* 275

Muckelroy, K. *Maritime Archaeology* (Cambridge University Press, Cambridge, 1978)

Nafziger, J.A.R. 'Finding the Titanic: Beginning an International Salvage of Derelict Law at Sea' (1988) 12 *Columbia-VLA Journal of Law & the Arts* 339

Nafziger, J.A.R. 'Historic Salvage Law Revisited' (2000) 31 *Ocean Development & International Law* 81

Nafziger, J.A.R. 'International Legal Protection of the Underwater Cultural Heritage' in Phelan, M. (ed.) *The Law of Cultural Property and Natural Heritage: Protection, Transfer, and Access* (Kalos Kapp Press, Evanston, Illinois, 1998) Chapter 2

Nafziger, J.A.R. 'The Titanic Revisited' (1999) 30 *Journal of Maritime Law and Commerce* 311

O'Connor, N. 'Ireland' in Dromgoole, S. (ed.) *Legal Protection of the Underwater Cultural Heritage: National and International Perspectives* (Kluwer Law International, The Hague, 1999) 87

O'Keefe, P.J. *Commentary on the UNESCO 1970 Convention on Illicit Traffic* (Institute of Art and Law, Builth Wells, 2nd ed., 2007)

O'Keefe, P.J. 'Second Meeting of Governmental Experts to Consider the Draft Convention on the Protection of Underwater Cultural Heritage: Paris, UNESCO Headquarters (April 19-24 1999)' (1999) 8 *International Journal of Cultural Property* 568

O'Keefe, P.J. 'Archaeology and Human Rights' (2000) 1 *Public Archaeology* 181

O'Keefe, P.J. 'Gold, Abandonment and Salvage' (1994) (February) *Lloyd's Maritime and Commercial Law Quarterly* 7

O'Keefe, P.J. 'International Waters' in Dromgoole, S. (ed.) *Legal Protection of the Underwater Cultural Heritage: National and International Perspectives* (Kluwer Law International, The Hague, 1999) 223

O'Keefe, P.J. 'Protection of the Underwater Cultural Heritage: Developments at UNESCO' (1996) 25 *International Journal of Nautical Archaeology* 169

O'Keefe, P.J. 'The European Convention on the Protection of the Archaeological Heritage' (1993) 67 *Antiquity* 406

O'Keefe, P.J. 'The Law and Nautical Archaeology: An International Survey' in Langley, S.B.M. & Unger, R.W. (eds) *Nautical Archaeology: Progress and Public Responsibility* (BAR International Series 220, 1984) 9

O'Keefe, P.J. 'Protecting the Underwater Cultural Heritage: The International Law Association Draft Convention' (1996) 20 *Marine Policy* 297

O'Keefe, P.J. 'The Implementation of the 2001 Underwater Convention' in González, A.W., O'Keefe, P.J. and Williams, M. 'The UNESCO Convention on the Protection of the Underwater Cultural Heritage: a Future for our Past?' (2009) 11 *Conservation and Management of Archaeological Sites* 54.

O'Keefe, P.J. 'The International Law Association Draft Convention on the Protection of the Underwater Cultural Heritage' in Vedovato, G. & Borrelli, L.V. (eds) *La tutela del patrimonio archeologico subacqueo* (Istituto Poligrafico e Zeccadello Stato, Rome, 1995) 39

O'Keefe, P.J. "Commercial Exploitation': Its Prohibition in the UNESCO Convention on Protection of the Underwater Cultural Heritage 2001 and Other Instruments' (2013) XVIII *Art Antiquity and Law* 129.

O'Keefe, P.J. & Nafziger, J.A.R. 'The Draft Convention on the Protection of the Underwater Cultural Heritage' (1994) 25 *Ocean Development and International Law* 391

O'Keefe, P.J. & Prott, L.V. 'Analysis of Legislation in Individual Countries of the Council of Europe' Annex III in *The Underwater Cultural Heritage: Report of the Committee on Culture and Education, Parliamentary Assembly* (Council of Europe Doc.4200. Strasbourg, 1978) 91

O'Keefe, P.J. & Prott, L.V. (eds) *Cultural Heritage Conventions and Other Instruments: A Compendium with Commentaries* (Institute of Art and Law, Builth Wells, 2011).

O'Keefe, P.J. & Prott, L.V. 'Final Report on Legal Protection of the Underwater Cultural Heritage' Annex II in *The Underwater Cultural Heritage: Report of the Committee on Culture and Education, Parliamentary Assembly* (Council of Europe Doc.4200. Strasbourg, 1978) 45

O'Keefe, P.J. & Prott, L.V. *Law and the Cultural Heritage: Volume I: Discovery and Excavation* (Professional Books, Abingdon, 1984)

Oxman, B.H. 'The Third United Nations Conference on the Law of the Sea: The Ninth Session (1980)' (1981) 75 *American Journal of International Law* 211

Peltz, R.D. 'Salvaging Historic Wrecks' (2000) 25 *Tulane Maritime Law Journal* 1

Price, L. 'The Canadian Law of Treasure and Wreck' (2000) *Nautical Year Book* 67

Pringle, H. "Smithsonian Shipwreck Exhibit Draws Fire from Archaeologists" *Science Insider* 10 March 2011: <http://news.sciencemag.org/scienceinsider/2011/03/smithsonian-shipwreck-exhibit.html>

Prott, L.V. (ed.) *Finishing the Interrupted Voyage* (UNESCO, Institute of Art and Law; Paris, Builth Wells; 2006).

Prott, L.V. & O'Keefe, P.J. 'International Legal Protection of the Underwater Cultural Heritage' (1978-79) *Belgian Review of International Law* 85

Prott, L.V. & Srong, I. (eds) *Background Materials on the Protection of the Underwater Cultural Heritage* (UNESCO &The Nautical Archaeology Society, Paris & Portsmouth, 1999)

Prott, L.V., Planche, E. & Roca-Hachem, R. (eds) *Background Materials on the Protection of the Underwater Cultural Heritage* (UNESCO & Ministère de la Culture et de la Communication (France), Paris, 2000)

Bonifácio Ramos, J.L. O Achamento de Bens Culturais Subaquáticos (Livraria Petrony Editores, Lisbon, 2008)

Rigambert, C. *Le Droit de l'Archéologie Francaise* (Picard Editeur, Paris, 1996)

Roach, J.A. 'Sunken Warships and Military Aircraft' (1996) 20 *Marine Policy* 351

Robol, R.T. 'Legal Protection for Underwater Cultural Resources: Can We do Better?' (1999) 30 *Journal of Maritime Law and Commerce* 303

Rodrigues, J. 'An Amnesty Assessed. Human Impact on Shipwreck Sites: the Australian Case' (2009) 38 *International Journal of Nautical Archaeology* 153

Sinclair, J. 'Threats to Underwater Cultural Heritage – Real & Imagined' in Stemm, G. & Kingsley, S. (eds) *Oceans Odyssey 2: Underwater Heritage Management & Deep-Sea Shipwrecks in the English Channel & Atlantic Ocean* (Oxbow Books, Oxford, 2011) 17

Skowronek, R.K. & Fischer, G.R. *HMS Fowey Lost and Found* (University Press of Florida, Gainesville, 2009).

Staniland, H. 'South Africa' in Dromgoole, S. (ed.) *Legal Protection of the Underwater Cultural Heritage: National and International Perspectives* (Kluwer Law International, The Hague, 1999) 133

Stemm, G. & Kingsley, S. (eds) *Oceans Odyssey 2: Underwater Heritage Management & Deep-Sea Shipwrecks in the English Channel & Atlantic Ocean* (Oxbow Books, Oxford, 2011).

Stemm, G. "Comment on Shipwreck Resources Management Issues" presented to the U.S. Commission on Ocean Policy, 22 February, 2002: <http://www.oceancommission.gov/publicomment/floridacomments/stemm_comment.pdf>

Stemm,G. & Kingsley, S. (eds) *Oceans Odyssey: Deep-sea Shipwrecks in the English Channel, Straits of Gibraltar& Atlantic Ocean* (Oxbow Books, Oxford, 2010).

Stemm, G. 'Differentiation of Shipwreck Artifacts as a Cultural Resource Management Tool' paper delivered at the Ocean Intervention 2000 Conference, Houston, Texas, 25-27 January 2000

Stemm, G. "Virtual Collectors and Private Curators: A Model for the Museum of the Future" in Stemm, G. & Kingsley, S. (eds) *Oceans Odyssey 2: Underwater Heritage Management & Deep-Sea Shipwrecks in the English Channel & Atlantic Ocean* (Oxbow Books, Oxford, 2011) 27.

Stevenson, P. "A Titanic Struggle: An Update. Salvage Beyond the Scope of the UNESCO Underwater Cultural Heritage Convention" (2011) 16 *Art Antiquity and Law* 305

Stoddart, S. & Malone, C. 'Editorial' (2001) 75 *Antiquity* 233, 234-236

Strati, A. 'Deep Seabed Cultural Property and the Common Heritage of Mankind' (1991) 40 *International and Comparative Law Quarterly* 859

Strati, A. 'Greece' in Dromgoole, S. (ed.) *Legal Protection of the Underwater Cultural Heritage: National and International Perspectives* (Kluwer Law International, The Hague, 1999) 65

Strati, A. 'The Protection of the Underwater Cultural Heritage in International Legal Perspective' in Kassimatis, G. (ed.) *Archaeological Heritage: Current Trends in Its Legal Protection* (Sakkoulas Bros., Athens,1995) 143

Strati, A. *Draft Convention on the Protection of Underwater Cultural Heritage: A Commentary Prepared for UNESCO, April 1999* UNESCO Doc. CLT-99/WS/8

Strati, A.*The Protection of the Underwater Cultural Heritage: An Emerging Objective of the Contemporary Law of the Sea* (Martinus Nijhoff Publishers, The Hague, 1995)

Sweeney, J.C. 'An Overview of Commercial Salvage Principles in the Context of Marine Archaeology' (1999) 30 *Journal of Maritime Law and Commerce* 185

Symmons, C.R. *Ireland and the Law of the Sea* (Round Hall Sweet & Maxwell, Dublin, 2000)

Tolson, H. 'The Jacksonville 'Blue China' Shipwreck & the Myth of Deep-Sea Preservation' in Stemm, G. & Kingsley, S. (eds) *Oceans Odyssey: Deep-sea Shipwrecks in the English Channel, Straits of Gibraltar & Atlantic Ocean* (Oxbow Books, Oxford, 2010) 145

Vadi, V.S. 'Investing in Culture: Underwater Cultural Heritage and International Investment Law' (2009) 42 *Vanderbilt Journal of Transnational Law* 853

Varmer, O. 'The Case Against the 'Salvage' of the Cultural Heritage' (1999) 30 *Journal of Maritime Law and Commerce* 279

Varmer, O. & Blanco, C.M. 'United States of America' in Dromgoole, S. (ed.) *Legal Protection of the Underwater Cultural Heritage: National and International Perspectives* (Kluwer Law International, The Hague, 1999) 205

Veccella, R. 'The Gran Underwater Inventory of French Polynesia' in Prott, L.V. (ed.) *Finishing the Interrupted Voyage* (UNESCO, Institute of Art and Law; Paris, Builth Wells; 2006) 77.

Waddell, P.J.A. 'Long Range Shipwreck Timber Storage' (1994) 18 *Bulletin of the Australian Institute for Maritime Archaeology* 1

Walker, J.E. 'A Contemporary Standard for Determining Title to Sunken Warships: A Tale of Two Vessels and Two Nations' (1999-2000) 12 *U.S.F. Maritime Law Journal* 311

Watts, G.P. 'C.S.S. Alabama: Controversial as Always, Yet Offering Opportunities for International Cooperation' (1987) *Underwater Archaeology: Proceedings from the Society for Historical Archaeology Conference, 1990, Tucson, Arizona* 75

Wei Jun 'Innovative Thoughts on the Preservation of Underwater Cultural Heritage in China: No.1 Nanhai as a Project Example' in International Meeting on the Protection, Presentation and Valorisation of Underwater Cultural Heritage – Chongqing, China (23 to 27 November 2010): <http://www.unesco.org/culture/underwater/pdf/uch_publication_chine_en.pdf>

Williams, M. "War Graves' and Salvage: Murky Waters' (2000) 5 *International Maritime Law* 151

Yorke, R. "Introduction: Protection of Underwater Cultural Heritage" in *International Waters Adjacent to the UK – a JNAPC Perspective 21 Years On"* in Yorke, R. (ed.) *Protection of Underwater Cultural Heritage in International Waters Adjacent to the UK: Proceedings of the JNAPC 21st Anniversary Seminar, Burlington House, November, 2010* (Nautical Archaeology Society, Fort Cumberland, 2011) 1

Yormak, S.R. 'Canadian Treasure: Law and Lore' (1999) 30 *Journal of Maritime Law and Commerce* 229

Zarza Alvarez, E. 'Spain' in Dromgoole, S. (ed.) *Legal Protection of the Underwater Cultural Heritage: National and International Perspectives* (Kluwer Law International, The Hague, 1999) 143

Zhang Wei 'Exploring History Underwater: The Development and Current Status of Underwater Archaeology in China' in Prott, L.V. (ed.) *Finishing the Interrupted Voyage* (UNESCO, Institute of Art and Law; Paris, Builth Wells; 2006) 81

INDEX

'Activities directed at' underwater cultural heritage,	33, 36, 38, 40, 49, 51, 56
see also Rules concerning 'activities etc...'	
as distinct from 'activities incidentally affecting'	33, 36, 49, 51
'Activities incidentally affecting' underwater cultural heritage	33, 36, 49, 51
Adoption of Underwater Convention	1, 21, 22, 55
Aircraft	35, 77
see also State vessels and aircraft	
Alabama	52, 58
Amnesties in relation to underwater cultural heritage	9-10
Archipelagic waters	56-60, 71, 112
'Area', as defined in Underwater Convention, definition of	2
protection of underwater cultural heritage in	74-76
reporting and notification in	72-73
Armada	37, 139
Batavia	4, 43, 151
Belitung	41, 91, 129-130, 143
Benin Bronzes	3
Bilateral agreements relating to underwater cultural heritage	52-55
Birkenhead	52, 58-59
Cables, cable industry	30, 33, 36, 45
Cape Gelidonya	3-4
Central America	6, 30, 45, 92
Chuuk Lagoon	32, 93
Code of Ethics for Diving on Underwater Cultural Heritage Sites	23
Commercial exploitation	23-24, 39-42, 124-132, 150, 152, 159,
definition of	124-125
in practice	125-127
Titanic	131-132
Contiguous zone	2, 61
Continental shelf, legal definition of	2
physical description of	1
protection of underwater cultural heritage on	67-71 and see 12-13, 17-18, 20-21
reporting and notification of	62-66
Council of American Maritime Museums	127, 129, 131
Definition of underwater cultural heritage	1-2, 33-36
Disposition of underwater cultural heritage	86-89
Disputes concerning Underwater Convention	104-108
Divers	3, 16, 19, 23, 31, 93, 95-96, 154
Divers, Code of Ethics for Diving on Underwater Cultural Heritage Sites	23
DOALOS, see United Nations Division of Ocean Affairs and Law of the Sea	
Exclusive economic zone (EEZ), definition of	2, 20-21
protection of underwater cultural heritage in	67-71 and see 12-13, 17-18, 20-21
reporting and notification in	62-66
Finds, law of	48-50
Fowey	59, 146
Funding for underwater archaeology under Rules for 'activities directed at etc...',	139-141
Geldermahlsen	4-5, 80
Grenier, Robert	4, 96, 121, 140
Victory	40-41, 126, 159
Human remains	42-43, 133
ICOMOS International Committee on the Underwater Cultural Heritage	4, 15, 96, 117, 121, 140
Illicit export/recovery of underwater cultural heritage	78-81
Inland waters	111, 10, 57
Internal waters	2, 15, 31, 56-60, 83, 112
International Counci8l of Museums (ICOM	128, 129, 151

International Council on Monuments and Sites (ICOMOS)	19, 20, 34, 98, 115, 127, 132, 135
see also ICOMOS International Committee on the Underwater Cultural Heritage	
International Centre for the Study of the Preservation and Restoration of Cultural Property (ICCROM)	95
International Congress of Maritime Museums	127, 130
International Court of Justice	106, 109
International Law Association (ILA)	11-12, 14-16
International Law Association Draft Convention	14-16, 34, 49, 57, 87, 91, 115, 117, 157
International Seabed Authority	72, 74
International Tribunal for the Law of the Sea	106, 108
Interpretation of Treaties	27-28
Inventory of underwater cultural heritage	98-99
Invincible	139
Law of the Sea, United Nations Convention on (UNCLOS)	2, 12-14, 17-18, 21, 24, 45-47, 157-159
Looting	31-32, 40, 67, 70, 74
Lund, Carsten,	17, 21, 44
Manual for Activities Directed At Underwater Cultural Heritage (UNESCO)	22, 23, 120, 126, 144, 151, 159
Mary Rose	4, 31, 43, 97, 140, 145, 154
Multilateral agreements relating to underwater cultural heritage	52-55
Museums Association, United Kingdom	128
Nautical Archaeology Society	17, 95
Odyssey Marine Exploration	40-41, 119, 121, 125-127, 159
Operational Guidelines	22-23, 31, 65, 66, 71, 72, 73, 101
Preservation *in situ*	4, 30-32, 38-39, 51, 57, 121-124, 137
Public access to underwater cultural heritage	19, 29, 30, 43-44, 86, 134
Public awareness of, education regarding, underwater cultural heritage	93-94, 145-146, 154
Recovery of underwater cultural heritage, see illicit export/recovery of underwater cultural heritage	
Red Bay, Canada	4, 121, 123, 145-146, 155
Regional agreements relating to underwater cultural heritage	52-55
Retroactivity in treaty interpretation	28
Rewards in relation to underwater cultural heritage	9-10
Rules concerning 'activities directed at' underwater cultural heritage	56, 119-155
funding for underwater archaeology under Rules	139-141
methodology for project design	138
preliminary work for project design	137
project design for activities	135-136
Salvage, law of	6-12, 48-50
Sanctions for violations of Underwater Convention	84-85, 30, 78, 81
Scientific and Technical Advisory Body (STAB)	101-102, 115, 153, 158-159
Second World War	33, 34, 93
Seizure of underwater cultural heritage	86-89
Settlement of disputes concerning Underwater Convention	104-108
Sovereign immunity	77, 11, 40, 42
State vessels and aircraft	11, 33, 36-37, 42, 43, 56, 57-60, 71, 76
Territorial sea	56-61
Titanic	3, 7-8, 39, 45, 48, 52-53, 121-122, 130-132, 139, 148
Training in underwater cultural heritage	95-97
Treaty interpretation	27-28
UNCLOS	see Law of the Sea, United Nations Convention on (UNCLOS)
United Nations	23-25, 106, 107, 109, 118
United Nations Division of Ocean Affairs and Law of the Sea, DOALOS	17, 19-20, 30, 35, 42, 49
Value of underwater cultural heritage	2-3
Vasa	4, 31
Violations of Underwater Convention	84-85, 30
Warships	see State vessels and aircraft